Non-Sovereign Futures

Non-Sovereign Futures

French Caribbean Politics in the Wake of Disenchantment

YARIMAR BONILLA

The University of Chicago Press
Chicago and London

Yarimar Bonilla is associate professor of anthropology and Caribbean studies at Rutgers University.

The University of Chicago Press, Chicago 60637
The University of Chicago Press, Ltd., London
© 2015 by The University of Chicago
All rights reserved. Published 2015.

24 23 22 21 20 19 18 17 16 15   1 2 3 4 5

ISBN-13: 978-0-226-28378-4 (cloth)
ISBN-13: 978-0-226-28381-4 (paper)
ISBN-13: 978-0-226-28395-1 (e-book)
DOI: 10.7208/chicago/9780226283951.001.0001

Library of Congress Cataloging-in-Publication Data

Bonilla, Yarimar, author.
    Non-sovereign futures : French Caribbean politics in the wake of
disenchantment / Yarimar Bonilla.
        pages : illustrations ; cm
    Includes bibliographical references and index.
    ISBN 978-0-226-28378-4 (cloth : alk. paper)—ISBN 978-0-226-28381-4
(pbk. : alk. paper)—ISBN 978-0-226-28395-1 (ebook)   1. Labor unions—
Political activity—Guadeloupe. 2. Union générale des travailleurs de
Guadeloupe. 3. National liberation movements—Guadeloupe.
4. Postcolonialism—Guadeloupe. 5. Guadeloupe—Politics and
government—21st century.   I. Title.
    HD6595.9.Z65B66 2015
    322'.20972976—dc23
                                                        2015007462

CONTENTS

ILLUSTRATIONS

TIMELINE OF EVENTS

1789   French Revolution (1789–1799)

1791   Haitian Revolution (1791–1804)

1794   Slavery first abolished in Guadeloupe

1802   Slavery violently reinstated in Guadeloupe, leading to a massive anti-slavery insurrection

1848   French citizenship extended to Guadeloupeans, along with the second abolition of slavery

1854   Indentured workers from India begin to arrive in Guadeloupe (42,000 total arrived from 1854 to 1880)

1923   Citizenship and voting rights extended to indentured workers from India and their descendants

1925   Sugar workers strike at the Duval factory in Petit-Canal involving Indo- and Afro-Guadeloupean workers, resulting in six fatalities

1946   Départements d'outre-mer (Martinique, Guadeloupe, Guiana, Réunion) created

1946   French Union (1946–1958)

1952   Sugar workers strike in the Gardel Factory of Le Moule, resulting in four fatalities

1954   Algerian War of Independence (1954–1962)

1958   West Indies Federation (1958–1962)

1959   Cuban Revolution

1960   United Nations Resolution 1514, Declaration on the Granting of Independence to Colonial Countries and Peoples

1961   Front antillo-guyannais (FAG) created

1963   Groupe d'organisation nationale de la Guadeloupe (GONG) founded

1963   Bureau pour le développement des migrations intéressant les départements d'outre-mer (BUMIDOM) established (1963–81)

1967   Massacre of protesters in Point-à-Pitre during GONG labor strike

1968   BUMIDOM offices in Paris ransacked

1968   Eighteen activists tried for political crimes before the Court of State Security (Cour de sûreté) in France, with several sentenced to prison

1970   Union of Agricultural Workers (Union des travailleurs agricoles, UTA) created

1972   Union of Impoverished Guadeloupean Peasants (Union des paysans pauvres de la Guadeloupe, UPG) created

1973   UTA and UPA merge to create General Union of Guadeloupean Workers (Union générale des travailleurs de la Guadeloupe, UGTG)

1973   Sugar workers strike in Baie-Mahault, supported by Père Céleste's hunger strike

1978   Popular Union for the Liberation of Guadeloupe (Union populaire pour la libération de la Guadeloupe, UPLG) created

1980s   Armed Liberation Group (Groupe de liberation armée, GLA), Caribbean Revolutionary Alliance (Alliance révolutionnaire caribéenne, ARC), and Popular Movement for Guadeloupean Independence (Mouvement populaire pour la Guadeloupe indépendante, MPGI) created

1983   France under François Mitterrand declares May 27 to be Abolition Day, a commemorative holiday in Guadeloupe

1984   Luc Reinette, presumed leader of the MPGI, arrested and incarcerated by the French government

1992   Quincentennial of Columbus's arrival in the Americas

1996   Fiftieth anniversary of departmentalization

1998   150th anniversary of abolition celebrated in France

1998   UGTG public servants' strike; city services suspended for over six months

2001   France passes Taubira Law designating slavery a crime against humanity

2001   First Madassamy affair: UGTG leads demonstrations to commemorate Abolition Day; Michel Madassamy is arrested

2001   NONM group created

2002   First NONM memory walk

2004   Second Madassamy affair: Michel Madassamy is detained and carries out a hunger strike for thirty-two days

2005   Banlieue riots in Paris

2008   Death of Aimé Césaire

2008   Élie Domota is elected secretary general of the UGTG

2009   Liyannaj kont pwofitasyon (LKP, Alliance against Profiteering) created, leads forty-four-day general strike

Native Categories and Native Arguments

I do not remember the first time I heard the word "sovereignty." Growing up in Puerto Rico, an unincorporated territory of the United States, I grew accustomed to routinely hearing this term bandied about at cultural events and political rallies. On these occasions, whenever someone would call out "Viva Puerto Rico!" it would inevitably be followed by a collective response: "Libre y soberano!" (Long live Puerto Rico, free and sovereign.) I cannot claim that simply hearing this phrase repeated over and over gave me a full understanding of the meaning of these terms, or of their entwinement, but it did make it clear that these categories matter—particularly to those who feel acutely dispossessed of what they represent.

As Michel-Rolph Trouillot argues, native categories are not the terrain of false consciousness, but the language of routine; they are signposts for the relationships and institutions that shape daily life.[1] For my generation, coming of age politically in the Puerto Rico of the 1990s, the social relations that impacted daily life were routinely articulated as problems of sovereignty. We often heard from politicians that the issues that concerned us most—depressed incomes, high prices, unemployment, crime, violence, and government corruption—all hinged on resolving our sovereignty problem.[2]

This is not exclusive to Puerto Rico. Across and beyond the Caribbean, sovereignty serves as a native category for the bundle of relations that shape daily life, including access to goods, the valuation of labor, the prestige of vernacular forms, and the ability to forge culturally distinct landscapes, soundtracks, aesthetics, visions of the future, and testaments to the past. These issues are routinely debated and negotiated under the sign of sovereignty—food sovereignty, economic sovereignty, cultural sovereignty, and, in the words of the renowned Barbadian novelist George Lamming, the "sovereignty of the imagination."[3]

In Puerto Rico the sovereignty problem has long been tied to the "status question." Political parties have traditionally been defined by their position on Puerto Rico's status vis-à-vis the United States (pro-statehood, pro-commonwealth, or pro-independence), and local residents are routinely called upon to engage in elaborate opinion polls masked as referenda for change.[4] Contradictions seem to plague our current position as an *Estado Libre Asociado* (ELA), a legal term of art, usually translated as "commonwealth," which has been taken to mean that Puerto Ricans "belong to, but are not a part of, the United States."[5] Under this arrangement Puerto Ricans benefit from the mobility and access that a US passport provides, but we hold out our passports with a shaky hand, never feeling wholly represented or fully confident in a political membership that feels tenuous and unguaranteed.

Yet, despite the contradictions and uncertainties of our status quo, most Puerto Ricans are skeptical of change. Although some claim that becoming the fifty-first state would solve the problems of unequal incorporation, the marginalization and exclusion of Puerto Ricans in the mainland (not to mention the unequal place of other racialized groups within the United States) suggests otherwise. Moreover, although many Puerto Ricans have relinquished claims to political nationalism, there remains a shared feeling of "distinctiveness," what some describe as cultural nationalism, based on culinary, linguistic, and other cultural practices that some fear would be either lost or repressed in the context of US integration.[6] Nevertheless, political nationalism (understood as the search for formal independence) appears increasingly implausible and impractical. In an era of global economic integration, and at a time when most Puerto Rican families span beyond the confines of the Puerto Rican territory, independence has increasingly become a foreclosed option, or a "future past," even for those who still profess nostalgia for its promises.[7]

Still, notwithstanding the oft-cited government slogan that Puerto Ricans possess "the best of both worlds" (i.e., a distinct cultural identity and an advantageous passport), being non-independent feels like being shut out of the global system—denied a political right that one is told should be both universally allocated and unequivocally desired. For example, a friend once asked what it was like to be Puerto Rican, prompting me with the question, "Is it like being in purgatory?"

Underlying this type of discourse is the idea that non-independent societies suffer from a form of arrested development. That is, they are imagined as having failed to complete their historical ascension to national sovereignty, resulting in a state of unachieved modernity. Ultimately, the idea of being non-sovereign, non-emancipated, or non-decolonized carries the same moral connotations as being non-modern in that it goes against the proper norms, the promoted ambitions, and the cultivated desires of modern personhood and modern politics. It is for this reason, I argue, that sovereignty needs to be understood not just as a native category but as a particular kind of normative ideal, what Michel-Rolph Trouillot calls a "North Atlantic Universal"—a category that both seduces and disappoints in its attempts at transcending its provincial origins.[8]

It was Puerto Rico's political impasse that led me to turn my analytical gaze toward the French Antilles. In Puerto Rico we were often told that we were an anomaly—the sole place that got left behind in the postwar parade of decolonization.[9] In the years following World War II, however, as Puerto Rico was crafting its "free association" with the United States, the French Antilles were in the process of becoming overseas departments of France.[10] These societies have also been described as exceptional, paradoxical, and even pathogenic. Local intellectuals often lament the "colonial alienation" and "dependent mentality" they believe to be at the root of the disinterest in independence, while outsiders routinely accuse residents of having traded the pride of nation for the economic guarantees of a North Atlantic citizenship, engaging in what has been described as "self-advancement by self-negation."[11] Even the eminent Caribbean thinker C. L. R. James once quipped that Martinique and Guadeloupe constituted the "lost sheep" of the Caribbean.[12]

This book questions these discourses of lack and pathos, but does not replace them with a triumphant narrative of strategic cunning.[13] It would be easy to represent places like Puerto Rico, Martinique, and Guadeloupe as sites of pragmatic vision that have managed to skirt the postcolonial crucibles of structural adjustment, the difficulties of small-state economies, and the imperial dictates of global trade. But any romantic view of these societies as "protected" quickly fades when confronted with the multiple ways they and their residents have served as military cannon fodder, medical guinea pigs, toxic dumping grounds, and laboratories of warfare, biopolitics, imperial statecraft, technological off-shoring, and neoliberal economics.[14]

My goal is thus neither to celebrate nor to condemn the political status of societies like Puerto Rico and Guadeloupe. Instead, I wish to historicize their political arrangements and place them within the broader framework of the postcolonial Caribbean. For, in fact, the *majority* of Caribbean polities are non-sovereign societies; even those that have achieved "flag independence" still struggle with how to forge a more robust project of self-determination, how to reconcile the unresolved legacies of colonialism and slavery, how to assert control over their entanglements with foreign powers, and how to stem their disappointment with the unfulfilled promises of political and economic modernity.

I argue that in both the independent and non-independent Caribbean, there is a common feeling of disenchantment with the modernist project of postcolonial sovereignty, even while there is also a lingering attachment to its normative ideals. For, although it might seem as if the project of post-colonial sovereignty has led to a political dead end, many populations still find meaning and power in the right to nation and state.[15] National independence does not seem to guarantee sovereignty, but it is unclear whether societies without it can achieve what sovereignty—as a native category—has come to represent. Moreover, contemporary populations often lack the conceptual language with which to describe plausible (or even utopian) alternatives to the modernist projects of decolonization and national sovereignty. This is why Puerto Ricans routinely vote against political independence even while asserting a wish to see their island "free and sovereign" and why the Guadeloupean protagonists of this book repeatedly declare that they want sovereignty "even if it is under the French flag."

I use the term *non-sovereign politics* to describe these kinds of acts for two reasons: First, because they challenge the modernist premise of absolute sovereignty by revealing its insufficiencies. That is, they trouble the fiction of sovereign control by negotiating and navigating forms of entanglement that cannot—or perhaps should not—be easily broken.[16] Second, because they operate as forms of immanent critique: they are attempts to break free from the epistemic constraints of political modernity, even while still being compelled to think through its normative categories. Non-sovereignty thus needs to be understood as both a positive project and a negative place-holder for an anticipated future characterized by something *other than* the search for sovereignty.[17]

Native Voices, Native Arguments, and Non-Native Anthropologists

This book is the result of over a decade of close conversations with Guadeloupean workers, activists, artists, students, journalists, and scholars about the political projects they deem plausible and desirable.[18] In the pages that follow, I engage with their reflections not just as anecdotal evidence but as sources of analytic insight. This represents a concerted attempt at challenging the traditional role of "the native voice" in anthropology.

Within ethnographic monographs, native voices are all too often robbed of their "competency effect."[19] That is, ethnographers rarely demonstrate their interlocutors' ability to speak with analytic value about their own society—much less the societies of others. The voices of informants might be rallied as evidence within a scholar's argument, but the position of those informants within that argument—and their assessment of its *stakes*—are rarely explored.

Take for example Laura Bohannan's classic text "Shakespeare in the Bush," a favorite of many introductory anthropology seminars and texts.[20] First published in 1971, some claim it might be "one of the most anthologized anthropology articles of all time," rivaling even Horace Miner's "Body Ritual among the Nacirema."[21] In this essay the author relates her misguided attempt at narrating the plot of Hamlet to Tiv elders in the small village in Nigeria where she conducted her research. As she spins the tale, her interlocutors share their own take on the story's meaning—revealing a radically different interpretation of what the author had considered to be a story with universal meaning. However, the way Bohannan deploys the voices of her informants is not as sources of insight, but as evidence both of and for her argument regarding cultural difference. If anything, her informants are presented as *un*-insightful. As one commentator notes, it is the Tiv's unabashed certainty that their reading of Hamlet is the better one, the only possible one, which lends the story its "charm."[22]

Bohannan's piece is beloved because it fits well with one of the stories anthropology most likes to tell itself about itself: that the discipline can help make the familiar strange and the strange familiar. It does so, however, by ultimately placing Bohannan's informants on the losing end of a debate to which they were never privy.[23]

This use of the native voice is not uncommon. As Trouillot argues, within ethnographic texts, informants rarely emerge as full interlocutors; their voices are routinely rallied within arguments that are neither for nor about them.[24] Trouillot suggests that the ambiguous role of the native voice within anthropological texts is rooted in the discipline's failure to theorize both the "semiotic relevance" and the "epistemological status" of native discourse. As he provocatively asks: "Is native discourse a citation, an indirect quote, or a paraphrase? . . . Is its value referential, indexical, phatic, or poetic?"[25] With these provocative questions, Trouillot pushes anthropologists to think carefully about the role of the native voice not just in the narrated frame— that is, in our depictions of what informants do with words in the scenes we describe—but also in the narrative frame.[26] That is, he asks us to consider what *we* do with the words and concepts of our informants in the service of *our* story. This requires recognizing that native voices do not sing in unison or with singular clarity, but just as importantly, it also requires acknowledging that our interlocutors are never merely describing their world—they are perpetually analyzing their world and making arguments about it. The challenge then is not simply to incorporate native voices, but to engage seriously with native *arguments*.

The inability to engage with native arguments is a fundamental part of why anthropologists have had such a vexed relationship with local scholars, politicians, and activists—for it is difficult to deploy these types of voices as simple evidence of cultural patterns and beliefs.[27] But why? Why are these voices trickier than others? Whose voice can be deployed as evidence of culture? Whose as ideology? And whose as theory?

The problem lies not just in the untheorized semiotic role of the native voice, but also in the epistemological status of native discourse. What do our informants know and not know about their social world? And how much competency should they be granted when speaking about it?

Cultural anthropology has long straddled the social sciences and the humanities—but it has done so awkwardly, with little attention to either the value or the pitfalls of this interstitial position. Trouillot argues that anthropologists have a privileged vantage point—we are well positioned to study both human experience and the historical processes and institutional forces that produce and shape that experience. There are, however, some pitfalls—specifically around questions of authority and evidence.[28] The problem is that ethnographers tend to deploy the native voice in ways that make native theory either redundant or irrelevant. On the one hand, anthropologists often claim to be peering "over the natives' shoulders"—as Clifford Geertz infamously suggested—directly conveying our informants' stories and interpretations.[29] On the other hand, as in the case of "Shakespeare in the Bush," native voices are often deployed as evidence within a scholarly argument that precludes them; they provide texture, character, and "charm"—but rarely analytical insight.

In this book I purposefully engage with my informants as theorists—that is, as reflective actors who seek to make sense of their experiences in relation to the ideas and experiences of others. In deciding when to cite, quote, or paraphrase, I treat their reflections and arguments as I do those of other theorists: I cite when I wish to rally their authority; I quote when I think they have found *le mot juste* to describe a particular phenomena, and I paraphrase when I feel like I can articulate their vision more succinctly, or more accessibly, to my presumed audience.[30] Moreover, I engage with my informants as a literary critic might engage with an author's reflections about their oeuvre: that is, I grant them analytic competency over their own acts and forms of cultural production.

My efforts build on Trouillot's call for anthropologists to "face the native" rather than peer over their shoulders (or write on their backs).[31] Building on this idea, I suggest that we not just "face the native" but *theorize with them.* This is not a matter of a simple rhetorical flourish—such as the gesture of replacing the word "informant" with "interlocutor"—since this mere act has no inherent consequence for the semiotic role of native voices in the text. Nor is it a matter of reflecting afterward upon what happens when "they read what we write."[32] It is instead a methodological practice sustained at the two sites of ethnography: the field and the page. In the field, this involves not reading over the natives' shoulders, so to speak, but standing alongside them, facing the action, and collectively reflecting on matters of mutual concern. On the page, it requires careful attention to the place of our informants' voices in both the narrated *and* the narrative frame, not by simply "giving them a voice" (itself a treacherous endeavor), but by taking seriously their arguments and their native categories: elaborating on them, theorizing with them, and questioning and departing from them as necessary—as one does with all theorists.[33]

Rethinking the place of the native voice within ethnography is, as Trouillot argues, a necessary part of breaking with the "savage slot" within which anthropology has traditionally operated. Anthropology was, and for the most part continues to be, predicated on the existence of a coherent category of "others" over which it can claim intellectual competency. This requires presuming that the study of Tiv mortuary practices, Mexican beauty pageants, and the lives of Swiss financiers are all collapsible and commensurable within the same slot. Trouillot understood that an important first step was to pluralize the native in order to break with the idea of anthropology as a discipline predicated on a coherent category that could hold "all of *them.*" The second step I would advocate, one about which Trouillot had less to say, is to think more carefully about the "otherness" of the anthropologist.[34] We must remember that the savage slot within which anthropology continues to operate is premised on a presumed relationship of alterity between a reified "them" and an equally reified "us."

This is not resolvable by simply calibrating the value of "insider" or "outsider" perspectives—for, as the slew of reflexive literature has demonstrated, anthropologists are always already positioned in complex ways to their informants and thus never truly insiders or outsiders in easy or uncomplicated ways.[35] Nor is it a matter of simply "studying up"—at least not in a way that depends on drawing a comforting relationship of otherness between the anthropologist and the reader, on the one hand, and the Swiss financiers, on the other. The point is, rather, to construct a premise—and a purpose—for anthropology based on something other than structural difference.[36]

Given the personal history discussed at the outset, my project has always been driven by an interest in the affinities I share with my informants rather than our differences. Although I experienced much of the cultural and linguistic estrangement of conducting fieldwork in a foreign context, I approached Guadeloupe as someone who was not foreign to its political terrain. As a result, while most commentators on the region have tended to represent the Antilles as states of exception and sites of political "otherness," I emphasize how Antillean struggles are emblematic of larger global politics. I say this not to privilege my own particular vantage point, but simply to assert the possibility and value of adopting an anthropological perspective that is not predicated on the study of otherness.[37] This book is thus purposefully framed not as a story about an exotic "them" but as a story about and for "us": those of us interested in the legacies of colonialism, those of us who wonder what forms of activism are necessary and possible in our contemporary moment, and those of us seeking, with anticipation, the political categories of the future. Embracing the virtues of anthropology's interstitial position, while remaining mindful of its pitfalls, I move across the terrains and methods of various disciplines, theorizing both native categories and projected universals alongside multiple interlocutors within and beyond academe. Throughout the text, I privilege both the concepts and the arguments of those I study and theorize closely alongside them. Indeed, I often find that my informants have the most useful perspectives for addressing the matters at hand, for they know all too well that the story of Hamlet—like that of Caliban—is a culturally specific tale, yet they are not ignorant as to why many have claimed otherwise.

In the early months of 2009, labor activists in the French overseas department of Guadeloupe launched the longest general strike in French history.[1] For a period of forty-four days, all schools and universities on this small Caribbean island were closed, major commerce was suspended, banks were shut down, government services discontinued, restaurants shuttered, hotel rooms emptied, public transportation came to a halt, barricades blocked major roadways, and gasoline distribution was interrupted throughout the island, forcing drivers to become pedestrians for over a month and a half. During this period, from January to March of 2009, Guadeloupeans took to the streets in unprecedented numbers, with as many as one hundred thousand people—one-fourth of the island's population—marching in support of the general strike.[2] Throughout the world, dramatic images flashed across television and computer screens of massive demonstrations, barricaded streets, overturned trash bins, and car carcasses in flames, with angry protesters chanting in the streets: "Guadeloupe is ours, not theirs! They cannot do as they please in our country!" Local observers claimed this was *du jamais vu*—something never before seen—and many long-standing nationalist activists declared that they could now die in peace because they had finally witnessed "the awakening" of the Guadeloupean people.

In some ways the 2009 strike can be interpreted as an echo of the rioting that shook the French *banlieues* in 2005, bringing the ethnic and economic disparities of the French Republic to worldwide attention.[3] It can also be seen as an early sign of the larger winds of discontent that would sweep the world during this period—from the *indignados* of Spain, to the demonstrators in Tahrir Square, to the young occupiers of Zuccotti Park, who would set up camp just a few months after the strike in the Antilles reached its resolution. Yet the mass strike in Guadeloupe also indexed a particular frustration, not just with global neoliberal economics, but with the modernist project of decolonization as experienced in the Antilles.

In 1946 the old sugar colonies, or *vieilles colonies*, of Guadeloupe, Martinique, Réunion, and French Guiana became overseas departments (*départements d'outre-mer*, or DOMs) of France—a status roughly similar that of Hawaii or Alaska in the United States.[4] This political status promised full integration into the French Republic, political representation in the National Assembly, the extension of French civic institutions, and a socioeconomic leveling with the citizens of mainland France. Yet, as their name suggests, the departments of the *outre-mer* remain marked as both geographically and categorically distinct: outside of, and separate from, the (unmarked) departments of the French Republic.

The grievances of the 2009 strike indexed the many social and economic disparities that persist between the mainland "hexagon" and the *outre-mer*, including steep price differentials in consumer goods, disproportionate rates of unemployment, and great variability in the cost, quality, and availability of public services. The strike also addressed the lingering social legacies of colonialism and slavery, particularly the racial hierarchies that persist on the island and the discrimination felt by local workers. The political platform for the movement was a list of 120 demands geared at offsetting these disparities by tackling what activists described as *la pwofitasyon*—a polyvalent Creole phrase that semantically unites profit, exploitation, and abusive power.[5] The strike focused on the high cost of living (*la vie chère*, or "the expensive life") and the lack of purchasing power in the French Antilles by questioning the abusive profit margins enjoyed by local employers and foregrounding the long histories that have shaped the Antilles as sites of disproportionate profit and exploitation.

Within a matter of weeks parallel strikes developed across all the overseas departments—marking the first time that these societies engaged in a shared political project since the moment of their incorporation in 1946.[6] French president Nicolas Sarkozy responded to the strikes by emphasizing the importance of the DOMs to the French Republic, repeatedly declaring that political independence was "out of the question." However, local activists stressed that independence was not their goal. As Raymond Gama, one of the spokespersons for the 2009 movement in Guadeloupe, explained:

> People like us, the little populations [*les petits peuples*] who were integrated into the big collectives [*les grands ensembles*], are currently in the process of creating new relationships. But we don't yet have the transcript of the future. . . . We are creating something that has already been promised but has

never been seen. Only we can imagine it because we feel it, we live it, even if we don't have the concepts with which to define it. . . . Right now the only slogan we have is independence. That is why we do not cling to it—because we know it is empty. You can have independence and be *dans la merde*.[7] That is why we are not committed to any slogan—we are committed to life. We want to transform our lives, even if it's under the French flag. The nationalists were guided by a single idea—not a desire for social change, but a desire for the nation. We do not cling to the nation. We want sovereignty but only if it comes with social transformation.

This book examines how contemporary labor activists in Guadeloupe wrestle with the conceptual arsenal of political modernity—including the seductive but constraining categories of freedom, sovereignty, nation, and revolution. As Gama's words suggest, contemporary political actors in the French Antilles are well aware of the limits of national independence: they realize that one can be independent and still be *dans la merde*. However, although they might be suspicious of nationhood, they still find themselves asserting a desire for sovereignty—even if it comes under the French flag. This book is thus both an ethnography of Guadeloupean labor activism and an exploration of how Caribbean political actors navigate the conflicting norms and attendant desires produced by the modernist projects of decolonization and postcolonial sovereignty. It examines the political and historical imaginaries that have emerged in the wake of postcolonial disenchantment and shows how, in an era of seemingly exhausted political options and vocabularies, contemporary activists strive to forge new visions for the future through a categorical apparatus inherited from the past.

As French citizens since 1848, Antilleans have long contested their colonial status through the search for full political and economic equality with mainland France, a search that culminated with departmentalization in 1946.[8] Although this political project might seem at odds with the generalized turn toward independence in the colonized world, it is important to remember that before the 1960s, various political forms—including the African Union and the West Indies Federation—were often imagined as plausible, and perhaps even preferable, alternatives to political independence, particularly for small Caribbean societies.[9] It was only after the 1960s that political independence was cemented as an intrinsic right and necessary historical stage for colonized populations throughout the world—as epitomized by the 1960 United Nations Declaration on the Granting of Independence to Colonial Countries and Peoples (see table 1).[10]

French Antillean actors were not immune to these global shifts. From the 1960s to the 1980s, numerous activists responded to the seductive call of modern sovereignty by attempting to develop a political project of national liberation. Drawing inspiration from other decolonization struggles—particularly in Algeria, Cuba, and Vietnam—Antillean activists both at home and in mainland France created new political organizations that sought to replicate the model of national liberation through armed struggle. However, by the end of the 1980s these actors faced a different landscape. Departmentalization had failed to fully transform their colonial economies or their marginal place in the French nation. Yet the promise of postcolonial sovereignty as a vehicle for economic development and prosperity for their Caribbean neighbors was also increasingly coming into question. Thus when Nicolas Sarkozy asserts in 2009 that independence is "out of the question," his words are less a warning for Antillean separatists than a recognition of the contemporary political horizon: one characterized by a profound disenchantment with the modernist projects of decolonization, postcolonial sovereignty, and national revolution.[11]

In this book I examine how, as the "national liberation" model lost its plausibility and promise, Guadeloupean militants found themselves reconceptualizing their anticolonial movement as a workers' movement. This new form of labor activism combined the institutional strength of the French labor tradition with the ideological and tactical legacies of anticolonialism, resulting in a new kind of postcolonial syndicalism.[12] The "post" in this postcolonial formation represents not just the temporal marker of a transformed colonial status, but also the mark of a transformed landscape of political possibility, distinct from a previous era of armed struggle and national revolution. The term "syndicalism," in turn, signals a particular approach to labor organizing that views labor struggles as sites for broader social transformation. As opposed to a more restrictive form of unionism that centers on workplace conditions, syndicalism seeks to transform the social fabric by utilizing labor conflicts as sites for broader political mobilization. The result is a social movement that infuses labor struggles with battles over historical memory, Creole-language use, racial and ethnic politics, and the search for alternative forms of political and economic autonomy. In the chapters that follow, I examine the political and historical repertoire of this movement, which includes the use of labor strikes, hunger strikes, memory walks, and the strategic use of media, rumor, gossip, and myth.

Three analytical goals drive this study. The first is to examine labor activism as a process of subject formation. I approach Antillean labor struggles not as the expression of a new political consciousness, but as a site for its development. As Raymond Gama suggests above, contemporary activists do not have "the transcripts of the future." They are in the process of prefiguring worlds that they cannot describe, much less guarantee, through the categories of modern sovereignty. I thus view the methods and tactics of labor activists not as simple means to clearly articulated ends, but as generative forms of prefigurative politics through which participants can imagine, conjure, and inhabit (even if only temporarily) alternative social and political forms.[13]

The success or failure of social movements has most often been assessed through the evaluation of material outcomes such as wage increases, policy changes, and other tangible and quantifiable metrics of success. However, as I show, even participants in "failed" or "disappointing" forms of social action are often transformed by their involvement. Political participation, even in a failed strike, conditions expectations of social struggle, shapes hopes and aspirations for the future, and influences the willingness to engage in collective action—both positively and negatively. I thus argue that the long-lasting effects of political struggle cannot be gauged through a simple measure of material and economic gains. Instead, they need to be more subtly rendered through a qualitative analysis of the affective and subjective transformations that characterize political life.

It has long been understood that the process of class formation encompasses emotional, sensorial, and corporeal experiences. In fact, some have argued that class consciousness and other forms of group affiliation are best understood as "structures of feeling," moral sentiments of shared exploitation, imagined solidarity, and collective readiness for action.[14] This book examines how these structures of feeling are forged through both the collective effervescence of mass action as well as through more quiet, intimate, and sensorial forms of political and historical engagement. Ultimately, I am concerned not with the organizational or institutional aspects of labor organizing, or even the material and economic gains of labor conflicts, but with the cultural, moral, and affective realms of political practice.[15]

The second goal of this book is to theorize the relationship between historical and political praxis. Building on a rich tradition of historically grounded Caribbeanist anthropology, I analyze how the relationships of the past—particularly those of slavery and slave resistance—are made salient to the political project of contemporary labor activists.[16] French government bureaucrats and mediators in local labor conflicts are often puzzled by Antillean activists' insistence on carrying out negotiations in Creole (thus creating the need for French translators), setting up drum circles outside labor courts, and consistently invoking the history of slavery and colonialism in the context of labor disputes. As one exasperated mediator sent from mainland France exclaimed: "How can we establish a dialogue when all they will talk about is colonialism and slavery?"

Local critics of the union, for their part, often contend that this form of dwelling on the past is unproductive, unhealthy, instrumentalist, and perhaps even harmful to the collective psyche and economic future of Guadeloupe. "We are not going to make any progress by talking incessantly about slavery," said one local bureaucrat. "No one is exclusively to blame for that history. Let's leave the past in the past!"[17] For striking workers and their leaders, however, the histories of colonialism and slavery provide relevant categories for interpreting the political and economic relationships of the present. These colonial histories offer both a language of contestation and a categorical framework for reimagining contemporary forms of economic and social inequality.

In the pages that follow I explore how the legacies of the past give shape to contemporary political action, as well as how historical narratives themselves become sites of political intervention. Throughout, my emphasis is not simply on the politics of history or memory, but on the process of historical production. Using the tools of critical historiography, I examine how labor activists operate as both actors and narrators of history.[18] I show how Antillean historical narratives have shifted over time in response to changing political contexts and how various Antillean actors have sought to craft postcolonial histories in the absence of postcolonial sovereignty.

The third, and perhaps most fundamental, goal of this book is to place Guadeloupean labor movements within the larger context of Caribbean postcolonial politics. Most studies of the French Antilles have tended to describe these societies as political oddities, exceptions to the rule of postcolonial independence, and sites of paradox and contradiction.[19] The project of departmentalization itself has often been viewed as paradoxical and irreconcilable with the strident anticolonial writings of its political architect, Aimé Césaire. This book challenges these narratives by placing French Caribbean politics within a larger historical and analytical frame.

The fact is that in the contemporary Caribbean, *most* societies are nonsovereign societies (see table 1). The political topography of the region reveals a plurality of political forms (territories, departments, protectorates, municipalities, commonwealths, etc.) and overlapping zones of affiliation (including the European Union, the British Commonwealth of Nations, and the Kingdom of the Netherlands) that defy the state-centered moral geography of a clearly bounded nation defined by a distinct land, people, and state.[20]

Table 1 Political Forms of the Caribbean

Jurisdiction	Political Status and Important Historical Dates	Currency
Netherlands:		
Aruba	Constituent country of the Kingdom of the Netherlands. Seceded from the Netherlands Antilles in 1986 with plans for independence, but independence was postponed indefinitely in 1994. Associate status in the European Union since 2007.	AFL
Curaçao	Constituent country of the Kingdom of the Netherlands since 2010. Former seat of the Netherlands Antilles central government. Associate status in the European Union since 2007.	ANG
Sint Maarten	Constituent country of the Kingdom of the Netherlands since 2010. Part of the Windward Islands territory within the Netherland Antilles from 1954 to 1983. Associate status in the European Union since 2007.	ANG
Bonaire	Special municipality of the Kingdom of the Netherlands since 2010. Formerly part of the Netherlands Antilles. Associate status in the European Union since 2007.	USD
Saba	Special municipality of the Kingdom of the Netherlands since 2010. Part of the Windward Islands territory within the Netherland Antilles from 1954 to 1983. Separate island territory within the Netherland Antilles from 1983 to 2010. Associate status in the European Union since 2007.	USD
Sint Eustatius	Special municipality of the Kingdom of the Netherlands since 2010. Part of the Windward Islands territory within the Netherland Antilles from 1954 to 1983. Separate island territory within the Netherland Antilles from 1983 to 2010. Associate status in the European Union since 2007.	USD
United Kingdom:		
Anguilla*	Overseas territory of the United Kingdom. Formerly part of the British Leeward Island colonial federation as the colony of Saint Cristopher-Nevis-Anguilla. Became a province of the West Indies Federation in 1958. Following the collapse of the federation, the British government reconstituted Saint Cristopher-Nevis-Anguilla as an associated state, but in 1971 Anguilla seceded as a separate dependency. British Overseas Territories Citizenship was granted in 2002. Associate status in the European Union since 2007.	XCD
Bermuda*	Overseas territory of the United Kingdom. Self-governing colony since 1968, independence rejected in 1995 referendum, British Overseas Territories Citizenship granted in 2002. Associate status in the European Union since 2007.	BMD
British Virgin Islands*	Overseas territory of the United Kingdom. Formerly part of the British Leeward Islands colonial federation. Separate colony status established in 1960, British Overseas Territories Citizenship granted in 2002. Associate status in the European Union since 2007.	USD

Table 1 (*continued*)

Jurisdiction	Political Status and Important Historical Dates	Currency
Cayman Islands*	Overseas territory of the United Kingdom. Was part of the West Indies Federation as a Jamaican dependency. When the federation dissolved in 1962, chose to remain a British dependency. British Overseas Territories Citizenship granted in 2002. Associate status in the European Union since 2007.	KYD
Montserrat*	Overseas territory of the United Kingdom. Formerly part of the British Leeward Islands colonial federation, in 1958 became a province of the West Indies Federation. In 1996, following volcanic eruptions, residents were granted residency and working rights in the UK. British Overseas Territories Citizenship granted in 2002. Associate status in the European Union since 2007.	XCD
Turks and Caicos	Overseas territory of the United Kingdom. Was part of the West Indies Federation as a Jamaican dependency. Became a Crown colony following Jamaica's independence in 1962. Administered by the governor of the Bahamas until Bahamian independence in 1973. Plans for independence in 1982 were later reversed. British Overseas Territories Citizenship was granted in 2002. In 2009 direct rule was imposed due to evidence of government corruption, home rule restored in 2012. Associate status in the European Union since 2007.	USD
France:		
Guadeloupe	Overseas department of France since 1946. Residents have been French citizens since 1848. Considered an outermost region of the European Union.	EUR
Guiana	Overseas department of France. French penal colony between 1852 and 1939; full political integration in 1946. Considered an outermost region of the European Union.	EUR
Martinique	Overseas department of France since 1946. Residents have been French citizens since 1848. Considered an outermost region of the European Union.	EUR
Saint Barthélemy	Overseas collectivity of France. Formerly part of the Overseas Department of Guadeloupe, seceded from Guadeloupe through a referendum in 2003 and became an overseas collectivity in 2007. Considered an outermost region of the European Union.	EUR
Saint Martin	Overseas collectivity of France. Formerly part of the Overseas Department of Guadeloupe, seceded from Guadeloupe through a referendum in 2003 and became an overseas collectivity in 2007. Considered an outermost region of the European Union.	EUR
USA:		
Puerto Rico	Unincorporated territory of the United States. Ceded to the United States by Spain in 1898. US citizenship granted in 1917. Commonwealth status established in 1952.	USD
US Virgin Islands*	Unincorporated territory of the United States, consisting of the islands of Saint Croix, Saint John, and Saint Thomas. Sold by Denmark to the US in 1916, US citizenship granted in 1927, territorial status established in 1954. Since 1968 the US Virgin Islands have elected their own governor.	USD

Table 1 (*continued*)

Jurisdiction	Political Status and Important Historical Dates	Currency
Independent:		
Haiti	Independent state. Became independent from France in 1804. Occupied by the United States 1915–1934 and 1994–1995. United Nations stabilization mission (MINUSTAH) has been in operation since 2004.	HTG
Dominican Republic	Independent state. Became independent from Spain in 1821. Merged with Haiti in 1822. Became independent from Haiti in 1844. Occupied by the United States 1916–1924.	DOP
Cuba	Independent state. Became independent from Spain in 1898. Occupied by the United States 1898–1902. Member of the Soviet-led Council for Mutual Economic Assistance (Comecon) from 1972 to 1991.	CUP
Jamaica	Independent state within the British Commonwealth since 1962.	JMD
Trinidad and Tobago	Independent state within the British Commonwealth since 1962.	TTD
Barbados	Independent state within the British Commonwealth since 1966.	BBD
Guyana	Independent state within the British Commonwealth since 1966.	GYD
The Bahamas	Independent state within the British Commonwealth since 1973.	BSD
Grenada	Independent state within the British Commonwealth since 1974. Invaded by the United States in 1983.	XCD
Suriname	Independent state. Became independent from the Netherlands in 1975. Occupied briefly by the United States in 1941.	SRD
Dominica	Independent state within the British Commonwealth since 1978.	XCD
Saint Lucia	Independent state within the British Commonwealth since 1979.	XCD
Saint Vincent and the Grenadines	Independent state within the British Commonwealth since 1979.	XCD
Antigua and Barbuda	Independent state within the British Commonwealth since 1981.	XCD
Belize	Independent state within the British Commonwealth since 1981.	BZD
Saint Kitts and Nevis	Independent state within the British Commonwealth since 1983.	XCD

Note: AFL, Aruban florin; ANG, Antillean guilder; BBD, Barbados dollar; BMD, Bermudian dollar; BSD, Bahamian dollar; BZD, Belize dollar; CUP, Cuban peso; DOP, Dominican peso; EUR, Euro; GYD, Guyanese dollar; HTG, Haitian gourde; JMD, Jamaican dollar; KYD, Caymanian dollar; SRD, Suriname dollar; TTD, Trinidad and Tobago dollar; USD, US dollar; XCD, East Caribbean dollar.
* On UN list of non-self-governing territories.

Places like Guadeloupe, Puerto Rico, the Virgin Islands, Anguilla, Aruba, Bermuda, Bonaire, Cayman Islands, Curaçao, Saba, Saint Barthélemy, Saint Martin, and the Turks and Caicos all fall outside of the legal definitions of either independent states or formal colonies. In addition, the Caribbean also holds a large number of non-sovereign enclaves: military bases, privately owned islands, semiautonomous tourist resorts, free-trade zones, tax havens, wildlife preserves, satellite launching stations, detention centers, penal colonies, floating data centers, and other spaces of suspended, subcontracted, usurped, or imposed foreign jurisdiction that challenge the principles of bounded territorial authority associated with the Westphalian order.[21] I use the concept of non-sovereignty to describe this topography of power and to highlight the political relationships that characterize the region as a whole. Although the discourse of pathos surrounding non-independent societies has traditionally severed them analytically from theorizations of the nominally independent Caribbean, I would like to suggest, borrowing from Antonio Benítez-Rojo, that we can imagine the Caribbean region itself as a non-sovereign archipelago—a "discontinuous conjunction" within which certain socioeconomic patterns of constrained sovereignty can be said to "repeat themselves."[22] Representations of non-sovereign societies as sites of paradox and exception have only served to occlude these repetitions, masking the larger sociohistorical processes that shape the question of sovereignty in the region as a whole.[23] Moreover, these exceptionalist claims inadvertently lead to a view of the Caribbean as a site of problematic sovereignty, rather than to an exploration of sovereignty itself as a categorical problem.

We Have Never Been Sovereign

As Dipesh Chakrabarty has argued, the concepts and categories of political modernity and contemporary social analysis are reflective less of the concrete historical realities of Europe than of an abstract "hyperreal Europe."[24] That is, terms such as *freedom, democracy, revolution,* and even *modernity* and *universalism* itself speak not just to a European experience but more precisely to what Europe claimed and sought to be. These terms need to be understood as part of larger claims, debates, and arguments about the social, rather than as unbiased social descriptors. Trouillot names these master categories "North Atlantic Universals"—a label that indexes both their provenance and their pretensions.[25] These terms are inherently prescriptive, for they are embedded not just in sociohistorical contexts but in particular political and moral projects. As such, they do not seek to simply describe the world but to constrain its possibilities. As Talal Asad argues, these are the necessary terms in which "modern living is required to take place, and nonmodern peoples are invited to assess their adequacy."[26]

Such is the case with sovereignty. Our foundational theories of sovereignty are rooted in provincial debates and cosmological projections of power and authority. This includes the battle between divine right and popular sovereignty, the shift from the "manifest destiny" of sovereign imperial expansion to the universal right of "self-determination," and the more recent mutation of sovereignty from a right to autochthonous rule to a measureable capacity of governance—easily brought into question if a particular state or government is deemed morally, politically, or financially bankrupt.

My main concern here is the emergence of a particular form of postcolonial sovereignty as a normative ideal. I argue that we need to examine how the postwar project of decolonization operated similarly to other projects of political modernity, such as modernization and secularization. Like secularization—which as a project of government produced the idea of religions as discrete and transhistorical spheres of life—I argue that decolonization also operated as part of a larger project that sought to naturalize the idea of nation-states as discrete and necessary units of political and economic organization, while silencing and foreclosing other forms and alignments. It should be remembered that even at the height of the decolonization era, multiple political and economic formulas were the object of sustained debate and contemplation. And even today the nation-state is just one of many political forms operating throughout the world.

The political formations of the Americas have long challenged the dominant paradigms of modern sovereignty. These territories became polities at the precise moment in which the theoretical foundations of modernity were being drafted in the West and upended in its colonies. As a result, the Americas have long served as both laboratory and foil for the modern project. The United States itself—ostensibly the Americas' first postcolony—charted a political project that, from its inception, allowed for what we have now come to know as "graduated" or "variegated" forms of sovereignty.[27] This includes the tribal sovereignty of Native American populations, the federalist system of states' rights, and the multiple arrangements of stratified inclusion through which non-national populations throughout the world (from the Virgin Islands to American Samoa) have been integrated as associated states, unincorporated territories, "disembodied shades," and other legal terms of art.[28] This political project troubles the tenets of a singular, territorially bound political power based on a social contract of civic equality.

In a different vein, the political project of the Haitian Revolution—which many see as the foundational charter of sovereignty in the Caribbean—also brings into question our understandings of political sovereignty. The rebellious slaves' initial demands were freedom from the whip and more days to work their provision grounds.[29] It was only after colonial forces and local planters refused to recognize the rebels' political capacity that a slave revolt became a national insurrection. Even by 1801, when Touissaint Louverture issued Haiti's first constitution, the project envisioned was not that of a sovereign state but of an autonomous polity, "free and French," within the larger imperial formation of France.[30] France, however, refused to reckon with this novel arrangement, and Napoleon sent a military expedition to arrest Toussaint, end the revolutionary war, and restore slavery in the colonies—precipitating the final break. Since then, Haiti has remained constrained by the international community's refusal to recognize its modern revolution and its sovereign status. Caught in its own double bind of sovereignty, it was forced to pay indemnities to the French by securing massive loans from French banks that crippled its economy—effectively ensuring that its political sovereignty would come at the expense of its economic power.[31] It is surely not coincidental that the first black republic of the Caribbean is today emblematic of the failures, rather than the possibilities, of modern sovereignty in the region.

The Problems of Freedom and Sovereignty

In framing sovereignty as a problem, I draw on Thomas Holt's seminal book *The Problem of Freedom*, which examines how emancipation constituted an inherent problem for Caribbean societies. "Measured against the goal of bringing new self-determination, justice, and dignity to former slaves, emancipation had failed," Holt writes. This failure, he argues, was not a question of poor judgment or bad policy. Rather, it was rooted in the fact that "something was amiss in the very project of emancipation, in the very premises on which it was founded."[32] Saidiya Hartman has similarly argued that the failures of Reconstruction in the United States need to be located "in the very language of persons, rights, and liberties" of liberal individualism that underpinned the moral project of emancipation.[33] Both Hartman and Holt demonstrate that slavery—as a system and an ideology—was supplanted by new coercive forms of free labor that required cultural transformations of desires and aspirations, and the formation of a social environment capable of converting the formerly enslaved into a reliable working class. This was both the problem and the *project* of Freedom.[34]

The problem/project of postcolonial sovereignty has similarly entailed the advancement of a particular set of aspirations, attachments, ideals, and desires. The freedom of emancipation became equated with the freedom of the market, the right to work, and the naturalization of a desire for material rewards from toil. In a similar fashion, postcolonial sovereignty became equated with the right to a passport, a flag, a stamp, a coin, and the formation of a native state. It also became associated with a restrictive ideology that suggests that national borders can and should serve as containers for homogenous content. This has led to an emphasis on the policing of "national identity" at the expense of other social projects and to the presumption that those who lie outside the nation's fabricated borders—or those who disrupt the homogeneity of its contents—are not only alien to the national project but a threat to its stability.

As Sidney Mintz and others have shown, Caribbean peasantries responded to the problem of freedom by creating alternative spaces to the plantation system, building upon maroon traditions, the use of provision grounds, and other alternative forms of social and economic life that were either marginal or at odds with the system of slavery.[35] The postemancipation problem/project of freedom consisted of eliminating these alternatives, in order to channel the formerly enslaved into the emerging wage economy. This entailed the deployment of both legal constraints (vagrancy statutes, black codes, contract systems, apprenticeship systems, and anti-enticement laws) and moral compulsions to enter the wage system—the latter operating through the promotion of ideas of responsibility, self-reliance, and industriousness.[36] One can easily draw connections between this project of freedom and the postcolonial project of sovereignty, which itself produced a series of institutions, most notably the UN, and moral compulsions—including the establishment of self-determination as a right, goal, norm, and ideal. It also created a system of international debt and finance through which to "develop," "modernize," and "assist" emerging nations in their efforts at refashioning themselves into sovereign moderns.

Given these connections, as Holt and others have argued, the problem of sovereignty was met in the Caribbean with a distinct feeling of déjà vu. Indeed, I contend that throughout the Caribbean the problems of freedom and sovereignty are parallel and entwined: both have hinged upon abstract promises of codified equality accompanied by a careful escort into codified systems of intrinsic inequality. In fact, it is difficult to say where one project ends and the other begins. This is perhaps most obvious in the case of Haiti, where both individual citizens and the nation-state were simultaneously ushered into the free-market system of wage labor and the sovereign system of national debt. Haiti, however, is not unique; throughout the Caribbean the project of sovereignty and the problem of freedom have been entwined, with the former often arriving as a solution to the unresolved contradictions of the latter. Indeed, for many Caribbean populations decolonization came with the hope of finally attaining the promises of freedom that had been held out since the moment of abolition.

In the Antilles, the problem of freedom came bundled with the problem of inclusion. In 1794 slavery was abolished throughout the French colonial empire—partly as an effort to contain the emerging Haitian Revolution—and former slaves were declared (in principle at least) citizens of the republic.[37] As a result, French colonial administrators were charged with extending universal rights to the colonies while simultaneously ensuring the persistence of racialized and exploitative labor regimes that provided economic benefit to the nation. To assure the continuation of the plantation economy, colonial administrators created forms of coercion, compulsion, and surveillance that effectively forced the newly emancipated to continue laboring on their plantations with the promise, if not the actual disbursement, of monetary reward. This produced a form of "colonial universalism" wherein freedom and inclusion were extended in theory but denied, deferred, and constrained in practice.[38]

Colonial citizens in Guadeloupe contested their unequal inclusion by appropriating the emerging language of republican rights and strategically wielding their access to the legal regimes that constrained them but also recognized them as French citizens. As Laurent Dubois argues, these actions effectively transformed republican ideas on both sides of the Atlantic.[39] However, the new "colonial universalism" that emerged also laid the groundwork for the forms of governance that would characterize the French imperial nation-state into the nineteenth and twentieth centuries.[40] Like the postemancipation colonial administrators who had to extend freedom while maintaining colonial forms of exploited labor, the twentieth-century French government was tasked with the project of extending political equality while sustaining the socioeconomic inequalities that condition the place of the Antilles in the French Republic. Decolonization, and its disappointments, thus produced as much déjà vu in the French Antilles as in other parts of the postcolonial Caribbean.

In the pages that follow, I examine how contemporary activists continue to wield their access to French legal forms and institutions (notably labor laws and syndical traditions) while simultaneously pushing at the limits of their political arrangement. I argue that like the newly emancipated slaves—who worked both within and against the constraints of the project of freedom—contemporary Antillean actors are working within and against the constraints of postcolonial sovereignty. It is for this reason that I describe their political project as the search for a *non*-sovereign future. I see this as an effort to break free from the epistemic binds of political modernity, even while still being compelled to think through its normative categories.

Organization of the Chapters

This book is organized into two parts. Part I offers a political history of Guadeloupe and an examination of the shifting landscape of historical production. Chapter 1, "The Wake of Disenchantment," discusses how different political generations in the French Antilles have sought to address the political imperatives of their time. I analyze the oft-misunderstood project of political integration championed by Césaire, the rise of anticolonial nationalism following departmentalization, and the formation of a new postcolonial syndicalism from the 1970s onward. Chapter 2, "Strategic Entanglement," asks how and why contemporary labor activists theorize their movement through the history of slave resistance. I examine how marronage has served as a metaphor for thinking through the possibilities of sovereignty, autonomy, and self-determination in the Caribbean and show how its narrative contours have changed over time in keeping with the shifting political landscape.

Part II provides a close ethnographic analysis of the political tactics, historiographic practices, and semiotic repertoires of contemporary labor activism in Guadeloupe. Chapter 3, "Life on the Piquet," examines how labor strikes are both lived and theorized by Guadeloupean activists. I discuss the political potential of the strike as viewed by both workers and leaders and trace the afterlife of one striking community in order to examine what happens to the relationships forged during the strike once workers leave the piquet.

Chapter 4, "Public Hunger," centers on a hunger strike that was launched by an imprisoned labor activist of East Indian descent. I examine how union leaders strategically navigate multiple terrains and tactics of struggle, leveraging legal and mediatic tactics along with the use of rumor, gossip, and myth. I also discuss how this episode brought to the fore the otherwise rarely discussed history of indentured labor and the contemporary place of *Indiens* in the French Antilles. Chapter 5, "The Route of History," explores how labor activists tackle the problem of history in the French

Antilles through the production of memory walks. I argue that these events reconfigure the natural landscape as both site and source of historical evidence and give a new "route" and purpose to the events of the past through a sensorial engagement with the landscape. During these events, historical knowledge is not transmitted through discursive engagement alone, but also through sensorial and material experiences. As a result, the past is both "lived" and "felt." The final chapter, "Hope and Disappointment," focuses on the general strike of 2009. I argue that the general strike stirred collective hopes, leading to unprecedented forms of political engagement, but it also led to widespread disappointment when it failed to meet the new expectations it itself generated. I caution, however, that the disappointment felt by those who participated in the strike should not be read as a simple sign of political failure, but as evidence of the possibilities and expectations that can arise in the wake of disenchantment.

PART I

Historical Legacies

ONE

The Wake of Disenchantment

On April 17, 2008, one of the Antilles' most famous literary and political figures, Aimé Césaire, passed away at the age of ninety-four in a small hospital on his native island of Martinique. Throughout the world, Césaire was known for his literary masterpieces and strident anticolonial writings, most notably *Notebook of a Return to a Native Land*, *A Tempest*, and *Discourse on Colonialism*. In the French Antilles, however, Césaire was equally known for his political legacies. Aside from serving forty-eight years in the French National Assembly and fifty-six years as mayor of Fort-de-France, Martinique's capital, Césaire was also, infamously, one of the principal architects of the 1946 *loi d'assimilation*, which transformed the French Antilles into overseas departments (DOMs) of France. The commemorations surrounding his death were a testament to this profound and complex legacy. Statesmen, dignitaries, literati, and popular masses alike gathered at his memorial service—the first French state funeral held outside the hexagon—and during his four-day public wake, thousands of mourners flooded the streets of Fort-de-France to bid farewell and offer their thanks to "Papa Césaire," Martinique's version of the "father of the nation."

As with the death of any father figure, Césaire's passing became a moment of reckoning. The "sons of Césaire"—even the self-declared "rebel sons," such as the *creolité* writers who had long decried his politics—suddenly found themselves forced to come to terms with the legacies of Martinique's great man.[1] Novelists, poets, scholars, and politicians offered up personal reflections asserting the admiration they felt for his lyrical mastery and uncompromising commitment to his homeland, all the while expressing ambivalence, if not disdain, toward his political project.[2] At a public event in Paris, for example, celebrated Martinican novelist Patrick Chamoiseau paid poignant tribute but described himself as Césaire's *fils d'erreur* (son by mistake). Chamoiseau has often puzzled over why Césaire never advocated political independence. That night in Paris, as if by way of exculpatory explanation, Chamoiseau exclaimed that if Césaire had belonged to *his* generation, surely he would have been an *indépendantiste*.

Chamoiseau's commentary recognizes that the political possibilities Césaire could entertain were conditioned by the political and historical moment he inhabited. Born in 1913, Césaire was part of a larger cohort of Francophone poets and politicians—including Léopold Senghor (1906–2001) from Senegal and Léon Damas (1912–78) from Guiana—that came of age at the height of the French colonial project. This generation experienced firsthand both the dehumanizing effects of the colonial enterprise and the liberatory promises of its proclaimed end. For them, colonialism represented something that could be toppled, transformed, and perhaps even overcome in the short run, and decolonization was still an open question, to which national independence had yet to emerge as a definitive answer. Césaire's immediate successors—the generation of Frantz Fanon (1925–61) and Édouard Glissant (1928–2011)—also held faith in the possibility of overcoming colonialism—though for intellectuals like Fanon, only a full-scale revolution would do. Despite their differences, however, these various political actors—from Césaire up to Chamoiseau—all imagined colonialism as a temporary stage rather than a lasting condition.

Today's activists inhabit a radically different landscape. They realize that political integration will not erase the disparities created by colonialism, but they do not share Chamoiseau's faith in the possibility (or necessity) of independence. For them, the future is once again an open question. In this chapter, I examine the history of Antillean activism from Césaire's generation to the present. I show how succeeding cohorts have crafted social projects shaped by the imperatives of their times and how contemporary actors struggle to develop new political projects in the wake of their own disenchantment.

The Search for Equality

From a contemporary vantage point, the Antillean project of political integration might seem like an anomaly within postcolonial history.[3] But when first charted, for many, departmentalization represented the logical outcome of a century-long quest to end Antilleans' unequal inclusion.[4] Although France had extended citizenship to the Caribbean colonies after the final abolition of slavery in 1848, Antillean residents had remained "citizen-subjects" for over one hundred years, lacking democratic representation and full access to the political rights and economic entitlements enjoyed by the citizens of mainland France.[5] The early extension of citizenship provided black and mulatto elites with access to the French educational system and entry into civil service. But economic power remained firmly under the control of the white planter class.[6]

By the early 1900s, Antilleans increasingly began to demand full civic and juridical inclusion as a way of gaining greater economic and legislative protection. Their demands included agrarian reform to break the monopoly of the planter class and the replacement of colonial governors with French prefects, in hopes of stemming the widespread corruption and racial discrimination characteristic of the time.[7] Placed in its proper context, the search for assimilation can thus be viewed as an Antillean civil rights movement comparable to that of African Americans in the United States, wherein the nation's marginalized citizens contested their unequal political and civic inclusion.

The main constituency that opposed integration was the béké planter class, which feared that extending French labor rights and legislation to Antillean workers would spell trouble for the sugar economy.[8] Since the eighteenth century, the békés had repeatedly threatened to break with France whenever French policy appeared to impinge upon their economic dominance. In 1794, for example, the Martinican plantocracy "escaped" the reforms of the French Revolution (including the abolition of slavery and the infamous guillotine) by coming under the jurisdiction of the British.[9] Planters in Guadeloupe attempted a similar move but were thwarted by an alliance of white republicans, free people of color, and insurgent slaves.[10] In 1946, as departmentalization was being debated, the white elites openly discussed joining the United States to avoid the consequences of integration—a threat that carried with it the possible importation of Jim Crow legislation.[11]

For Césaire's cohort of anticolonial intellectuals, meanwhile, France posed a radical alternative to the United States, which was then gaining ascendancy as an imperial white-supremacist nation. Immediately following the Second World War—which France fought with great assistance from Antillean and African soldiers—debates raged in the metropole over how to politically and socially transform the French Empire. Numerous forms of political organization were entertained, including formulas of local self-rule that would allow for the creation of the French Union: a multiethnic federation of over ten million citizens, of whom only four million would reside in the French mainland.[12] It was partly the promise of this multicultural, decentered France that drove Césaire's generation to embrace departmentalization.[13] In addition, the postwar years appeared to be an opportune moment of political experimentation. As a new coalition of leftist parties took control of the French government they unleashed an ambitious project of reconstruction that included nationalizing banks and industries, creating extensive state welfare programs, establishing national health care, and extending trade union rights and women's suffrage—all in the hopes of forging a new social democratic model.[14]

The possibilities afforded by a leftist government in France, combined with the legacies of a century of colonial citizenship and the plantocracy's threats of either succession or US annexation, made full integration the most promising vehicle not only for decolonization, but for the larger project of social justice in the Antilles. The report (drafted by Césaire) that accompanied the bill for departmentalization stated explicitly that the goal was not abstract equality, but a concrete *egalité de salaire* (wage equality). This, together with the extension of the nationalization efforts already under way in France, was viewed as the only viable means of dismantling the local plantocracy.[15]

Departmentalization was not without its critics in the French government. Some argued, using Montesquieu's climatic theory of race, that French laws were ill-suited for the residents of the tropics.[16] Césaire countered this by strategically drawing on Montesquieu's denunciation of slavery and his insistence on equality under the law. [17] Césaire stressed that the goal of departmentalization was *égalisation* (equalization)—which he saw as a search for equality, not a search for sameness.[18]

Still, Césaire was not oblivious to the pitfalls of assimilation. In an interview with filmmaker Patrice Louis, he explained that he was initially reticent to undertake the project of assimilation because of its undertones of racial and cultural superiority. "Assimilation means to become similar," he stated, "but I felt that for us, Martinicans, the descendants of Africans, that type of assimilation is a form of alienation. And I could not be in favor of alienation." For Césaire, the *loi d'assimilation*, as it was titled by the French Communists, was a misnomer. "What the people really wanted," he argued, "was equality with the French. So to speak of assimilation was to deploy an inappropriate terminology." Césaire, a renowned poet and wordsmith oft lauded for his ability to reshape and transform the French language, decided to tackle this terminological problem by coining a new term.[19] "I told myself, 'OK, then, I will ask for what you call assimilation but what I call departmentalization.' The word did not exist in French," he asserts. "It was I who imposed it."[20]

Césaire's *réforme vocabulaire* carried the promise of potentially refashioning the nature of the French departmental system itself. This promise, however, quickly faded. Soon after the departmentalization law was passed in 1946, the left-dominated government was replaced by a succession of mainly centrist coalitions, and the efforts to build the French Union lost impetus. At the same time, throughout the world decolonization became narrowly construed as the search for political and economic independence—rather than the project of "equalization" that Césaire had championed.

The 1946 law officially transformed the former colonies of Guadeloupe, Martinique, Guiana, and Réunion into full departments of France, and decreed that their political systems would be equal to those of the metropolitan departments—but for exceptions specified by law. This final clause opened the door to precisely the kind of "colonial" or "tropical" exceptionalism that Césaire had sought to prevent. For example, unlike mainland prefects, the overseas prefects that replaced the colonial governors were responsible for defense against possible foreign invasion; they could thus declare a state of siege, deploy military forces, and expel foreigners. They could also modify tariffs and taxes and fix certain prices, and they had "implicit diplomatic attributions" that gave them authority over relations with neighboring states.[21] These exceptional powers gave rise to enduring conflicts between the prefects and the general councils, with local elected members continually demanding greater administrative authority and autonomy.[22]

In the end, what resulted was a form of *assimilation assouplie* (flexible, relaxed integration), wherein most French laws were adapted, or simply deferred, for the DOMs. As a result, social security benefits, pensions, family assistance, and even the minimum wage remained lower in the DOMs than in the mainland late into the twentieth century.[23] This legislative "relaxation" was strategically leveraged by local employers who to this day often refuse to abide by national labor standards, claiming that these must be "adapted" to the special circumstances of the DOMs. The French labor protections and economic guarantees that had been sought through departmentalization thus arrived only partially, and what were once described as "disparities" became increasingly justified as "adaptations."[24] Meanwhile, the cost of living in the DOMs soared as the price of food, clothing, and other imports steadily climbed, due to high taxes and the monopolies of local merchants.[25]

By 1956, just ten years after departmentalization, Césaire conceded that the project of departmentalization had perhaps been naive in attempting to abolish inequality without eradicating the colonial regime itself.[26] One could, he argued, read departmentalization as a "ruse" on the part of the colonizer: an offer of abstract and ultimately unattainable equality meant to quell separatist sentiment. But, Césaire speculated, perhaps in the end "le ruse de l'histoire" would reveal the naiveté of the colonized as ruse, and the ruse of the colonizer as naiveté.[27] Indeed, it was only after the DOMs achieved full juridical inclusion that a new nationalist sentiment was stirred in the French Antilles—fueled in part by massive disappointment in the failed promises of departmentalization.

The Rise of Postcolonial Nationalism

Antillean residents initially celebrated the attainment of departmental status. In little more than a decade, however, the political landscape shifted dramatically. By 1959 the political Right had returned to power under the rule of Charles de Gaulle and the project of the French Union was abandoned, giving way to a new era of decolonization through independence. The outbreak of the Algerian War in 1954 and the Cuban Revolution of 1959 gave rise to new political scripts of self-determination that were markedly distinct from the separatist project once championed by the békés. By 1960 the United Nations would adopt Resolution 1514, the Declaration on the Granting of Independence to Colonial Countries and Peoples, which defined self-determination as a fundamental human right. This shifting context—which would also impose a new form of nationalist ideology as an integral element of the decolonization project—gave new shape to the political and social demands emerging from the Antilles.

The disappointments with departmentalization were felt almost immediately once Antilleans began pouring into mainland France to study, work, and engage in the process of rebuilding after the war. As famously documented in Frantz Fanon's searing *Black Skin, White Masks* (1952), Antillean migrants quickly confronted experiences that belied the promises of French universalism and inclusion.[28] Although full French citizens, they were the targets of racial discrimination and soon developed strong affinities with colonial "foreigners"—particularly African and North African students—thus becoming increasingly attuned to liberation struggles in the remaining French colonies, most notably Algeria.

Antillean residents who remained on the islands also grew frustrated with the slow application of French legislation and quickly realized that the shift from colonial governor to republican prefect would have little impact on the rampant political and economic corruption of the planter class—which proved surprisingly resilient to both juridical and economic shifts in the postwar era. The agrarian reform that Césaire had hoped would weaken the békés' monopoly served only to strengthen their dominance, as planters began taking advantage of French farm restructuring initiatives to sell off their less profitable sugar holdings to real estate developers, mechanizing their production to reduce their payrolls, and reinvesting their capital in the import-export industry.[29] Through this process, former agricultural lands were rapidly transformed into airports and shopping centers as agricultural production steadily gave way to a service-based economy centered on tourism, commerce, and a bloated government bureaucracy. The impressive infrastructure that arose after departmentalization—schools, roads, hospitals, and shopping malls—provided an impressive facade of prosperity for the underlying economic stagnation that ensued.[30]

As a result, the French Antilles saw a sharp rise in social conflict during the 1950s and 1960s. In 1959 a traffic accident involving a white *pied noir* recently resettled from Algeria to Martinique and a black Martinican on a motor scooter escalated into a violent encounter, drawing a crowd of hundreds that was then violently dispersed by French CRS riot police. The event was followed by three days of unrest in Fort-de-France; protesters looted and burned white-owned businesses, and French gendarmes shot and killed three young Martinicans.[31] In March 1967 a similar incident occurred in Guadeloupe when a *pied noir* shoe-store owner unleashed his dog upon a black cobbler who had set up his workbench near the store. This provoked several days of massive rioting, with demonstrators burning down the shop owner's vehicle and property, leading to widespread police violence directed at Guadeloupeans.[32] There were also numerous labor strikes and protests, accompanied by increasing calls for industrialization and economic reform to quell the tide of rising unemployment.

During this period of unrest, the French government sought to calm the growing dissatisfaction by promoting migration to the mainland. In 1963, it created the Bureau for the Development of Migration from Overseas Departments (Bureau pour le développement des migrations intéressant les départements d'outre-mer), popularly known by its acronym, BUMIDOM, which recruited over 160,000 workers from the DOMs before it was shut down in 1981. The BUMIDOM program aimed to stabilize the political and economic climate of the DOMs, while also addressing the purported "demographic boom" of the *outre-mer* population.[33] Antillean migrants were viewed as a cheap labor force that could fill the low-paid public sector jobs which foreign immigrants were unable to secure and mainland French citizens actively avoided. Although BUMIDOM recruitment materials promised advanced job training and high-paying government jobs, most migrants were offered little assistance upon arrival. The promised job training consisted mostly of acculturation lessons, including French language courses, domestic training for the women (consisting of lessons in how to cook, clean, and care for children according to French standards), and vocational training for the men to prepare them for work in heavy construction and instill in them "the French work ethic."[34]

Many BUMIDOM migrants were disappointed with the working conditions they faced. The French government supplied only a one-way ticket, however, so most of them settled permanently in France, quickly filling low-level janitorial and service positions in government agencies, including the postal service, transportation department, public hospitals, and sanitation. They also found positions in the booming construction industry, helping to build (and eventually inhabit) the new low-income housing projects (*Habitations à loyer modéré*, or HLM) that began dotting the Parisian suburbs in the 1950s.[35]

In the Antilles this cohort of migrants is often described as "the BUMIDOM generation." Many of them became politically involved with mainland labor unions and civic associations, initially working to improve migrants' reception and living conditions in France. Their emphasis, however, quickly turned towards improving working conditions back home in order to put an end to organized migration from the Caribbean and to shut down BUMIDOM, which had itself become a symbol of the unfulfilled promises of integration.[36] In fact, BUMIDOM offices were seized and ransacked by Antillean activists in May 1968, and in both the Antilles and among migrants in France, "À bas le BUMIDOM" became a central slogan for change.

During the same period, as Antillean migrants increasingly headed to the metropole in search of education and employment, bureaucrats from mainland France were increasingly arriving in the DOMs to fill positions as administrators, civil servants, technocrats, and cadres in the enlarged government bureaucracy. In contrast to the BUMIDOM migrants, bureaucrats from mainland France were offered numerous enticements to move to the DOMs, including a 40 percent wage increase, paid vacations, housing subsidies, and other benefits geared at offsetting the "hardships" of residing overseas.[37] These initiatives led to a massive influx of French bureaucrats—often described by locals as *chases primes* (benefits chasers). Césaire decried this combination of government-sponsored outward migration of young Antillean workers and inward migration of French *fonctionnaires* as "genocide by substitution."

During this period, Césaire and other local intellectuals increasingly began to express concern over the cultural and psychological consequences of political integration. Meanwhile, a new nationalist movement began to develop among students and workers in mainland France. Influenced by the Cuban and Algerian revolutions, the rise of Pan-Africanism, and the political climate leading up to the May 1968 movement in Paris, Antillean students in France came together under both new and reinvigorated student associations such as the General Association of Guadeloupean Students (Association générale des étudiants guadeloupéen, AGEG), the Association of Martinican Students (Association générale des étudiants martiniquais, AGEM), and the Union of Guianese Students (Union des étudiants guyanais, UEG). These organizations were closely tied to Catholic youth groups that had developed in France during the early stages of postwar migration, most notably the Federation of Antillean and Guianese Catholic Students (Federation antillo-guianese des étudiants catholiques, FAGEC).[38] Together, these groups founded a new spate of journals—including *Alizés*, *Trait d'union*, *Patriote guadeloupéen*, and *Matouba*—that detailed the difficulties émigrés encountered in France, the economic problems plaguing the DOMs, and the new political movements unfolding across Africa, Asia, and the Caribbean.

Although this nationalist current was sparked in the diaspora, it did not flourish in isolation from Antillean communities back home. The hexagon-based student activists of the AGEG, AGEM, and UEG frequently returned to the Antilles, particularly during summer vacations, when they would often work as volunteers among agricultural workers and carry out Maoist-style surveys (*enquêtes*) to better understand the conditions of life and political predispositions of workers back home.[39] This led to the formation of political organizations that bridged the Antilles and the diaspora, such as the Organization of Young Martinican Anticolonialists (Organisation de la jeunesse anticolonialiste de la Martinique, OJAM) and the Guadeloupean National Organization Group (Groupe d'organisation nationale de la Guadeloupe, GONG).

Both OJAM and GONG had strong ties to the revolutionary forces in Algeria; some participants had abandoned their military service, refusing to serve on the French side of the Algerian war. They also had strong ties to the Fidel Castro government in Cuba, where some had trained alongside Nicaraguan Sandinistas and other insurgent groups. Lastly, they were also strongly influenced by Maoist political thought, which at the time was seen as more favorable to anticolonial politics than French Communist doctrine.

French government officials began to suspect—with reason—that the influences of both Algeria and Cuba, combined with the rising social tensions in the Antilles, could lead to a nationalist uprising. They turned to a 1960 ordinance authorizing overseas prefects to dismiss and expel from their departments any civil servant who criticized French policies or threatened the "territorial integrity" of France. Under this ordinance, the French state carried out heavy surveillance of suspected activists, dismissed militants in government positions (including numerous educators), censored radical publications (such as the student magazines mentioned above), and forced numerous activists into exile, including the novelist Édouard Glissant, who at the time belonged to the Antillean-Guainese Front (Front antillo-guyanais, FAG), which had been banned by the French government in 1961 for advocating an independent federation for the French Antilles.

As a result, nationalist activity during this period became increasingly criminalized. In 1963, OJAM members were arrested for distributing a manifesto that called for political independence and for putting up posters with the slogan "La Martinique aux Martiniquais" (Martinique for Martinicans) on the walls of public buildings, schools, and churches in Fort-de-France during the anniversary of the 1959 riots.[40] Thirteen of the manifesto's eighteen signatories were tried in mainland France and sentenced to prison terms ranging from ten months to three years. In May 1967, police opened fire on demonstrators during a GONG-supported labor strike among construction workers in Pointe-à-Pitre, leading to three days of rioting and police violence that left numerous Guadeloupeans dead.[41] In the days that followed, activists and militants were rounded up, arrested, and charged with treason. Eighteen of these activists were tried for political crimes before the Court of State Security (Cour de sûreté de l' état) in mainland France and sentenced to long prison sentences for their presumed involvement in the nationalist struggle.[42]

The Politics of Cultural Nationalism

In the face of state repression, the nationalist movement that had emerged among Antillean students and workers in mainland France splintered. In Guadeloupe, GONG militants were divided over how to proceed after the imprisonment of numerous leaders in the wake of the 1968 trials. At the time the GONG was a self-described "propaganda movement" focused on drafting revolutionary texts that would inspire "agitation." Its goal was to stir political discontent in the hope of inspiring a nationalist revolution. But after the 1968 trials, a small group, which would become known as the démissionnaires (resigners) of the GONG, refocused its energies on forming a new populist movement.

In the tradition of the Maoist movements of the time, they set out to politicize the peasantry, carrying out literacy campaigns in the countryside and setting up night schools where they taught agricultural workers basic reading and math skills. They worked with cane cutters to obtain the extension of the local minimum wage (which at the time was still 20 percent less than on the mainland, and not applied to agricultural workers) and they helped small-scale peasants restructure their compensation, which until then had been based not on the amount of cane delivered but on its *sucricité*, that is, the amount of sugar it yielded.[43]

The other currents within the GONG disparaged these efforts as "economistic," arguing that the organization's priority should be the creation of a revolutionary nationalist movement rather than the search for small material gains. The *démissionnaires,* however, believed that workers would not become politicized through propaganda alone. As Rosan Mounien, one of the principal figures of the movement at the time, explained to me, "We felt that the people would not go to battle over ideas that resided in the minds of others." Mounien recounts that early on they realized that labor strikes were a particularly fertile mode of political praxis.

> The strike became our preferred mode of struggle, partly because it is the most natural way for workers to achieve their goals, but also because it is a highly potent form of ideological mobilization. The strike puts workers face to face with the system. And it is in the course of political action [*en mouvement*] that workers arrive at an understanding of that system.

Mounien stressed that for the *démissionnaires* "lived experience"—rather than political propaganda—was the key to social transformation.

> The capacity to absorb [*la faculté d'acquisition*] is not based primarily on ideas. Lived experience [*le vécu experientiel*] is the main source for the acquisition of knowledge. Thus, it is in practice [*en pratiquant*] that the worker comes to realization [*il se rend compte*]. Because in a meeting you can explain to him that the system is a colonial system, and you can explain what makes it colonial, but when he finds himself in the midst of struggle—face to face with his employer—it is *then* that he will understand, through his struggle, the workings of the system. He will see that every time there is a strike, the prosecutor will arrive, the police will arrive, the repressive forces will arrive—he is able to see the totality of the colonial state [*il globalise ce qui est l'état colonial*]. It is then that he will realize that he is part of a system, and that he must battle that entire system in order to affirm himself. That is why the strike is the best political school [*école de formation*].

While the GONG had focused on the production of political pamphlets and propaganda campaigns, the *démissionnaires* sought to involve peasants directly in social struggle. Unlike their critics, they did not see labor activism as a reformist project but as a site of revolutionary pedagogy.

These efforts led to the creation of a new series of trade unions, including the Union of Agricultural Workers (Union des travailleurs agricoles, UTA) in 1970 and the Union of Impoverished Guadeloupean Peasants (Union des paysans pauvres de la Guadeloupe, UPG) in 1972—these two unions merged into the General Union of Guadeloupean Workers (Union générale des travailleurs de la Guadeloupe, UGTG) in 1973. In addition, a nationalist teachers' union was formed in 1976 along the same ideological line as the UGTG—the General Education Union of Guadeloupe (Syndicat général de l'éducation en Guadeloupe, SGEG).[44]

The leaders of these new unions described their approach as a "syndicalisme nouveaux" (new-wave syndicalism) for two main reasons: First, because at the time they were the only unions in the Antilles that were not connected to a nationally recognized trade union federation.[45] Second, because they saw their role as not strictly economic but as more broadly political and cultural—they explicitly advocated political independence and infused their labor struggles with new forms of cultural and historical politics.

Originally, the new unions were based mainly in rural areas. This was partly because of the centrality of sugar to the Guadeloupean economy at the time, but it also reflected a view of the peasantry as the site of an authentic "folk culture" that could be rallied into a Guadeloupean "national culture."[46] During this time local cultural practices and traditions—particularly Creole language and gwoka music—became increasingly viewed as both tools for and emblems of the formation of a distinct Guadeloupean national identity.[47] As a result, the new syndicalism of the 1970s was closely tied to the work of cultural nationalists who sought to revitalize, codify, and refashion the cultural practices of the Guadeloupean peasantry.

For example, in association with the UTA, Guadeloupean sociologist and linguist Dany Bébel-Gisler founded the Bwadoubout Center for Popular Education (Centre d'éducation populaire bwadoubout), where both children and adults could gain Creole literacy along with political training.[48] Bébel-Gisler grew up in an agricultural milieu in Guadeloupe before completing training in sociology, ethnology, and linguistics in Paris. Her doctoral dissertation examined the sociological impact of French-language use in Guadeloupe, and as a student she participated in several experimental adult literary programs with immigrants from Algeria and other parts of Africa—an experience that inspired her political work after returning to Guadeloupe. In 1971, she published *Kèk prinsip pou ékri kréyòl*, one of the first Creole orthography books produced in Guadeloupe, as part of a broader effort to develop Creole as an autonomous language.

The emphasis on Creole language among these activists was essential for organizing the mostly Creole-speaking peasant population. But beyond its utilitarian role, the use of Creole was also highly symbolic. Although Creole was often spoken in the home among agricultural workers, it was banned from public schools, where it was seen as an obstacle to linguistic mastery of French, and stigmatized in places like the church as a sign of backwardness.[49] Even in the home, Creole was increasingly being replaced by French—particularly among middle-class families who wanted to secure their children's education and future class mobility.[50] Women were especially discouraged from speaking Creole, which was seen as vulgar and unladylike, but even men who grew up in the post-departmentalization era often confessed that they learned to speak Creole from their peers *an la ri* (on the street) because their parents would not allow it at home. Thus, while cultural activists celebrated Creole as the "true" and "authentic" language of the Guadeloupean people, they simultaneously feared that Guadeloupe was experiencing a process of de-Creolization and that French would soon become the first language of most residents.[51]

Along with the use of Creole, the cultural activists of the 1970s strongly emphasized folk practices such as traditional gwoka music and dance. *Gwoka* is an umbrella term for various Afro-Guadeloupean musical practices, referring both to a family of hand drums and the music created with them. As with Creole, gwoka was increasingly devalorized during the post-departmentalization search for economic and cultural modernity. Often described as "mizik a yé nèg" ("old black people's music"), it was shunned by the aspiring middle classes in favor of the beguine and the *chanson française*.

In the 1970s, the UTA sought to politicize gwoka musical traditions and to integrate them into its organizing efforts. A key figure in this effort was Gérard Lockel, who had been a successful jazz guitarist in France before resettling in Guadeloupe. Like the linguists who sought to both document and promote Creole by producing dictionaries and pedagogical tools, Lockel worked to develop a new form of musical notation for gwoka and a new musical tradition he described as *gwoka modèn*.[52] Lockel apprenticed with master gwoka singers in the countryside, working to steer their music in a more politicized direction. He strongly opposed musical traditions that he felt were too "Europeanized" while promoting what he saw as the more "authentically African" strands of Guadeloupean music.[53] Under Lockel's guidance the union began organizing *léwòz* (drumming parties) during union meetings. Today drum circles are an essential part of union life, and the union flag, created by Lockel in the 1990s, is emblazoned with a picture of a ka drum and a rising fist. Lockel also composed a song that became the union's anthem, *Chanté a Lendépandans*, which is still sung at the end of all events and rallies.[54]

Given the cultural nationalists' focus on promoting an ostensibly autochthonous peasant culture, one might expect the new generation of rural-based syndicalists to have rejected "European" religion in favor of syncretic folk practices. However, they disparagingly described folk religion as *magie* or "superstition," associating it with a mentality of *assistance* (public assistance/charity) which, to their mind, ran counter to the ideals of self-sufficiency and self-determination they sought to promote. Catholicism, by contrast, was viewed as a culturally adaptable religion that could be easily integrated into the nationalist agenda. Local priests and Catholic groups—influenced in part by the work of the religious organizations that had emerged among migrants in mainland France during the 1950s—thus became increasingly involved with both the syndical work and the cultural revival work of the 1980s, spearheading the development of a Guadeloupean version of liberation theology.

The most notable figure in this movement was the Catholic priest Chérubin Céleste, who rose to prominence during the 1973 UTA sugar strikes, when he carried out a hunger strike that was central to the strike's resolution. Céleste had completed his theological training, along with studies in sociology and economics, in Lyon—where he was Frantz Fanon's college roommate. In 1961 he returned to Guadeloupe, where he led the Rural Movement of Young Christians (Mouvement rural de la jeunesse chrétiene, MRJC; initially known as the Catholic Agriculture Youth, or Jeunesse agricole catholique, JAC).[55] Along with Céleste, other Catholic groups began adopting a similar position, viewing Catholicism as a natural ally of the nationalist agenda; these groups included Christians for the Liberation of the Guadeloupean People (Chrétiens pour la libération du peuple guadeloupéen, CLPG, or KLPG in Creole), Young Christian Workers (Jeunes ouvriers chrétiens, JOC), and the Christian Group for Research and Action (Groupe chrétien de recherche et d'action, GCRA).

For these nationalist activists, folk beliefs in *la magie* promoted a mentality of *assistance*, while Catholicism encouraged self-determination and self-sufficiency. In a 1983 interview in *Les Temps Modernes*, Céleste explained, "In the Christian faith, if you receive something from God, it's the product of your own personal act, acts for which you are responsible." By contrast,

he argued, "In *la magie*, what I obtain, I obtain from someone else by following their rules."[56] Céleste argued that superstitious beliefs made people
feel powerless in the face of the forces that surrounded them, thus leading
to fatalistic thinking—the opposite of the kind of hope in social change
he sought to inspire.

However, Céleste conceded that he understood why Guadeloupeans
might feel as if external powers were acting upon them. In the post-
departmentalization era the peasants in his parish had witnessed rapid societal changes over which they had little control: families were torn apart by
migration, young people vanished to the mainland, and agricultural jobs
slowly disappeared. Yet money appeared to be flowing, almost magically,
from the outside. His stated goal was to help Guadeloupeans get out of
the *"religion d'assistés"* (religion of assistance/charity) by empowering them
through a religion of self-determination and self-sufficiency.

As Bébel-Gisler writes, during the 1970s a whole host of social and political categories underwent a profound transformation in Guadeloupe. "Creole,
gwoka, religion, Guadeloupe, liberation, independence," all took on a distinct meaning within the broader context of Guadeloupean society.[57] These
efforts had a lasting impact on the cultural and political fabric of the Antilles.
For example, many credit the union activists of the 1970s for being among
the first to speak in Creole on the public airways. Today, Creole is employed
across broad sectors of society: billboards promoting McDonald's in Creole
dot public roadways, and even the French-controlled RFO radio has a Creole
summary of the news on the morning broadcast.[58] Gwoka also experienced a
strong resurgence in the last several decades. In the late 1970s former AGEG
militants founded the Festival de Gwo Ka, an important yearly event in the
town of Saint-Anne, that attracts musicians and dancers from across the island and beyond—serving as an important reference point for a new generation of artists. Today popular singers like Dominik Coco and dancehall artists
like Admiral T often incorporate elements of gwoka into their music. In addition, new forms of "urban ka" have developed among artists like François
Ladrezeau, who push back against the "folklorization" of gwoka by trying to
maintain its dynamism as an evolving musical form.[59]

Many in Guadeloupe credit the UGTG for "rescuing" these cultural
practices, and this is a strong point of pride for many union members. For
example, during a union seminar I attended one of the UGTG delegates
remarked,

I've been noticing that the politics of the UGTG have really affected people's
thinking. Even the politicians, they all speak Creole now. There isn't a single

politician who doesn't speak Creole! And they use the same terms the UGTG
uses and the same political line—they all use it now in their campaigns. . . .
And even among the wider population, you can see it too. That should serve
to show us that the ideals of the UGTG have really made inroads [*ca ka fé
chimen*] in Guadeloupe!

Labor activists do not see this as a form of cooptation but as evidence of
their success.

The Path of Armed Struggle

By the late 1970s, Guadeloupe's nationalist unions had developed a strong
following, achieving important economic gains for agricultural workers,
while also engaging in larger social struggles. But there was an emerging
frustration among some nationalists that the "new syndicalism" was not
paving a clear path toward political independence. Opinions were split on
whether to engage in electoral politics. Most activists agreed on boycott-
ing national elections (presidential and legislative), but some supported
participating in municipal and cantonal elections, with the goal of elect-
ing a pro-independence politician as the head of the General Council.[60]
To this end a new political party, the People's Union for the Liberation of
Guadeloupe (Union populaire pour la libération de la Guadeloupe, UPLG),
was founded in 1978.

Some disagreed with this electoral tack, advocating armed struggle as
the best means of obtaining political independence. In the 1980s these
radicalized activists came together to form a new series of clandestine
pro-independence guerrilla groups such as the Armed Liberation Group
(Groupe de libération armée, GLA), which in turn spawned the Caribbean
Revolutionary Alliance (Alliance révolutionnaire caribéenne, ARC) and the
People's Movement for an Independent Guadeloupe (Mouvement populaire pour la Guadeloupe indépendante, MPGI). These groups claimed responsibility for over sixty bombings throughout the Antilles and mainland
France during the early 1980s. Their targets included hotels, department
stores, airline companies, automobile clubs, banks, prisons, restaurants, police stations, and tax offices.[61]

These activists did not emerge out of the political tradition of the AGEG
or the GONG. They were slightly younger than the BUMIDOM generation
and had not participated in the political movements of the 1950s and '60s.[62]
The movement's main figure was Luc Reinette (born in 1950), who became

a popular hero in the 1980s after he escaped imprisonment in Basse-Terre, where he was serving a sentence for his presumed involvement in the ARC bombings. After escaping, Reinette eluded the authorities for three years, living *en marronage* in Guadeloupe. He was eventually arrested in St. Vincent in 1987, when he left Guadeloupe to seek political asylum. He was then extradited to France and sentenced to thirty years in prison but was pardoned in 1989 by François Mitterrand.

This new generation of militants claimed to be engaging in armed struggle, but their use of violence was mostly symbolic. In its 1987 manifesto, the ARC cited the 1960 UN Declaration on the Granting of Independence to Colonial Countries and Peoples as both the legal justification and the guiding principle for its tactics. They outlined three criteria for obtaining UN recognition as a non-self-governing territory: geographic distance from the governing power, cultural and ethnic difference from the governing nation, and evidence of a national liberation movement. Arguing that the first two conditions were clearly met in the French Antilles, the ARC stated that its goal was to provide evidence of a separatist movement.[63]

These activists were more focused on creating international pressure for decolonization than on building nationalist consciousness, yet they managed to gain respect, if not mass support, from local residents who viewed them as devoted to the noble (if not necessarily viable) cause of national independence. As the Guadeloupean novelist Maryse Condé once quipped, Reinette's ability to hide on an island as small as Guadeloupe for three years is in and of itself testament to the support he received.[64] By the time Reinette was released from jail in 1989, however, the political landscape was shifting. After the US invasion of Grenada in 1983 and the fall of the Sandinista government in Nicaragua in 1990, armed struggle seemed less and less viable.[65]

In her reflections on the political possibilities of the 1980s, Bébel-Gisler writes that the squabbles over electoral participation versus armed struggle were ultimately pointless. Drawing from her ethnographic research and the oral histories she collected in the countryside, she argues that the peasantry had little interest in supporting the nationalists in either their electoral campaigns, or in their search for political independence. On the electoral front, they had grown accustomed to the clientelist tactics of the elected officials and had become adept at navigating and skirting the system.[66] More importantly, Bébel-Gisler suggests that most of the quotidian challenges the peasants faced—illiteracy, unemployment, inadequate housing, etc.—could not be resolved by simply raising a sovereign flag. In a stray footnote she cites an emerging "désenchantement nationale" (a disenchantment with nationalism) taking root across postcolonial societies, as postcolonial projects of modernist development increasingly eroded the promises of the decolonization era.[67] Indeed by the 1990s, political independence would increasingly become a "future past": a once contemplated but no longer imaginable political option.

The Wake of Disenchantment

When the new syndicalism emerged in the 1970s, it consisted of small, mostly agricultural unions which local employers often refused to recognize as collective-bargaining partners. In subsequent years the UGTG slowly expanded in keeping with the larger shifts in the Guadeloupean economy. With the agricultural industry's decline, many former farmworkers found employment in the expanded French bureaucracy—though without the same privileges as the *fonctionnaires* hailing from the metropole. In the 1980s the UGTG began organizing workers in sanitation services, hospitals, and school cafeterias, along with other low-ranking civil servants, to obtain collective agreements and full benefits. It also expanded into the tourism industry, unionizing hotel workers (housekeepers, cooks, groundskeepers, etc.), many of whom complained that tourism reproduced the servile relations of slavery. As the service sector grew, the union also expanded into commerce, organizing workers in shopping centers, fast-food franchises, and gas stations.

Today, the UGTG is the largest labor union in the French Antilles, with over six thousand members. Guadeloupe has much higher union density in general than mainland France, with 18 percent of the working population unionized, as opposed to 7 percent on the mainland.[68] The UGTG represents 30 percent of those unionized workers and is responsible for over 70 percent of all labor strikes on the island.[69] In most industries, the UGTG is the majority union, and it also holds the majority of seats in the Conseil de prud'hommes (labor court).[70]

When I began my fieldwork in 2002, the local prefecture estimated that in the previous year there had been over two hundred labor conflicts. That same year, the French magazine *L'Express* declared Guadeloupe "l'île chaudron" (the boiling-pot island), and the popular travel guide *Le Routard* began warning tourists of the heated social climate and of the radical union activists who would frequently paralyze the island.[71] Since the mass strike of 2009, the image of Guadeloupe as an "island of strikes" has only solidified. The frequency of strikes, and their prominent role in the collective imagination, has led commentators in both local intellectual circles and the French national press to argue that Guadeloupe is plagued by a particularly conflictive social climate—or, in the words of French journalists, a "conflictualité singulière."

Within this context the UGTG looms large. This is partly because of its size and its ability to mobilize workers on a massive scale, but also because it uses highly confrontational tactics, including roadblocks, slowdowns, and the prolonged suspension of public services. The UGTG has also become known for engaging in struggles that extend beyond the workplace—such as battling to establish Abolition Day as a local holiday or going on strike to force multinational companies to sell their franchises to Guadeloupean workers rather than foreign interests.

Although the UGTG enjoys broad support, it is also the target of much criticism for its "hard-line tactics"—particularly its roadblocks and long-term strikes, which deprive residents of goods and services (as discussed in chapter 3).[72] Critics also fault the union for its political agenda, which many feel oversteps the bounds of traditional labor struggles. These criticisms often hinge on a distinction between "le social" (the socioeconomic realm), which is the recognized terrain of labor struggle, and "le politique" (the political realm), which is seen as the terrain of political parties and elected officials. Even those who criticize the UGTG's incursion into the political realm, however, often recognize that, following the nationalist movement's decline, local politicians have failed to produce new visions for Guadeloupe. They see the UGTG's initiatives as a response to the existing political vacuum, but view the union as a threat to the mainstream. As I discuss in chapter 6, local politicians in particular often view the union as a challenge to their already weak authority.

There are others, however, who contend that the union does not do enough in the political realm. Some argue that the UGTG is too reformist, and that it should do more to promote political independence, echoing the early criticisms of UTA activists as "economistes." Others believe that the union should formally enter the electoral arena—rather than carrying out politics "undemocratically" from the streets. Particularly after the success of the 2009 strike, it was common to hear many Guadeloupean residents express a desire to see UGTG leaders running for public office. Even among those who would welcome the union's incursion into politics, however, there is still a looming fear of "antidemocratic" practices—often associated with the legacies of authoritarian governments in neighboring Caribbean islands.[73]

Contemporary UGTG leaders insist that trade unionism is itself a form of politics and that their activities need not be confined to the realm of *le social.* For example, during a training session for union delegates, Max, an important leader in the union, encouraged the delegates to embrace their political potential, asking them,

> What exactly is the political responsibility of a *syndicaliste*? Is it that in order to have power, in order to reach people, in order to transform Guadeloupe, to start a revolution in this country, we need some kind of political mandate? Is it that by doing trade unionism we can't do politics?

He further questioned the idea that social change could be effected only through the political realm, asking provocatively,

> Do you really think the Regional Council is the only site through which you can reach people and talk about transforming Guadeloupe? At the end of the day, who do you think has brought more changes—more concrete, material, changes to the Guadeloupean people—politicians or the UGTG?

As Max suggests, many important political and cultural changes in Guadeloupe—the increased visibility of Creole, the raise in the minimum wage, the extension of labor rights and regulations, the recognition of local holidays—have resulted from strikes and collective mobilizations. He further argued: "Labor contracts are the foundations of a society. Through the establishment of collective agreements we create new legislation, new social relations, new social practices. *We* are building a new society."

Max's comments reflect a vision of political action that is neither driven nor constrained by the search for a transformed political status or the seizure of state power. Indeed, when he asks "who has brought more changes," his words index a skepticism regarding what can actually be obtained through the traditional channels of governance in Guadeloupe. When I pushed him on this point and asked why the union still officially favored independence given that it was able to make so many gains through the current system, he simply shrugged and said, "*Beh*, to not be French!"

Max's final remark speaks to the challenges faced by the contemporary political generation in the French Antilles. Contemporary activists are dissatisfied with their social and political conditions and wish to forge a new political future, but they are still struggling to think beyond the categories of the past. They are unable to articulate a strong case for political independence but still rally behind it as the only existing alternative to "being French."

These actors find themselves at the wake of a previous political generation. They are ready to bid farewell to the failed projects and unfulfilled
promises of the previous era but have yet to bury the conceptual frameworks, political expectations, and historical legacies of their forebears.
Theirs is a moment of categorical uncertainty. But it is also an era rife with
emergent possibilities.

TWO

Strategic Entanglement

On a sunny afternoon in the fall of 2005, I sat at on the veranda of a seaside café in the beach town of Gosier engrossed in heated conversation with Lukas, a consultant for the UGTG. Lukas worked as a middle-school teacher in the public school system but, according to his own account, had completed numerous university programs, earning degrees in law, business, and anthropology. He was also a judo champion and claimed to have put himself through college by working as a bodyguard for high-ranking French diplomats. I had arranged our meeting that day to discuss his plans for economic development and entrepreneurship in Guadeloupe, specifically his efforts with workers interested in forming cooperatives to develop their own businesses.[1] However, as we waited for our meal, the conversation strayed, and we suddenly found ourselves passionately debating the prospects of political independence for Guadeloupe. Right as the waitress arrived with our sampler of local delicacies Lukas declared,

> It's not that I don't believe in independence for Guadeloupe. It's that I don't believe in independence! It doesn't exist—anywhere! You're always dependent on something: on those who are more powerful, on those who have what you need. Political independence has no meaning without economic independence.

I was surprised by Lukas's comments given that the UGTG is generally regarded as a bastion of cultural nationalism and pro-independence sentiment. Lukas, however, saw things differently.

> Those people who propose independence are charlatans! These are people who have clearly never looked around the Caribbean. They don't understand

the power of a country like the United States and how it rules the region. Heck, they don't even understand a little country like France!

I was initially taken aback by Lukas' categorical rejection of the possibility of independence in the Caribbean, and his seeming acceptance of French integration. "What about autonomy?" I asked. "What about a certain *indépendance d'esprit*, if nothing else?" When I mentioned this search for an alternative form of autonomy, he smiled knowingly and said,

> Let me tell you about where I come from: my ancestors were *nèg mawons* [maroons, fugitive rebel slaves]. . . . Do you know about the nèg mawons? Do you know that they escaped the system of slavery and created their own independent states?

I nodded and he continued, "How did they do this, you ask? Well, by using the same tactics as the UGTG, by being a guerrilla force." He further explained,

> What did the nèg mawons do? . . . They fled and went into the depth of the forest. But they did not remain isolated—they would return regularly to the plantation and take what they needed. There was no "social dialogue," no negotiations.[2] . . . It was guerrilla warfare. And, you know, that's what the union does here. Every time there is a period of calm—bam! A new strike is unleashed. Every time the employers think they have won—guerrilla!

He slammed the table for emphasis as he uttered these final words, then leaned back in his chair, while nodding repeatedly. After a short pause he placed his hands on the table and leaned forward once again as he whispered, almost conspiratorially,

> But the thing is that the UGTG doesn't realize what they're doing. They do it spontaneously—without even knowing that they are being driven from within. Truly, it is history at work.

Lukas's remarks reflect a common tendency in Guadeloupe to associate the tactics and actions of contemporary labor activists with the practice of marronage and the figure of the nèg mawon, or rebel slave.[3] The term *marronage* refers to the broad range of practices through which enslaved populations contested the system of slavery across the Americas. This includes permanent acts of flight and the formation of large-scale maroon communities, but it also encompasses what has been described in French as *petit marronage*: provisional acts of fugitivity during which the enslaved would temporarily escape their confines to visit relatives in a neighboring plantation, recover from injury or illness, avoid being punished or sold, carry out illicit trade, or plot larger actions of revolt.

When Lukas invokes the figure of the nèg mawon, he argues that rebel slaves did not simply depart from the plantation. Instead, he suggests that they engaged selectively with the dominant system, drawing from its resources when needed. It is in this sense that he imagines contemporary labor activists as rebel slaves and guerrilla warriors. Lukas argues that union activists deploy maroon tactics when they strategically pillage French trade unionism using tools such as the labor strike while refusing to engage with the logics of mediation and "social dialogue." This approach is imagined as a form of marronage in that it allows political actors to temporarily break, circumvent, and contest the norms of a system from which they are unable to fully disentangle.

Lukas's reading of marronage as a form of strategic entanglement is just one of the many ways that rebel slaves have figured in the political imagination of the Americas. Maroons have been represented in fluctuating and at times overlapping ways as criminal outlaws, romantic heroes, tragic victims, and guerrilla warriors.[4] These varying representations speak to both the complexity of the sociohistorical processes of slavery (and slave resistance) as well as to the complexities of the ongoing and overlapping process of historical narration. As Michel-Rolph Trouillot argues, "What history is changes with time and place or, better said, history reveals itself only through the production of specific narratives."[5]

In this chapter, I examine how different political generations in the Antilles have approached the figure of the maroon through shifting ideas of autonomy and self-determination. I argue that these historical narratives are situated within conceptual and ideological milieux, or "problem-spaces," from which particular questions emerge and within which particular answers find resonance.[6] Indeed, it is not coincidental that in my conversation with Lukas, he turned to marronage precisely as an answer to the question of autonomy in an era of foreclosed political independence.

As I show, for political activists and intellectuals from the 1960s through the 1980s, marronage was imagined as a form of permanent flight and absolute rupture. This narrative corresponded to a particular moment when questions of freedom and sovereignty were being actively shaped by the imperatives of postcolonial nationalism. This view contrasts with how marronage is invoked by both Aimé Césaire, who preceded the nationalist project, and by the UGTG activists who succeeded it.[7] I argue that in these non-nationalist visions, marronage represents a form of strategic entanglement: a way of crafting and enacting autonomy within a system from which one is unable to fully disentangle. Even within these contexts, however, maroons are still imagined as artful political subjects, able to challenge the institutional and categorical confines of their society. For these various Caribbean political cohorts, marronage thus represents the hope and evokes the possibility of transcending the epistemic limits of one's place and time.[8]

Marronage: A Complex of Resistance

Throughout the Americas, wherever the system of plantation slavery was instituted, enslaved subjects challenged its confines. On slave ships, at auction sites, in plantation fields and labor camps, captive populations were a constant flight risk. The size, scale, and duration of their acts varied widely depending on the ability (both financial and logistic) of planters and colonial officials to surveil, retrieve, and imprison runaways. It also varied according to the geographic terrain. Maroons most often found shelter in dense forests, swamps, or mountainous areas where thickets and uncleared brush could offer protection from bounty hunters and colonial authorities. In places like Jamaica, Suriname, and Brazil, large-scale settlements were established, and today their descendants continue to assert rights and demand recognition as autonomous communities.[9] In flatland societies, permanent encampments were more difficult to sustain, but enslaved populations still managed to flee and form small groups. Of these impermanent communities, little remains other than place names, local lore, and passing references in the colonial records that document their punitions.

It has often been argued that marronage was not a significant practice in the French Antilles.[10] However, although large-scale, permanent settlements were uncommon, temporary acts of flight were so frequent that a lexicon emerged to distinguish these acts according to their duration: long-term escape was described as *grand marronage* and short-term escape as *petit marronage*.[11] The legal codes governing slavery in the Antilles reveal a taxonomy of crime, reward, and penalty based on the duration and frequency of these absences: a monthlong absence justified a severed ear, a repeat offense merited a slashed hamstring. If the absence exceeded six months, a leg might be severed, and if the offender was female a nose could be sliced, ensuring permanent mutilation.[12] At each instance a fleur-de-lis was to be seared on the flesh, becoming both the brand of escape and a visual reminder of the likelihood of capture.

The bounty for runaways was also measured against the duration of absence: one hundred and fifty pounds of sugar for a maroon who had been absent up to two months, six hundred pounds for one gone six months, and one thousand pounds if they had been missing up to three years. That the catalog of reward ends at three years suggests that perhaps at this point marronage was considered "grand." In 1672 the Sovereign Council in Martinique ruled that slaves engaged in marronage for over three years should be put to death and their owners reimbursed for their value.[13] Whether or not this was strictly enforced, it suggests that long-term marronage was of concern not just to plantation owners but also, and perhaps to an even greater degree, to the colonial state, for which maroon communities posed the threat of an alternative polity.

If long-term marronage was seen as a looming threat, short-term absences appear to have been an accepted fact of colonial life.[14] French historian Gabriel Debien has argued that in the context of the French Antilles, acts of petit marronage constituted a form of sustained *va-et-vient* (coming and going) to which planters were forced to accommodate. Absences of a week or less were usually pardoned, and Debien suggests that these small and mostly individual acts did not constitute marronage "proper," describing them instead as a form of "marronage léger."[15] There are, however, records that attest to significant incidents of long-term escape in the French Antilles. For example, one notorious maroon leader, Mocachy, known as *le roi de bois* (king of the forest), spent over twenty-five years *en marronage* before being captured.[16] Mocachy had led the Kellers, a community numbering over 2,800 in the area of Petit Bourg.[17] The existence of such a large, if impermanent, maroon community in a society where grand marronage ostensibly did not exist brings into question how marronage has traditionally been imagined and evaluated.

The distinction historians have drawn between petit and grand marronage (which is itself based on the taxonomy of colonial planters) hinges on duration, but it also implies an assessment of motives and goals. Petit marronage has been described as a temporary departure with the intent of return, whereas grand marronage has been deemed "grand" in both its duration and intent.[18] This distinction has also hinged on a presumed difference between the search for personal freedom and the struggle for social transformation; short-term marronage is thus often characterized as a form of individual escapism, while grand marronage is viewed as more politically ambitious.[19]

In thinking about these categorizations, we should bear in mind that any attempt at gauging the political significance of maroon struggle will be inherently fraught, given not only the problems of archival evidence but also the difficulty of assessing slave acts through contemporary categories of political action.[20] The categories through which marronage is read, the questions asked of that history, and the various claims made of and through it are necessarily informed by a broader intellectual and political context. For example, the Haitian Revolution has been famously described as "the only successful slave revolt in history," but this claim only makes sense within a political context in which state overthrow is viewed as a singular measure of accomplishment.[21]

Across the Americas, maroons often undertook political projects that were predicated on forms of coexistence, interdependence, and noninterference—with varying degrees of success.[22] In Jamaica and Suriname, for example, maroons chartered treaties with colonial authorities that allowed their coexistence within the colonial order. Under these treaties maroons agreed to restrict their settlements within certain boundaries, to abstain from recruiting members from the surrounding plantations, and to return (repatriate, so to speak) future runaways in exchange for territorial recognition and economic assistance.[23] These treaties could be viewed as an effort on behalf of the colonial state to contain the growth of maroon settlements—and indeed they significantly constrained maroon sovereignty. Yet these negotiated forms of strategic entanglement also enabled maroons to carve out spaces of autonomy within the colonial system, assuring their communities' persistence into the present day.

The point here is not to engage in an exercise of revisionism but rather to foreground the evaluative frameworks that underlie these historical narratives. Similarly to how postwar "methodological nationalism" led to the conflation of anticolonialism with the search for political independence, the abolitionist project of freedom and the decolonizing project of postcolonial sovereignty have also imposed particular narrative frames onto the history of slave resistance.[24] "Treaty maroons" and small acts of petit marronage have often been characterized as politically insignificant compared with the "uncompromising" political project of grand marronage. Yet, I would like to suggest that these narratives are closely tied to a particular moment of historical production, one when ideas and questions about freedom and sovereignty were being shaped and guided by the imperatives of postcolonial nationalism.

The Postcolonial Maroon

In the Antillean popular imagination the maroon has not always figured as a rebel, warrior, or hero. In the nineteenth and twentieth centuries, the most

common image of the maroon was that of a dangerous criminal or bandit—
someone on the lam from the authorities. Nèg mawons were constructed
as shadowy figures, bogeymen summoned up to frighten wayward children.[25] It was not until the 1960s that the figure of the maroon was refash-
ioned as a symbol of pride and an emblem of resistance.

In the literary realm, Édouard Glissant's 1958 novel *La lézarde* is said to
mark the arrival of the romantic maroon protagonist in Antillean literature.
Previously, maroons had figured only at the margins of literary texts rather
than as central characters, and maroon acts were associated with ancestral
African tradition—not the formation of a new Caribbean community.[26] It
is with Glissant and the later generation of *creolité* writers, such as Patrick
Chamoiseau and Raphaël Confiant, that marronage emerges as a central
theme for imagining Antillean political possibility. Indeed, these authors
have at times been taken to task for engaging in *marronisme*, by deploying overly romantic masculinist celebrations of maroons as symbols of
Caribbean resistance.[27]

In the political realm, the syndicalists and cultural nationalists of the
1970s also celebrated maroon practices. As described in chapter 1, during
the 1970s Antillean Creole and gwoka music were increasingly affirmed not
just as the language and music of slaves but as the communicative tools of
slave resistance, with gwoka in particular often referred to as the *téléfonn a nèg
mawon*.[28] The nationalist teachers' union SOGED produced numerous pedagogical manuals during this time that sought to decenter the abolitionist
history of freedom by recasting rebel slaves as the protagonists of their own
emancipation. Texts such as *A pa Schoelcher ki libéré nèg*, for example, sought
to explicitly displace the figure of the French abolitionist Victor Schoelcher
by placing rebel slaves at the center of the history of Freedom.

Although the turn to the maroon was generalized, it was not the new syndicalists who became most associated with marronage. Instead, it was the
armed struggle groups that emerged in the 1980s—ARC, GLA, and MPIG—
that explicitly took on the label of "the modern maroons." As discussed
in chapter 1, these activists arrived on the political scene in the late 1970s
and quickly became frustrated with the labor movement—which in their
view was not charting a clear and direct path toward national independence.
They advocated armed struggle and carried out a number of strategic attacks,
placing bombs in public buildings throughout the Antilles and mainland
France. Their movement did not focus on producing historical narratives per
se, but they launched a radical newspaper titled *Neg Mawon* and referred to
themselves in their manifestos as "the modern maroons."[29] The association
with the maroons was further cemented when their leader, Luc Reinette,

2.1. Cover of April 1984 issue of the ARC newspaper *Neg Mawon*. Source: *Magwa: Magazine Gwadloupeyen Anticolonialiste,* special supplement, 1987.

escaped from the Basse-Terre prison, eluding authorities for three years by going into "marronage."

The association of marronage with the nationalist movement was not exclusive to the French Antilles. Throughout the Caribbean, intellectuals during this period began to turn to the figure of the maroon as a protonationalist hero. As Richard Price writes in the preface to the seminal collection *Maroon Societies*, "Rare was the Caribbean intellectual or artist of the 1960s, 1970s, or 1980s who failed to compare himself to a maroon."[30] In Cuba the figure of the maroon was associated with the "new man" of the revolution following the publication of Miguel Barnet's *Biography of a Runaway Slave* in 1966.[31] As Barnet would later write, in the aftermath of the revolution, "it was necessary to record history from a new perspective." Although Esteban Montejo, the 103-year-old man at the center of the Barnet's oral history, had lived through various important periods in Cuban history, it was his experiences as a *cimarrón* that carried the most pressing lessons for 1960s Cuba, according to Barnet. "The rest," he argued, "is a grey and murky life, as 'normal' as that of any other citizen or worker."[32]

In Jamaica the postindependence moment also inspired a reexamination of the history and figure of the maroon. This led to the consecration of the maroon leader Nanny as a national heroine, and the appropriation of cultural symbols like the Abeng cow horn as an emblem of anticolonial resistance and political thought. Indeed, *Abeng* was taken up as the title of a radical newspaper founded by the New World Group in 1968.[33] That same year in Haiti the Duvalier government commissioned the now iconic monument to the "unknown maroon." The statue serves as a visible marker of the larger historiographic debates brewing at the time over the importance of marronage in the development of the Haitian Revolution.[34]

These efforts were part of a larger search for a new Caribbean political and ideological ground. These actors sought to break with European narrative frames by recentering Caribbean subjects as the protagonists of New World histories of freedom and sovereignty. Their attempts were, however, inherently shaped by the conceptual and ideological terrain of the time— particularly by the project of postcolonial nationalism, which was predicated on the formation of independent polities bound by a shared language, territory, and cultural tradition. As a result, the representations of marronage that emerged during this period hinged on the celebration of grand marronage as a form of both ideological and political rupture.

In the Antilles, writers and activists would often claim that they were "rescuing" the forgotten or silenced figure of the maroon. What was finding voice in their narratives, however, was not necessarily the figure of the maroon itself but rather a narrative frame that could recast marronage as a form of political rupture. Indeed, although the *indépendantistes* would claim to depart sharply from the previous generation of "assimilationist" thinkers and writers, we can find among the previous generation, particularly in the work of Aimé Césaire, numerous references to marronage as a metaphor for a Caribbean political subjectivity. Yet, as I show below, Césaire's model of marronage is not premised on absolute rupture. It is less a celebration of grand marronage than of marronage as a form of coming and going—an epistemic *va-et-vient* with the categories and institutions of the dominant system.

The Verb "Marroner"

Si vous voulez savoir ce que je suis, je ne suis pas le Maire de Fort de France: JE SUIS UN NEGRE MARRON. Mentalement, je suis un nègre marron; je refuse de baisser la tête devant qui que ce soit. Je refuse les grands frères. Je refuse les tontons. Je refuse que l'on me montre la route. La route je la trouverai moi-même avec mon peuple.

[If you want to know what I am, I am not the mayor of Fort de France, I AM A *NEGRE MARRON*. Mentally, I am a *nègre marron*; I refuse to lower my head before anyone. I refuse the big brothers. I refuse the uncles. I refuse to be shown the way; I will find the way myself, with my people.]

—Aimé Césaire[35]

Césaire was often proclaimed—and proclaimed himself—*le nèg fundamental* and was considered to be, in the words of Patrick Chamoiseau, "maître-marronneur en connaissance" (the masterful marooner of knowledge). Yet Césaire's maroon politics have traditionally been set apart from the broader literary canon of Antillean *marronisme*.[36] This is partly due to the analytical reduction of marronage to an abstract search for freedom through acts of grand-scale rupture, flight, and retreat, but it is also due to a miscasting of Césairean politics and to the tendency to view Césaire the politician in opposition to Césaire the poet. Even those who have tried to bridge these representational divides have often fallen back on a view of Césaire as ultimately "ambivalent" and "incoherent"— hindered by his misguided commitment to the paradoxical demands of the people he was elected to represent.[37] As Chamoiseau states, "C'est au nom de Césaire que nous nous battions contre la politique de Césaire!" (It is in the name of Césaire that we fight the politics of Césaire!).[38]

This seeming paradox comes about partly because Césaire's vision of marronage is not predicated on nationalist models of political or cultural purity. Indeed, Antillean intellectuals such as Raphaël Confiant have often chastised Césaire for writing in French rather than in Creole, suggesting that this represents a devalorization of local vernacular forms.[39] These criticisms, however, assume that Césaire simply adopted the French language rather than recognizing how he worked both within and against French—precisely through acts of pillaging, marooning, and reinvention.[40]

In his writings, Césaire repeatedly flouted the traditions and norms of the French literary canon. His poetry defies the constraints of the printed page, featuring long run-on sentences that challenge publishing conventions. Unconstrained by dictionaries, Césaire consistently engaged in a "politics of neologism" through which he fabricated his own innovative vocabulary, breathing new life into discarded archaisms, inventing new words out of whole cloth, and infusing French with an Antillean rhythm and sensibility that rendered it unfamiliar to metropolitan speakers.[41]

As Césaire himself stated in a famous interview with the Haitian poet René Depestre, he approached French as a tool with which to create what he described as a new language: an "Antillean French" or a "Black French."[42] His efforts are reminiscent of what reggae musicians have called "versioning," what the Barbadian writer Kamau Brathwaite has described as "calibanization," and what the poet and scholar Nathaniel Mackey has termed "artistic othering"—practices that self-reflectively address the kind of "social othering" to which their practitioners have been subjected.[43]

Césaire's most famous neologism is *négritude*, which was itself a form of linguistic marooning or artistic othering. As a young student arriving in France, Césaire was confronted with the insult of *nèg* and decided to seize it and refashion it into a combative stance.[44] In his interviews with filmmaker Euzhan Palcy, Césaire clarified that negritude was less an assertion of racial pride than the declaration of a rebellious posture. "It was not a triumphant or glorious negritude," he said. "It was a trampled negritude, it was the trampled *nèg*, the oppressed *nèg*, the rebel *nèg*—that is negritude."[45]

Césaire further suggested that his vision of negritude was necessarily distinct from that of his comrade in literary arms, the Senegalese poet and politician Léopold Senghor. Césaire argued that the negritude of an Antillean subject "a la reconquête de son être" (seeking the recovery/reconquest of his being) was necessarily different from the negritude of someone "enraciné dans son être" (someone rooted in their sense of being). Césaire's negritude had no essentialist core; it was not a longing for an authentic African identity but a particularly Antillean stance toward both Africa and Europe—each

2.2. Aimé Césaire in 1982. Photo by Sophie Bassouls, courtesy of Corbis Images.

of which constituted impossible homelands, both intimately familiar yet ultimately denied. Césaire's politics and poetics consistently moved across these denied homelands, refusing to relinquish either. Although he has often been cast as the founder of an Afrocentric cultural negritude—which is seen to stand in contradiction with his support for a Eurocentric assimilationist political project—his oeuvre is perhaps best understood as a form of both political and literary marronage.

Césaire himself described his literary practices as a form of marooning in a poem originally published in *Présence Africaine* in 1955 under the title "Reply to Depestre, Haitian Poet: Elements of an Ars Poetica." A revised version of the poem later appeared under the title "The Verb Marroner" in the 1976 collection *Noria*. In this poem, Césaire criticizes Depestre for accepting the French Communist Party's dictum that politically engaged poets should abandon surrealist exploration in favor of Soviet-style social realism. Rather than adopting the clarity of form and content that the French Left demanded, Césaire purposefully deploys a baroque, impenetrable style, which he links directly to maroon strategies of resistance and subterfuge.

Césaire begins the poem by writing from "a Seine night" to his comrade Depestre, who was exiled in Brazil at the time, urging him to ignore the call for French formalism and to join him instead in an evocation of the memory of the rebel Boukman. In the poem, Césaire asks Depestre with a hint of accusation if "the rains of exile" had "slackened the drum skin" of his voice. He urges Depestre to remember that as Antillean poets their blood was tinged with bad manners, leading them to occasionally "unlearn" how to count with their fingers and bow. But he also suggests that "blood is a thing that comes and goes." Thus, for Césaire, French norms are both learned and unlearned, intimately familiar but routinely rejected.

Césaire does not ask Depestre to turn his back on the French cultural establishment but to mock it, to disrespect it, and to not let himself be restrained by it. He implores him, "Rions, buvons, et marronnons!" This phrase has traditionally been translated as "Let's laugh, drink, and escape like slaves!" Césaire, however, does not urge his fellow bard to simply flee or abandon the French literary tradition, but to "maroon" it. Moreover, as the title of the poem suggests, Césaire's goal is to fashion a verb out of the noun *marronage*, that is, to imagine it as an ongoing activity rather than a discrete act.[46] Thus, a more accurate translation would be "Let's laugh, drink, and turn maroon!"

In the original version of the poem, Césaire declares: "Marronnons-les Depestre, Marronnons-les / comme jadis nous marronions nos maîtres à fouet" (Let's maroon them, Depestre, let's maroon them / as in the past we marooned our whip-wielding masters). In the later version, Césaire shifts from the exhortation "Let's maroon *them*" (i.e., the slave drivers, the party line) to an interrogative future form: "Marronnerons-nous?" (Shall we turn maroon?) It has been suggested that this change transforms marronage from a singular moment of flight into an ongoing act of escape.[47] Indeed, the first version suggests a more definitive assertion of rupture and abandonment—an attempt at deserting and leaving the master marooned and stranded—while the second version suggests an internal act—an epistemic break from within.

Césaire's poetics and his literary strategies have often been cast as disconnected from and discordant with his political project. His calls for rupture from Eurocentric norms and aesthetics have been placed in opposition to his efforts at incorporating the Antilles into the French Republic. However, one can view the political project of departmentalization as an example of his efforts at pillaging, othering, or marooning. For, as Césaire himself explained, the term *departmentalization* was itself one of his neologisms. He described it as "a reform in vocabulary," a way of reimagining what French Communists had named "the law of assimilation," a term he felt had humiliating cultural connotations. He described departmentalization as a *mesure technique*—a form of tinkering, a rearrangement, or a kind of legal "versioning." He did not see it as a permanent state, but rather as something that could be infinitely reworked. Moreover, he argued that what mattered most was not the word but the political project encapsulated by the word: the Antillean desire for social change. Thus, although for his "rebel sons" Césaire's political and literary contributions might seem contradictory and at times frustrating, his vision speaks directly to that of a later generation, for which marronage is also imagined as a form of strategic entanglement.

Lespri Kaskod

Though rarely compared to Césairean poetics, the political project of contemporary labor activists in Guadeloupe is often described as inherently contradictory in ways that echo the criticisms launched at Aimé Césaire. For example, UGTG activists are often chided for demanding the application of French labor laws while simultaneously promoting political and cultural rupture with France. For most union members, however, this seeming contradiction poses little problems. As Jackie, an active union delegate, explained,

> They say we are French. We don't want to be French. But fine, if you say we are French, then apply French law. Pay us minimum wage. Give us our rights, since we are supposedly French.

Most union leaders and members describe the union's use of the French legal system in similarly nonchalant ways, presenting their relationship to French law as a clearly calculated and strategic move. Max, one of the main leaders, put it this way:

> You need to understand our frame of mind: we are not constrained by legal decisions. That is, we are not bound by them. We have one political goal: to mobilize people for social change [*mobilizer les hommes pour transformer la vie*]. There are certain obstacles that have to be surpassed in order to arrive at that goal—we will surpass them. They place juridical barriers in front of us, legal barriers, they make use of the law just like they make use of the police and the media. The law poses an obstacle, but one that we will completely

overcome, because we know very well how they operate, we understand their means and ends. The barrier of the law is not new. The law has always been an obstacle, but it is only an immediate obstacle. The challenge is to be able to master the law [*le matriser*] without losing our orientation [*sans perdre le fil*].

Max's assertions echo the arguments of numerous Antillean scholars who suggest that French law has long been associated with social hierarchy, racial discrimination, and economic exploitation in the French Antilles.[48] These authors suggest that contemporary relationships with the legal system are conditioned by the importance of past forms of jurisprudence such as the *code noir*, the document that legally codified the slave economy, and postemancipation vagrancy laws, which often forced emancipated slaves to return to their former plantations against their will. They argue that the importance of these legally codified forms of exploitation and hierarchy in the past have led to particular understandings of liberty and freedom in the present, wherein liberty is understood as freedom *from* the law rather than a freedom guaranteed by law.[49]

This notion of freedom as an escape from the law is said to construct legal interactions as moments of individual ruse and acts of *débrouillage*.[50] The French term *débrouillage* refers to acts of resourceful cunning. A *débrouillard* is someone who is able to fend for themselves and deftly skirt obstacles and problems. In the Antilles, the Creole concept of *débrouya* often refers to unlawful or unconventional forms of resourcefulness that, although illicit, play an important role in daily life.[51] As the popular Creole proverb suggests, *débrouya pa péché* (the *débrouillard* is not a sinner). In other words, skirting and maneuvering the law does not conflict with the moral order of the contemporary Antilles.

This detached relationship to the law is said to lead Guadeloupeans to systematically avoid "legalizing" their lives, preferring to remain on the margins of the legal system.[52] As a result, acts such as squatting or appropriating land, constructing illegal or unapproved housing, driving without a license or car insurance, and *le travail au noir* (unreported labor and income) all become acceptable and normalized forms of behavior.[53] What matters is not abiding by the law, but being able to elude it.[54] As Guadeloupean sociologist Georges Trésor argues, this instrumental relationship to the law is deepened by the sense of exteriority or foreignness that French law holds in the Antillean context. He argues that

French laws, regardless of their content or contribution . . . continue to smack of exteriority. They intervene certainly in the internal organization of

Guadeloupean society, but we interpret them in our own way, we instrumentalize them for our own benefit, never having the feeling that they are the product of our own sovereignty or our own legislative power.[55]

The idea of "instrumentalizing" the law has long been an important part of the UGTG's legal strategies. Although its activists often use French labor laws to justify their claims, they also often demand (and receive) rights and benefits that go beyond the prescriptions of the French labor code. Thus on the one hand they will demand *egalité* (equality) with mainland French workers when it is materially beneficial—such as in the case of the thirty-five-hour workweek that was established in France under François Mitterrand. Yet at other times they will insist that the *specificité* (particularity) of Guadeloupean workers be recognized through the implementation of local holidays (such as Abolition Day, Carnival Week, and Whitmonday) or the application of regionally specific labor contracts that provide a different set of rights and compensation from those afforded to workers in mainland France.

Employers frequently fault the union for this selective use of the legal code, but they themselves also deploy similar tactics by claiming to be exempt from certain labor regulations based on the *specificité* of entrepreneurship in the Guadeloupean context.[56] UGTG activists counter employer claims to exceptionalism by unequivocally demanding the full application of the law; hence one of their more memorable battle cries during the 1990s: *la loi, toute la loi, et rien que la loi* (the law, the whole law, and nothing but the law).

Max explained the union's shifting position toward the law as follows:

> Our labor struggle operates on two different levels. First: 'The law, the whole law, and nothing but the law'—that was our mantra in many conflicts. But we mean the law as long as it serves us. As soon as the law holds us back, we break with the law, we create our own laws—that is the tradition of the nèg mawon.

Max further explained that the union uses the French labor code to "maré" the employers. In Creole *maré* can mean to restrain, halt, tie down, or physically prevent someone from doing something, but it can also refer to a spell or hex through which one controls the actions and desires of another. He explained,

> The labor code is supposed to *maré le patwon* [restrain the employers], but if the labor code *nou maré* [restrains us], we break with it as well. That is the

principle of *kaskod*, of rebels, of rebellion, of the maroons, of marronage. In other words, we conform to the law as long as it is working for us, but as soon as it stops working, *kaskod*!

For Max, the union engages in maroon politics not when it abandons the French system but when it uses it strategically. In other words, he doesn't let the French system "restrain" him but rather uses it (the master's tools, so to speak) to "restrain" the employers and government bureaucrats. His use of the term *kaskod* is significant here. *Kaskod* is a polyvalent Creole word that means "to break free" both in the sense of escape (to break from) and that of rupture (to break with). By engaging in kaskod politics, labor activists use the French labor system but remain unrestrained by its norms and constitutive logics—they effectively pillage trade unionism to achieve their ends but just as easily retreat from its logics when, as Max explains, those logics no longer work in their favor.

This form of political entanglement constitutes a significant shift from a traditional anticolonial ideology premised on complete rupture with the colonial system. Unlike previous models of postcolonial sovereignty, which hinged on the search for economic and political rupture, kaskod is predicated on acts of selective engagement and strategic retreat. It is in this sense that the union's politics can be said to constitute a form of guerrilla warfare (as Lukas suggested) or a modern-day form of marronage.

Union members generally described these practices as the realization of a deeply rooted spirit of rebellion that they describe as "lespri kaskod." They would often tell me that they had been drawn to the union precisely because of this rebellious spirit. Most reported that they had always been a bit rebellious; before coming to the union many of them had served as community organizers, cultural activists, and student leaders, or had been involved in athletic clubs, religious groups, neighborhood associations, or other types of civic groups. These might not seem like overtly political organizations, but in the context of the Antilles, cultural and civic associations and religious groups (particularly those informed by liberation theology) have long been closely linked to activism—indeed, it was precisely these kinds of groups that came together for the general strike of 2009.

Even those who hadn't been formally involved in organizations or associations would say that they had always been the voice of dissent among their family, friends, or colleagues. Their experiences varied, but the constant theme throughout their stories was that of a predisposition for confrontation and defiance, which they described as "lespri kaskod." They would often say that they had always been nèg mawons but just hadn't found a proper channel for their rebelliousness until joining the UGTG. In this narrative the UGTG emerges as a haven for these individual rebels. If union members are imagined as "runaway slaves," then the UGTG represents their refuge, their maroon community, their alternative society.

History at Work

When Lukas described the UGTG's actions as a form of guerrilla warfare, he suggested that their evocation of maroon practices was "spontaneous" and that labor activists engaged in these actions without knowing that they were being "driven from within." His comments seemed to suggest that the union's turn to the slave past was the result of an embodied and unarticulated memory of past forms of struggle. However, although the metaphor of unionism as marronage was common among many union members (and even among the union's critics, who often described the UGTG as radical, untamed nèg mawons), the use of marronage as a political category, and as a way of rethinking autonomy and sovereignty in the French Caribbean, is not simply the result of history working unconsciously through its subjects, but of present-day agents putting historical narratives to work.

Several months after my original conversation with Lukas about marronage and independence, he invited me to participate in a series of historical workshops he was organizing for the union. He named the workshops *atèlyé simawon—atèlyé* being the Creole word for workshop and *simawon* being Lukas's own Creole neologism. When I asked him about this term, he said that he wanted to move away from all this talk of nèg mawon and to go back to the Spanish root, *cimarrón*. He felt that a return to the word's etymological origins would help disentangle what he saw as the valiant history of marronage from the current misuse of *nèg mawon* as a catchall for all things rebellious.

Lukas's motivation for this workshop was partly rooted in his dismay at the release of a popular film titled *Nég Maron*, which he argued served only to perpetuate stereotypical images of the maroons. The film features music stars Stomy Bugsy and Admiral T in the lead roles as residents of a poor urban slum who find themselves on the wrong side of the law. Their characters (Josua and Silex) embody the figure of the *djobber*, the urban trickster whom some see as the modern-day avatar of the nèg mawon—floating from one odd job to the next, carving out a living on the fringes of the urban economy.[57] When the film opens, the lead characters appear as masterful navigators of the urban informal economy, engaging in questionable economic practices and carrying out illicit tasks for the island's powerful béké elites without questioning the role of these white elites in the island's racial and economic history. As the film progresses, the characters acquire a new political consciousness. Midway through the film they are hired to break into the home of a powerful béké to steal some documents. When they first arrive they amuse themselves by enjoying the trappings of the béké's wealth: they raid the refrigerator and eat their spoils while watching movies on the big-screen TV. But when they enter the béké's personal library, they discover framed pictures on the walls featuring iconic images of slave ships carrying human cargo. They also find slave records with the surnames of contemporary béké families listed as slave owners. At this point they are no longer enjoying the spoils of the béké's wealth. They trash the home and accidentally shoot the man who had sent them there, after which they flee the urban *cité* to find refuge in the rural countryside.

The film's director, Jean-Claude Flamand-Barny, explained his intentions in bringing together the history of marronage with the contemporary urban social landscape as follows:

> The *nègre marron* was the first *contestataire* of the law of slavery. It was he who liberated himself from his chains and took back his freedom. Refusing the degradation of the sugar plantations, he regains his dignity by finding refuge in the forest, protected from a system that was imposed upon him. The choice of the title *Nèg Maron* is a tribute to those uprooted men who fought in isolation, against an entire society, and who have been denigrated or forgotten. The title also draws a parallel with certain disaffected young people, who have no frame of reference, who have not found their place in this society, and who refuse to abide by its laws.[58]

In Flamand-Barny's description we can see an attempt at bringing together multiple, overlapping, at times contradictory narratives of marronage. He weaves a vision of grand marronage as rupture, isolation, and combat aimed at "an entire society" together with that of the urban trickster pillaging the system for individual profit and refusing to abide by its laws. Although the film might appear to be celebrating the djobber as the modern-day nèg mawon, it is only after the two protagonists make the historical connections between the contemporary wealth of the békés and their direct role in the slave trade that they come to embody the spirit of marronage. Further, the film's subtitle, *Ni chenn an pyé, ni chenn an tèt!*

2.3. *Nèg Maron* movie poster. Courtesy of Syncroteam Films.

(Chains on our feet, chains on our minds!), echoes a popular folk saying in Guadeloupe cautioning that although the physical chains of slavery have been broken, the psychological chains remain. Thus, although the film might appear to celebrate the petit marronage of the urban trickster, it suggests that the chains of slavery can only be broken through a psychological awakening. In other words, to qualify as marronage, these acts must be tied to a political and historical consciousness. In this sense the film directly echoes the historical debate over the distinction between petit and grand marronage as one based not just on duration but on political intent.

Lukas took great issue with the film, which he thought inappropriately celebrated urban youth as modern day nèg mawons and resurrected the representation of maroons as bandits on the lam.

> Who are the nèg mawons in that film? Drug addicts, delinquents, thieves, thugs! Once again the media and the government—because it is the government that financed this movie, the Regional Council, etc.—seek to promote the vision of nèg mawons as thieves, criminals, and bandits.

He argued that the movie represented an extension of the same discourse propagated by slave owners who had sought to tarnish the image of the nèg mawons.

> Who were the real maroons? The maroons were human beings who upon arriving in the Americas decided that they wanted nothing to do with the logic of the white man, and because of that they left and installed themselves on the outside and declared war on that system. They were not delinquents—they were warriors! When they say that those folks fled the system—that isn't what they did! They didn't just flee the system, they declared war on that system!

Lukas decided to organize his atèlyé simawon to educate union members about the "true" history of marronage and to dispel popular myths and stereotypes about that history. For his first workshop he brought together a group of construction workers for whom he had been a consultant during recent contract negotiations. On the day of the event, I joined the group of about a dozen male workers around the conference table at the union headquarters. Lukas stood at the front of the room with a large map of the Americas taped to the wall behind him.

Although he modeled the workshop on the union's popular-education-style discussion sessions, he ran it more like a traditional classroom, posing questions that he would call upon us to answer (though he would frequently cut us off and answer them himself). He began the session by offering a brief lecture on the history of the slave trade and the historical origins of the word cimarrón. He explained that the original term meant "he who escapes" (celui qui s'enfui). The term, however, referred not just to anyone who fled, he argued, but specifically to those who fled the imprisonment of slavery. He explained,

It is important to understand that these folks didn't just take off. They didn't just hide. Once they declared kaskod, they would come back regularly to liberate other slaves. And they declared war on the slaveholders.

He suggested that it was the white elites who began calling these runaway slaves "nèg mawons." Because, he insisted, "nèg is an insult."

You need to remember that a nèg was like a dog. There was a difference between an *homme de couleur* and a nèg. The word nèg does not refer to color, nèg doesn't mean "noir," and it doesn't just mean "slave." So those whites, they concocted this expression, based on *nèg* and *cimarrón*, and they called them *nèg marrons* and then later *marron* became in and of itself a verb: to *marroner*. . . .

At one point Lukas asked us how maroons were recaptured after they had run away. Answering his own question, he stated that it was other slaves, specifically trained by their owners for that purpose, who would bring them back to the plantation, where they would then face public punishment.

The other slaves who didn't kaskod, either because they were scared, didn't have the strength, or didn't want to leave their families—when they saw that others had left, they couldn't be comfortable with themselves as they continued to be slaves. So they started to denigrate those who left and to create this negative image of the nèg mawons.

The participants in the workshop responded by offering their own examples of negative images and stories they had heard as children about the nèg mawons. Slowly they began to recount how, indeed, escaped convicts and rapists were described as "maroons" and how the maroon had been evoked as a bogeyman figure to scare them when they were young. They shook their heads and looked at each other in amazement—it was as if they had almost forgotten that past.

Lukas encouraged the participants to connect these negative images of maroons with contemporary criticisms of the UGTG. "And what happens today? People call the UGTG vandals, delinquents. They criticize us and denigrate us . . . in the same way. It is the same story." By linking narratives about eighteenth-century maroons to contemporary anti-union discourse, Lukas used the workshop to offer not simply a lesson about the past, but to model ways of using the past to think about the present.

The conversation that day—the different ways the past was narrated and queried—evidenced the plausible interpretations of marronage that were available at this particular place and time. On the one hand, participants offered hazy recollections from their childhoods of parents equating maroons with bandits and escaped convicts—but it was clear that this narrative no longer resonated for them as an adequate frame for that history. The romantic image of the nèg mawon as a radical and noble *contestataire*, on the other hand, still had resonance and appeal. Yet the filmic portrayal of maroons as unlawful urban tricksters showed that a different, less heroic, model of marronage was also in play. The trickster's failure to, in Lukas's words, "declare war on the system" was, however, a source of disappointment.

In his presentation, Lukas wrestled with these different models. He asserted that rebel slaves had turned their backs on the logic of the West but he also recognized that they sustained complicated entanglements with the dominant system. He argued that they tried to liberate others, but were betrayed. They attempted to forge new political projects, but were criticized and denigrated. They were valiant, but challenged. They were not tragically doomed, but neither were they entirely triumphant.

The various narratives that emerged in Lukas's workshop speak to the particularities of their context of production. They index a moment when total rupture from the dominant system appears implausible, but simply navigating the system's contradictions feels inadequate. Ultimately, these narratives assert the value of engaging in forms of strategic entanglement, that is, of brokering terms and asserting control over political, economic, and historical ties that are not easily broken.

PART II

Emerging Transcripts

THREE

Life on the Piquet

During my time in Guadeloupe, when I would ask someone outside the UGTG what they thought of the infamous labor union, they would almost invariably criticize its disruptive and violent methods. "I'm not against the union in principle," they would insist. "The problem is the methods." They would assure me that they supported the union's efforts to improve the economic conditions of workers, but just wished that its labor struggles could be successfully carried out through other, less disruptive, means. In rejecting the union's methods, these observers would try to draw a neat distinction between the means and ends of political struggle. In this chapter, I would like to question whether such a distinction is possible.

I focus here on the most emblematic form of UGTG action: the labor strike. Most critics who denounce the union's methods point to strikes—and their accompanying suspension of sales and services—as its most reprehensible form of action. I thus begin by discussing how strikes are viewed and experienced in the public sphere as moments of economic and social disruption that threaten the prevailing social order. I then explore how strikes are lived by striking workers as moments of liminality and suspension, during which the economic and social relationships of daily life are brought into question.

In some ways, the story I tell might appear to be a romantic tale in which "all that is solid melts into air" and workers discover their class allegiances and political capacities.[1] As I demonstrate, however, the results of strikes are often ambiguous, sometimes negative, and almost always disappointing. Promises are made, agreements are signed, but harsh consequences often follow. I thus suggest that the effects of political struggle cannot be assessed through a simple measure of material and economic gains; rather, they need to be more subtly gauged by analyzing the affective and subjective transformations that take place during collective action.

Spectacles of Disruption

Although strikes may have become a rarity in other parts of the world, they are common occurrences in Guadeloupe. In 2002, the local prefecture estimated that in the previous year there had been over two hundred labor conflicts—a remarkable number for an economy of Guadeloupe's size.[2] Guadeloupe has much higher union density in general than mainland France, with 18 percent of the working population unionized, as opposed to 7 percent on the mainland.[3] The frequency of strikes, and their prominent role in the collective imagination, has led commentators in both local intellectual circles and the French national press to argue that Guadeloupe is plagued by a particularly conflictive social climate. As a result, tourists are often steered away from vacationing in this Caribbean "hot spot" and encouraged instead to spend a placid holiday in Saint Barthelemy, Saint Martin, or at least in Martinique, where the labor activists are said to be less virulent.

One reason labor strikes in Guadeloupe generate such a discourse of crisis is that, unlike traditional factory strikes that focus solely on disrupting production, Guadeloupe's strikes also disrupt forms of circulation and consumption. Striking workers typically paralyze their workplaces, block access to goods and services, and interrupt both local and transnational flows of capital. For example, during a government workers' strike in 1998, public servants shut down all local *mairies* (city halls), effectively suspending a wide range of city services—from the issuing of birth certificates to garbage collection—for over six months. During the infamous *grève d'essence* (gasoline strike) of 2001, workers in the petroleum industry, such as truck drivers and gas station attendants, blocked Guadeloupe's central point of gas distribution, cutting off the petroleum supply to the entire territory for three days while generating spectacular lines at gas stations. The *grève d'essence* has become part of local lore, and stories abound of commuters spending the night stranded in their cars or camping out at local gas stations to wait for a new supply. As a result, any mention of a strike—regardless of workforce sector—will send Guadeloupean commuters straight to the pumps to stock up.

During strikes workers also set up roadblocks by placing trash bins, lumber, rocks, and anything else they can gather in the middle of the road. These barricades are often quite spectacular in and of themselves, creatively reappropriating the tools and trappings of the workers' industry. For example, during a strike at the Carrefour megastore, workers gathered all the shopping carts from the parking lot and fenced off the entrance with row upon row of carts. At a local construction company, workers used the company's forklifts to pile up debris (including a burned-out car) in front of the company's entrance.

Striking workers also spill out onto the streets, blocking intersections, disrupting traffic, and cutting off access to strategic areas. The rallying call for such actions in Creole is *baré chimen*, which means "to block paths." Since blocking public roads is not a legally sanctioned form of trade union activity, workers get up at dawn to set up the barricades, then leave before the morning rush hour to avoid confrontation with the police and possible arrest. Although authorities eventually dismantle the barricades, their temporary placement successfully disrupts morning traffic and can easily bring the already-congested main coastal highway to a near standstill. Given that Guadeloupe has only one major highway, which circles the perimeter of the entire territory, a strategically placed barricade—combined with frantic traffic reports on the morning radio—can appear to paralyze the entire society.[4]

When I interviewed Rosan Mounien, one of the UGTG's first secretary-generals, he explained that the union had "invented" the barricades in the 1970s, during the sugar workers' struggles in Baie-Mahault. At the time, sharecroppers were being evicted from their homes by large sugar estates, which claimed that the workers had no legal claims to the property and that the owners had no legal responsibility to help them secure new housing. The first barricade was constructed out of a small, one-room creole *kaz* (house) that belonged to the sharecroppers, which was set up on logs and dragged to the main intersection with a tractor. At the time there were few side roads in Guadeloupe, so by blocking the main intersection they effectively cut off the two sides of Guadeloupe—Basse Terre and Grand Terre—from each other. After just one day of the *barricade a kaz*, workers signed agreements with employers and government officials that resulted in the construction of homes for former sugar workers in the Moudong sector of Baie-Mahault.[5]

Mounien proudly proclaimed that after that incident the UGTG's members became "barricade experts." He explained that the secret to a good barricade is to have something moveable in order to allow "priority vehicles," such as ambulances, to come through. He described barricades as sophisticated machinery that had to be carefully managed. "Not everyone knows how to build a proper barricade," he cautioned. "You have to master it. Otherwise you can end up *piégé* [trapped] by your own barricade." When I asked how they managed to move the original *barricade a kaz*, he laughed and said, "Exactly!" Apparently, at the time they hadn't yet refined their technique, so they ended up having to demolish the little *kaz creole*.

Over time, Mounien explained, the union continued to adapt its tactics to the changing landscape. As the French road system expanded, union militants began taking advantage of its features, particularly the ubiquitous traffic circles that dot the island. When a large-scale barricade isn't feasible, workers organize what they call an *opération escargot* (snail operation) in which they target a traffic circle and drive around it in separate cars as slowly as possible, slowing traffic down to a snail's pace while other workers pass out leaflets to surrounding drivers.

For example, in December 2003, bank workers for the Association française des banques (AFB) organized this type of slowdown to distribute leaflets explaining the details of their grievances in the business district of Jarry.[6] This commercial district sits on a peninsula that can only be accessed through two points on the main highway. By slowing down traffic in these two spots, workers effectively blocked all commercial activities in Jarry that morning, while also shutting down most of the banking system with their strike.

Given their frequency of use, barricades have become iconic symbols of union protest, serving as contentious smoke signals that announce the launch of an important conflict.[7] The main goal of these actions is to disrupt daily life, creating a sense of urgency and large-scale crisis. Barricades and slowdowns characterize the initial phases of conflict, often described as *le déclenchement*, meaning start, trigger, or release (as in the outbreak of a war or revolution). They represent a moment of rupture or breach, a "symbolic trigger of confrontation" in the larger social drama of the strike.[8] During strikes, a breach occurs not only between workers and their employers— through a suspension of their labor contract—but also between workers and the general public, through a suspension of the rules that govern social production and consumption. Critics widely cite the blocking of traffic (or *la circulation* in French) as the union's most offensive crime. Suddenly the ability to move, to circulate, and to consume becomes an inalienable right, and the suspension of such movement is experienced as a social crisis.

The Politics of Entrepreneurship

During my fieldwork, I interviewed Maryse Mayeco, the spokesperson for the Guadeloupean chapter of the Mouvement des entreprises de France

(MEDEF), an organization that represents employers, or as she described it, "l'UGTG des patrons." Mayeco was a middle-aged Afro-Guadeloupean woman, a former bank manager, and a self-described "boss" (*patron*) in the cement industry. She was charismatic and commanding, decidedly brash and outspoken, and clearly enjoyed representing the Guadeloupean business community. When I visited her in the offices of the MEDEF, located above a gas station in the Jarry industrial zone, she greeted me warmly and spoke openly about how she viewed the landscape of industrial relations in Guadeloupe. "You see," she said,

> here in Guadeloupe the international model of the relationship between employers and workers takes on a particular connotation. Everywhere else the boss has employees regulated by a contract, etc.—that is a Western kind of thing. But here the boss is still seen as the *chef négrière* [slave overseer], as the *colonialiste*, and they see themselves not as workers but as the slaves of the employer. Something that everywhere else is a normal relationship, here gets all tied up with slavery.

What Mayeco failed to mention was that most businesses in Guadeloupe are owned and operated by white families—either *blanc pays* (local whites), white béké elites from Martinique, white *métropolitain* managers and operators from mainland France, or the descendants of Syro-Lebanese immigrants who control major commercial sectors and are often grouped with the békés.[9] It is with local employers such as these that the union has the most heated conflicts, since they are the most reluctant to conform to French labor laws and the most resentful about having a union presence in their companies. As Colette Koury, the head of the Confédération générale du patronat des petites et moyennes entreprises (CGPME), put it during a public labor forum, rather than dealing with a union, they much prefer to resolve things "en famille."

These elites often imagine themselves at odds with the French state, and tend to argue that French economic and labor policies are ill-suited for the Caribbean context. They see themselves less as a bourgeoisie than as an aristocratic class with status and rights that precede and surpass the French state's authority.[10] They also maintain their distance from local politicians, whom they regard as more interested in courting votes than building the economy. As Mayeco told me, "Politicians don't work for the economy, because the economy doesn't vote." Her comments reflect a broader tendency among business leaders to dismiss political activism as banal and futile populist amusement. They argue that business leaders are the only ones who are serious about creating wealth and prosperity in Guadeloupe, and that labor activists and politicians seek only to increase Guadeloupe's dependency on the French state by hampering economic growth.

"This shows you the employers' attitude," said Urbain Martial Arconte, the director of the local labor department. "They say that if there is a strike, it is not because their company does not respect the law or because workers seek certain advantages. No, it is because the union wants to sink the economy!" Martial had spent several years documenting the labor problem in Guadeloupe and produced numerous statistical studies on the cause and nature of its labor conflicts. In 2003 he found that 73 percent of the strikes carried out during the previous year were fueled by demands for enforcement of existing labor legislation.[11] Local employers contend that French labor laws are unsuitable to the local context, constantly exclaiming, "We're not in Europe!" Willy Angèle, president of MEDEF during the 2009 strike, once explained to me, "We're a little piece of Europe in the Americas. Our development model doesn't correspond to our societal structure. We are seven thousand kilometers from the economic bloc to which we belong. You simply can't expect to apply the same model here!"[12]

During labor strikes these employers often appear on local television in order to put public pressure on workers to return to work. They routinely stress how hard they work, how many obstacles and difficulties they face, and how difficult it is to be an entrepreneur in the Guadeloupean context.[13] They argue that the union wants to break them, drive them to bankruptcy, and destroy the local economy. Employers also often challenge the strikers to try to run their own businesses so they can see for themselves just how hard it is.

At one point the union actually did try to encourage workers to take over their own companies, trying (in their words) to turn proletarians into entrepreneurs. The targets for these initiatives were not businesses run by local elites, but those belonging to what the union describes as *affairistes*: foreign investors seeking tax havens in the overseas territories. Labor leaders argue that *affairistes* often refuse to settle a labor conflict so that they can declare bankruptcy, collect assistance from the French state, and set up shop somewhere else. Union officials decided that instead of sitting around waiting for these conflicts to be resolved, they would occupy their workplaces and keep them running.[14] Keeping businesses open offered a way of generating income for the strikers while training them as managers, and in this way no one could argue that the union was destroying the economy. In addition to the workplace takeovers, the union also began organizing worker-run

cooperatives. However, these efforts were short lived, partly because workers lacked access to the necessary networks of capital and credit, but also
because of the union's reputation.

This became clear to me during a chance encounter with a high-ranking
Exxon-Mobil executive whom I happened to sit next to during a flight out
of Guadeloupe. As our plane took off we exchanged introductions and
engaged in some good-natured teasing about Caribbean rivalries (he was
from the Bahamas and I from Puerto Rico). He explained that he had been
in Guadeloupe on business, promoting Exxon's new On the Run conve-
nience store franchises. I told him that I was sure he would have no problems finding potential buyers for his franchise, particularly in Guadeloupe,
where gas stations serve as popular gathering spots. He smiled but said he
was a little disappointed after his trip. He had hoped to find enterprising
young locals looking for a business opportunity, but instead the only interested parties had been white elites. He said he was of humble background,
that his father had been a sugar worker, but he himself had risen in the
Bahamian social ranks thanks to education and business opportunities. I
smiled and told him that I knew plenty of "enterprising locals" quite interested in buying franchises—particularly service stations. He was surprised
to hear this and said that the white elites he met with had claimed that local
blacks were simply uninterested in entering into the business sector, as if
this were some kind of cultural preference. We laughed and became excited
about the opportunities that lay ahead. However, when I explained that
these were unionized workers seeking to buy franchises with the support of
their union, the conversation came to a halt. "Oh no!" he said. "We want
nothing to do with those unions!"

I had a similar encounter, during a different trip, with the regional op-
erations manager of McDonald's Corporation. We were both sitting at the
departure gate, waiting for our American Eagle flight to Puerto Rico to begin
boarding, when I overheard him talking on the phone and immediately
recognized his Puerto Rican accent. As soon as he finished his conversation, I made my way over to him and expressed my delight at encountering
another Puerto Rican in Guadeloupe. After exchanging pleasantries he told
me that he had been in Guadeloupe checking on the McDonald's franchises
and making sure that everything was up to standards. I started asking him
about the process of buying a franchise and what it entailed. He described
it all in excited detail, but when I told him that I worked with local labor unions, his tone changed and the conversation shifted. He said it was
impossible for a group of workers to buy a McDonald's franchise. Even if
they had the necessary capital and undertook training, they would still lack

expertise. He said that to have a McDonald's franchise, one needed a business degree and significant experience. "We can't sell our franchises to just anyone," he explained, "because before you know it they'll have *bokits* on the menu!"[15] As we parted he reached into his pocket for what I expected to be his business card—instead it was a coupon for a free Big Mac at the airport McDonald's in Puerto Rico.

Given the obstacles to entrepreneurship in Guadeloupe, labor disputes and negotiations emerge as the sole instance in which workers can voice not only complaints about their work conditions, but also recommendations and proposals for their industries. Negotiating sessions represent one of the few spaces where workers can act as managers and owners—and realize that they have the capacity to do so. Not coincidentally, one of the biggest challenges workers face is getting employers to sit at the negotiating table and let them have a say in their businesses.

Negotiations are highly ritualistic processes that involve spectacles of disruption followed by a longer process of dialogue.[16] The first several meetings are usually devoted to airing grievances and venting frustrations that have accumulated over years of workplace conflict. Workers will begin by stating their complaints and demands but will often veer off into a discussion of personal frustrations with how they are treated and how the company is run. These preliminaries allow workers to voice their grievances while also demonstrating their knowledge of the workplace and their ability to speak as competent professionals in their field. Employers usually respond by invalidating their claims, questioning their abilities, and devaluing their knowledge of the business world.

One of the labor disputes I witnessed was particularly revealing: workers had gone on strike to demand the reinstatement of a manager who had been fired after accusing the company's director of mishandling funds. As part of the strike the union had demanded an audit, which found that funds had indeed been mishandled, even if this did not point directly to the director. The conflict should have been resolved immediately after the audit, but the director insisted that the manager apologize for having made such accusations and the manager refused. During the negotiations the suspected theft was at the forefront of the discussions. Employees argued that they were tired of silently bearing witness to thievery, waste, and mismanagement in their workplace.

Only a handful of workers were allowed in the negotiations, so during each pause (i.e., when either party would dramatically storm out), the rest of the striking workers huddled around those of us who had been in the room to find out what had happened. They were shocked to hear that the union delegate had called the director a thief to his face. They turned to me looking for a witness, and when I played my tape back for them, they started screaming and cheering. At that point, none of the strike's material demands had been addressed, and it was still unclear whether the dismissed manager would be reinstated; but the simple fact of having voiced these accusations directly to company officials was already a significant reward for the long weeks of striking. It meant that their opinions and criticisms of how the company was being run were finally being heard.

Sucré: The Bittersweet Space of the Piquet Grève

Although the media and the public tend to view strikes as dramatic moments of disruption and confrontation, most workers in Guadeloupe experience them as moments of stillness. Whereas in the United States strikes usually take the form of workers chanting and marching single file, creating a picket line that one must decide whether or not to cross, in Guadeloupe the *piquet* is not a line in the sand but a space of suspension.[17] Most of the time on strike is spent waiting: waiting for employers to agree to negotiate, waiting for the labor courts to hand down a ruling, or simply waiting to see what will happen next. It is this experience of waiting and simply being *sur le piquet* (on the picket site) that distinguishes the *grèvistes*, striking workers, from the *non-grèvistes*, those coworkers who don't support the strike and who stay home, take sick leave, or perhaps work elsewhere until the strike ends.

At times picket sites can become spaces of heated conflict, especially when employers try to break the strike by hiring replacement workers or by otherwise intimidating and threatening strikers. In fact, employers often arrive at the piquet either armed or accompanied by armed guards, and at various points in Guadeloupean history, numerous workers have lost their lives on the piquet. However, despite these eruptions of violence, for the most part the *piquet grève* represents a space of community and solidarity.

The importance of the piquet as a site of community became clear to me through my ongoing conversations with striking workers at the Sucré production facility in Baie-Mahault.[18] Sucré is a large, internationally known food company specializing in dairy products and bottled beverages. It is one of several food franchise companies operating in Guadeloupe; these include the likes of Nestlé, Dannon, and Yoplait. Workers at the Sucré production plant had gone on strike to demand the application of the French thirty-five-hour workweek legislation and to establish a base salary for their delivery drivers, among other grievances.[19]

I spoke with these workers for the first time on the week before Christmas, when they were six months into their strike and preparing to face the holidays with no income, no savings, and no resolution in sight. They all said that the only place they found solace was on the picket site. As one of the workers remarked, "I only feel at ease when I'm here. When I'm at home I start to worry and get anxious—I start turning things over and over in my mind. But when I'm here I feel better, I get strength from the other *camarades.*"

Denis, the union delegate for their section, told me of the pressure and responsibility he felt in handling the strike. His initial smile faded as he spoke; he exhaled slowly, and his shoulders dropped, as if burdened by an invisible weight. In broken, unfinished sentences he began telling me about late-night phone calls and hushed conversations with his colleagues. He told me their stories of past-due accounts and fears of foreclosures, re-possessions, divorces, and Christmas without presents for their children. In the end he said, "I have to be strong for them. That's why I have to be here, because they give me strength."

When I asked Corinne, the only female grèviste in the Sucré strike, how she felt about being the sole woman on the piquet, she smiled and quickly responded, "I feel myself becoming stronger." She acknowledged that as a woman it was less acceptable for her to be on strike and that her participation had generated some jealousy from both her husband, who was not pleased that she was spending her days alone with a group of men, as well as from the wives and girlfriends of the other grèvistes, who treated her with suspicion when they visited the piquet. However, she insisted that she had to be there "to draw strength in order to continue," because if she stayed home she would drown in sorrow.

Corinne compared the experience of being on strike to a dreamlike state, with the piquet as her site of realization:

> You know, for months it felt like I was in a dream. I wouldn't realize that I was on strike until I got here. I would prepare my daughter for school, drop her off, and drive over here, and it wasn't until the moment I parked my car over there [outside the company's parking lot] that I would realize that I was going to the piquet and not to work.

She paused for a minute, then concluded, "I think you have to be in a dream, because if you realize what is going on, you won't be able to bear it." How-ever, she was careful to point out that it was "like a bad dream, not a night-mare, but a bad dream." When I asked her why she made this distinction, she responded without hesitation, "Because we laugh, we joke, and we play *la belotte* (a French card game)!"

As Corinne's comments suggest, some of the essential aspects of the piquet are food, alcohol, laughter, and play. In fact, with workers seated at
folding tables, playing cards, and often (especially in the case of female
grèvistes) with their children in tow, prolonged work stoppages might appear to foreign eyes more like family picnics than episodes of social crisis.
Playing cards and dominoes is important not just for passing the time but
also for channeling workers' energies and frustrations. Several strikers commented that playing cards helped them relax and release some of the frustration they felt about their economic difficulties. The piquet offered a space of
reprieve from the stress and tension of sustaining the strike. The long hours
were whittled away in competitive games and humorous storytelling.

Drinking was also an important aspect of socialization, since it helped
break down social barriers and encourage intimacy and sociality. At one
piquet site a women whispered to me that several of the men had lost their
girlfriends due to the financial difficulties of the strike. When I asked how
she knew this, she whispered softly, "They talk about it when they drink."

Despite the importance of alcohol, the mainstay of the piquet is collective food preparation, for which striking workers usually pool their resources. Often these meals involve traditional Guadeloupean foods made
of locally grown ingredients, many of which are offered to the strikers in
solidarity. Strikers insist that when you go on strike, you will never starve;
you may not be able to buy French cheese, but you will have plenty of green
bananas and *igname* (local yams). Food thus becomes an integral aspect of
being on strike, and in some ways an abundance of food signals a healthy
strike. For example, I once called a union delegate on the phone to discuss
a strike at her workplace. When I asked her how the strike was going, she
replied, "Oh, it's going wonderfully. We've received so much support—I've
already gained three kilos!"

During strikes workers place great emphasis on solidarity, often articulated around the Creole notion of *koudmen* (which can be loosely translated
as "giving a hand").[20] During traditional *koudmen* actions, neighbors and
friends would form collectives to help each other tend to their fields, particularly around the time of sugar harvests. The idea of *koudmen* evokes a
feeling of commonality and collectivity that is felt to have been lost with the
decline of the agricultural industry and the shift to a consumer-based economy. The time spent on the piquet provides the opportunity to not only
reflect on these past social forms but to reenact them, albeit temporarily.

The solidarity experienced during a strike pushes workers to rethink the
importance of community while also creating a new community among
the striking workers. Often workers will spend more time together during

a strike than they did during their normal workdays. Whereas before they would most likely know only the workers on their shift, on the piquet there are no shifts, no areas of production, and no hierarchical distinctions. Further, people who work nearby often stop in at the piquet to have a drink, buy a meal, or perhaps just honk their horn and wave as they drive by. One of the workers at a distribution center in Jarry remarked that the strike period marked the first time she had felt a sense of community in the industrial zone despite having worked there for seven years.

This opportunity for reflection on and experimentation with alternative social and economic practices is part of why union leaders emphasize that life on the piquet is the most important aspect of labor struggles, above and beyond the initial spectacles and public shows of force. This is when solidarity is forged, as workers discuss the problems they face together, including the individual problems and challenges of living for a prolonged period without a salary.[21] On the piquet, they share their experiences of having their cell phones cut off, losing their car insurance, taking the bus because they cannot afford gas, and having to pick up their children from school at lunchtime to feed them at home because they cannot afford to pay school cafeteria fees. This kind of support and camaraderie is essential for sustaining their movement because, as one of the workers explained, being on strike "destabilizes you on all sides." He explained that during this time your bills pile up, your spouse threatens to leave, your friends and family disapprove of your union affiliation, and your entire social world is brought into question.

Union leaders argue that this destabilization forces workers to reevaluate their relationships. The hardships of the strike unmask fair-weather friends while revealing the importance and power of other social ties. Most striking workers will admit that the only way they were able to endure long strikes was by relying on the support of their closest friends and kin. For example, one striking worker related a chance encounter with his cousin: the cousin complained about being unable to reach the worker on his cell phone; when the worker explained that his phone had been disconnected because he couldn't afford to pay the bill, his cousin immediately gave him the money to pay for it. A female grèviste compared these types of experiences to those of a new mother. "When you go on strike," she said, "you don't know how you're going to do it, but you always find help. It's like when you have a baby. You don't know how you're going to do it, but you do. Someone always shows up to help you, just when you need it the most!"

As they struggle for better wages, overtime pay, and other benefits, workers ironically find themselves without an income, depending on either their savings or (more likely) the help of those close to them. Therefore, although they are becoming empowered through collective action, they have great feelings of vulnerability and uncertainty, since they have no idea when the strike will end and cannot fully control its outcome. This creates a feeling of suspension, as their normal lives are indefinitely put on hold.

Corinne remarked that since the strike began, she had stopped thinking about the future and focused only on the immediate present.

> Since the strike, I don't have any projects—I live each day. I have no plans for the future. I simply endure the strike [*je ne fait que subir le grève*]. The only project I have is to buy my daughter's Christmas presents—because she is counting on that—but people ask me where I'm going to spend Christmas Eve, and I have no idea! Before, I had plans. I was thinking of buying some furniture for the living room. . . . But now I realize you can't really control your destiny [*on n'est pas maître de soi*]. You never really know what's going to happen. That makes you live life differently.

As Corinne's words suggest, being on strike not only makes workers reflect and see things differently, it also makes them live differently. Workers craft new forms of relatedness, new relationships to their community, new relationships to time and to the future, and even new relationships to money. As one striking worker explained, given the uncertain duration of a strike, even when they do get access to money they are hesitant to spend it. As another worker put it:

> If someone lends you money, you're going to spend it carefully. You're not going to spend two euros on a bottle of water or anything like that. Being on strike really makes you rethink the value of things.

Corinne remarked, "Now when my husband gives me money, I don't enjoy spending it as I did before—it's not the same as when I was earning it." She said her husband had given her one hundred euros to buy Christmas presents for their daughter, but she couldn't bring herself to spend it. She touched her purse and said softly, "I have it here, right here in my purse." She paused and looked at her purse, touching it hesitantly as if it were a foreign object. It was almost as if she had forgotten what it was like to have so much money in it. Or as if, coming out of a long fast, she had to slowly coax back her appetite for consumption.

In addition to reassessing their own social and economic relationships, workers on the piquet also reflect in detail on the economic relationships underpinning their strike. During this time, they prepare for negotiating sessions by meeting with union-affiliated accountants who present them with the organizational structure, financial flows, and corporate makeup of their company. In addition, according to French labor law, they should have access to the company's internal documents, payroll information, and financial reports. However, the fines that employers face if they refuse to turn these over are relatively small, and many employers prefer to pay them than to share their financial information with their workers. This was the case at the Sucré production facility. The manager's refusal to turn over the company's records, and the many financial burdens the company was willing to bear during the strike, were deeply revealing. As Denis, the union delegate for negotiations during the Sucré strike, recounts:

> This has been a real maturing process for all of us. At first we couldn't believe he [the manager] could do this to us. We thought we knew him, but we didn't know him at all. We respected him. He always acted like he was correct—right with the law—but he's not. And can you imagine how much money he must have, that he can afford to shut down for this long?! And he knows we can't afford it—he sees us here every day, he knows how hard it is for us. He says the company doesn't have the money to pay us what we deserve, but they have money to fly out a lawyer from Martinique for each negotiating session and to rent a meeting space, even though both the union and the labor department could provide one for free?

In addition to seeing their employers in a new light, workers also develop new relationships with each other, breaking down prior divisions among themselves. During the strike, Denis explained, workers in the different areas of production and distribution had come together to discuss each others' pay scales and benefits.

> Now we all know what everyone makes. There are no secrets between us anymore. We even know how much workers at the rival company make—they came here and met with us, gave us support, and told us what they were getting paid so that we could use that in our negotiations. We now know that we have to stick together, because they [the employers] stick together. You know, one time he [the manager] had us take some sugar over to their factory because they had run out—I think it was during the dockworkers' strike, I'm not sure. . . . But the point is, he sent them sugar! OK? And they're supposed to be competitors! What is that?

Thus, in preparing for negotiations, workers learn not only about their conflict but also about their workplace and their industry and often expand their notion of community to include workers in other companies.

Labor strikes generate a conceptual clearing by providing a break from the bodily hexis of quotidian life.[22] Strikes create a suspension of work, an engagement in new social relationships with coworkers and family, and a momentary rupture with the wage economy. "On the piquet you find yourself analyzing a lot of things," said Aline, a young preschool teacher who had been on strike for four months at the time of our conversation. "Usually during your daily life things just happen and you don't think twice about them, but here I've discovered things that I had never even thought of questioning."

As Aline's words suggest, the piquet provides a unique space for analysis. For union leaders, this is the main reward of a prolonged strike: not the spectacle of initial direct actions or the actual results of negotiation, but this space and time for discussion and reflection. Union leaders sometimes draw out strikes, or at the very least do not rush them to resolution, so that workers can revel in and fully experience this liminal space, betwixt and between the domains of labor and leisure, on the margins of the capitalist economy, and enmeshed in new forms of community with those around them.

Although temporary, the transformations experienced during this period are consequential. It has been argued that liminal moments can forge an "institutional capsule or pocket" that contains "the germ" for future social change.[23] Few, however, have explored how these potentialities can be organized and directed toward broader societal change. To understand this process, it is important to examine not only the experiences of striking workers but also the role of union leaders in shaping and directing the subversive potential of the piquet grève.

"All That Is Solid Melts into Air"

During my fieldwork, I visited many piquet sites with Max. We would often meet at the union office early in the morning and drive around all day in his beat-up white Volkswagen Fox, visiting different groups of striking workers. When he arrived at a piquet, everyone would rise from their chairs and make their way over to him. They all seemed to light up when he arrived: the men would shake his hand vigorously and offer him a drink, and the women would kiss his two cheeks, hugging him and tugging at him in a way that was both maternal and playful.

The grèviste, the true grèviste, is reborn after the strike. He's a new man after
the strike. There are losses—it's true that there are losses and there are people
who are destroyed after a long strike, who lose a lot, because they didn't organize themselves, they didn't prepare their families ideologically or in terms
of their personal finances. But the long strike which we [the UGTG] carry out
is a strike of construction. Through it we build new relationships, new bal-
ances of power, and also a new man.[26]

After the Strike: New Men and Women?

I met again with some of the Sucré workers during a return visit to Guadeloupe, two years after their strike had begun and one year after it had
reached its resolution. I was excited to see them, to learn how their conflict
had concluded, and to know how things changed for them once they left the
piquet. When I originally encountered them, six months into their strike,
I was struck by their unity and resolve. Although they spoke openly about
the challenges they faced, they also demonstrated a sense of empowerment
and pride in their actions. In fact, one of the workers suggested that they
had already won their battle. "Just being here as long as we have—that is
already a victory." They seemed like a textbook example of the kind of processes that Max described.[27] Before going on strike there was little solidarity
among them; there were deep cleavages between truck drivers and factory-
side workers and between the day and night shifts. But during their time on
the picket site, they had developed new bonds through their shared experiences. I was thus eager to know the outcomes of their strike: what did they
achieve? And what happened to the new relationships they developed once
they left the piquet? In addition, I was curious about the impact of their
experiences on their political engagement. After sustaining a yearlong strike,
how did they view the union and its methods?

Denis

I met with Denis, the Sucré union delegate, outside one of the large apartment complexes that line the entry to Pointe-à-Pitre's colonial district.
When I arrived, he led me through the maze of buildings and interior pa-
tios to a small, cozy office that belonged to the tenants' association. Denis
had been raised in this building and maintained a close relationship to
the community. Although he now lived with his wife and children in a

more spacious home in the suburb of Les Abymes, he still kept his parents' old apartment and was closely involved with the tenants' association.[28] The office was empty except for a large dining room table covered in a cheery madras-patterned tablecloth. We opened the windows to let in some fresh air and began discussing the strike as the neighborhood children played an impromptu game of soccer in the courtyard.

Denis was in his early forties at the time. He had held several odd jobs before coming to Sucré, where he had worked for over ten years. He was of average height but extremely muscular and tended to wear sleeveless shirts that highlighted his strong build and tattooed arms. Corinne once commented that his gruff appearance had made her hesitant to talk to him before the strike. However, on the picket site, she and the other workers had come to know him as a kind and gentle soul, and in fact he had become the main confessor for their group. This posed a bit of a problem for Denis, since it left him with no one in whom to confide his own problems.

> Voilà! That's the thing [c'est ça l'histoire]. I listened to everyone, but no one could listen to me. As a delegate, I also had financial problems, family problems, etcetera, but if people came to cry on my shoulder and I started to cry on their shoulders, it would have been over—we would have collapsed! It was important for them to see me as strong. If I confided too much in them, they would have thought I was weak, and they needed me to be strong.

Despite Denis's strength, the long strike took a significant toll on him and his family. At the time of our conversation, a year after returning to work, his marriage was still strained and he had few people to confide in. During our conversation he seemed nervous and unaccustomed to revealing his fears and worries. He kept his head down initially, staring at the table and shuffling through his stack of union papers as if a script for our conversation were to be found among the many press releases, faxes, and letters of the Sucré case. He had brought with him all the documents from the conflict, which he kept neatly arranged in a bright yellow portfolio. They were in pristine condition and carefully organized, with several passages highlighted in bright orange. Although it was clear that he had read them closely, he seemed to still be struggling to make sense of them, still searching for something in them that would explain the length of their strike, the stubbornness of their employer, and the apparent failure of their efforts. During our conversation he often handed me a document, hoping that perhaps the answer to my questions might be found there.

We began by discussing the end of the strike. When I had last spoken with him, over a year earlier, it had seemed as if both sides were deadlocked and refusing to make any concessions. After the initial round of negotiations, months had gone by with little progress and little contact with the employer. The long periods of silence were discouraging and made it seem as if the conflict would never end. However, the worst part came later, when the franchise manager started bringing in products from the production facility in Martinique. Denis recounted,

> That was the hardest part, watching him arrive with his products and with the gendarmes protecting him. It was insulting to us. You know, there are people who think that to insult someone is to use *grosse mots* [bad words], but it's not true—*le comportement* [actions] can be equally insulting. Every time we saw the gendarmes arrive on the piquet, we'd know that a new shipment had arrived. And the whole time we're sitting there on strike, with no money, and he's bringing in his products and making his money [*il fait son chiffre*]. That really affected the *camarades.* And on top of it, he would come by the piquet and harass us, saying, 'Aha, you think the strike is almost over, no? Well, you're wrong, you'll see, it's going to last a long time.' He would always try to provoke us like that. We wouldn't say anything, but still we would hear that, and that stays with you.

Denis explained that initially workers tried to block the trucks from delivering the imported goods, but they were sentenced to pay hefty fines for their actions and soon their bank accounts were frozen.

> Can you imagine what it was like when those bank papers arrived? Your account is blocked, and your wife sees that? Just imagine the problems it creates. . . . That's what they do—since they can't confront you physically, since they can't break you down, they try to mess things up for you at home. They try to make you give up, to make you think twice, and you think that maybe you *should* give in before you lose everything. . . . But you know there comes a time when you're in so deep that you just can't go back.

He smiled, glanced out the window at the children playing, and said,

> It's like if you're playing a game of soccer and it starts to rain. If you hadn't started playing already you might say, "I won't play, I don't want to get wet and dirty." But if you're already there, if you're already dirty, and it starts to rain, well, you might as well just keep on playing.

After several months of deliveries, the workers were discouraged, and Denis believes they let themselves fall into a trap.

> On that day, he [the manager] arrived in his car, all by himself. And behind him the truck arrived with just three people: a driver and two other people. There were no gendarmes, and the people in the truck, they weren't even—they were wearing T-shirts and jeans, like they were just out for the day. And when the boys saw that, they said, 'Oh! He arrived without gendarmes. We're going to take advantage!' So they called me—I was at the union headquarters—and they told me he had arrived without gendarmes and that they were going to mess with him [*le stresser, l'angoisser*]. But when they told me that, I told them not to do it. Because what were they going to accomplish? Not let him get his truck out? *Beh*, then he'd call the gendarmes and get it out anyway! So I told them not to do it. And they said, 'OK, Denis, *d'accord!*' But then immediately they called Max, who was sitting across from me at the same table, and they told him the same thing, and Max told them the same thing I did. So we hung up, laughed, and assumed that they hadn't done anything. But then when I returned to the piquet later that afternoon, I found them celebrating: they had barricaded the truck and started a fire. The firemen had come and everything! They were so happy, we were all happy. We needed a victory. But then in June they received a letter—that famous letter. Apparently one of the men in the truck was an off-duty police officer and had identified them. So, you see, it was a trap. The whole thing was a trap and a provocation! He [the manager] was smart [*malin*]. Once that happened he knew that we were in a weak position. Several months later he signed the end-of-strike agreements and then he went ahead and fired all those guys.

The "famous letter" Denis refers to is a dismissal letter that six of the workers received on the day they were supposed to return to work. Initially the union had sought to contest their dismissals, but in the end the workers accepted severance packages and moved on to other jobs. Denis explained that these dismissals soured the return to the workplace and made the strikers feel defeated.

> It was very bitter. We had waited so long that we just couldn't believe it was over. And then we weren't really proud, either, because of the *camarades* who were left out. We returned to work, because, well, you have to work, but there is no more love for what you do, because you are completely *déçu* [disappointed]. And also, there was a lot of tension with the *non-grévistes* when we came back. They never really knew what was going on. They weren't with us

on the piquet. When we came back they didn't know how to address us, and we didn't even want to talk to those people. What was really troubling is that they benefited from the strike—it was tough to be put down by these people [*te fait mépriser*] while knowing that you are struggling for them too. But that is the law—the French law.

Although the firings created a tense climate upon their return, the situation was somewhat defused by the massive cleanup task they faced. After being closed for an entire year, the Sucré factory was a mess. The stocked ingredients had gone bad, the stores of sugar had melted, and the entire plant was infested with vermin. "You can't imagine it," Denis said. "It was disgusting." All the workers pitched in for the cleanup and they even received bonus pay for their trouble. Denis said that this transition made them lose steam. Although union leaders had warned them that they needed to make sure their agreement was respected, the long period of cleanup and *redémarrage* (restarting) of the factory made them lose their momentum. They stopped holding union meetings and focused their energies on paying off their debts and patching things up with their families.

After the initial cleanup passed, it became clear that the employer had little intention of implementing the contract agreement. By then it was too late to enforce the agreement because the workers had already lost too much ground.

That is the drama in this place! If you go on strike, people accuse you of trying to strangle the *société*.[29] They say that strikes are unnecessary and that you need to dialogue—but where is the dialogue here? Every week we have delegate meetings with this guy and they are pointless. None of the agreements have been applied. But what are you going to do? Go back on strike? The strike lasted one year! What am I going to do? Go back on strike for another year so he will respect the agreement he signed?

Denis thought going back on strike was unlikely. He was biding his time, no longer doing his job with the same pleasure. He was actually making less money than before, though working fewer hours.

Before we were paid on commission, so we really hustled [*on se démmerdait*]. But now, after everything he said and everything he did, after he denigrated us like that . . . you have no desire to make any sacrifices, because you also have a family—he [the manager] privileged his family, no? So, you too—you have your children. So the new agreement says that we work a maximum of ten hours a day—so you begin at 5:30 a.m. and at 3:30 p.m. you're done. You go home to your family. In the end, that's what really matters. And you know, I tell myself that I wasn't necessarily born to be that man's *salarié* [wage worker]. My destiny is mine—it is in my hands. If tomorrow I don't have a job, life isn't over. There's much more to life than work.

Corinne

When I called Corinne on the phone, she immediately recognized my voice, and even though over a year and a half had passed since we had last spoken, she graciously offered to spend her day off with me. We met in the *zone industrielle*, at the lunch wagon across from the Sucré factory. From there I hopped into her two-door Fiat, and she drove me through the town of Sainte-Rose, up the winding roads leading to her home in the outer hills. During the drive we spoke of my deteriorating French skills, her daughter's newly acquired food allergies, and the fear of coming hurricanes—carefully avoiding the purpose of my visit. It was not until we reached her home and took our places across from each other at her kitchen table that we finally spoke of the strike. Suddenly it was as if the floodgates had opened and she rushed to fill me in on everything that had happened. But first she quickly slipped into the other room to fetch her stack of papers. Unlike Denis, she did not emerge with a neatly organized dossier but with a messy, unwieldy pile that she carried with both hands. Like Denis, however, she seemed to have pored over them looking for clues. During our conversation she kept turning the pages, flipping violently through them in search of answers.

Although more than a year had passed, to her it all still felt like a dream. The fact that the strike had ended exactly one year after it started added to that dreamlike feeling. She said it was as if suddenly she had awoken and the previous year had been erased—her husband was no longer mad at her, her family no longer disapproved, and she had returned to work as if nothing had happened. "It was like that year didn't exist," she said. "It was wasted. Nothing came of it. We had no victories. It was just over." During the entire year that followed, she kept reliving the strike—every day she would think back about what they had done on the piquet the previous year. She compared it to the mourning period that follows the end of a great love affair.

It's like when a relationship ends, and you mourn it for a long time, but eventually you let it go because you know that nothing lasts forever—everything comes to an end. Even those relationships that seemed so strong and sure, they disappear.

Part of the reason Corinne mourned the strike was that she missed the camaraderie and solidarity she had experienced. Although the strike had brought many economic and personal hardships, there was something magical about the experience itself. She said she now realized that the piquet provided a "cocoon" of sorts.

> It was like we were insulated from everything. We were in this cocoon, and we were like some sort of strike machine: strike, strike, strike! We didn't know anything else. The *non-grèvistes* would come talk to us, try to reason with us, but we couldn't conceive of anything else. We were locked into our own logic.

Corinne thought the cocoon somehow protected them from the hardships of the strike. She said it was like they were in their own alternate reality, and once the strike ended, their cocoon burst. Rather than emerging triumphant, however, they exited rather hesitantly, longing for what were in some ways easier days on the piquet.

However, unlike Denis, who said he no longer had the same love for his job, Corinne was relatively content to be back at work. She worked in Sucré's *labo* (production facility), and her job was to measure and mix the ingredients for the different food formulas. She said she and her coworkers had a lot of responsibility; if something went wrong, if someone got sick from eating their product, they would be held accountable. Something about that level of responsibility appealed to her. She confessed that she was not really qualified for her job, which she had gotten through a *filon* (connection) after her uncle had helped the franchise owner process some tax-relief forms through his government office. She was really only qualified to be a secretary—answer phones, make copies—but she said she could not imagine herself in that kind of job, which seemed painful and boring. She loved working in the laboratory, mixing ingredients and brewing concoctions; she seemed to fancy herself as a sorcerer or mad scientist at play.

Although she enjoyed her work and was glad to return to it, she felt increasingly exploited after the strike and mentioned several times that the békés were becoming rich at her expense. She also said her work conditions had worsened, particularly because the dismissed workers had not been replaced. After the initial cleanup, production tasks were redistributed among the remaining workers, and as a result they now all had increased duties and, in some cases, longer hours. Since their return, work conditions had deteriorated and the employer seemed more hostile than before. The boss even refused to repair an air-conditioning unit that had stopped working. There were no immediate plans for replacing the dismissed workers or for making repairs since (according to Denis) this would indicate that money was flowing again and would make it hard for their employer to keep stalling on the rest of the agreement.

Corinne argued that all these things happened without the workers realizing what was unfolding. She said they let themselves "s'en dormir" (be put to sleep or hypnotized) by their employer. During the cleanup period, the boss seemed accommodating and appeared happy to have them back at work, and they were so preoccupied with the task itself that they lost sight of their demands and didn't notice that management was ignoring the agreement. She admitted that Max had warned them that the employer's protocol was "nothing but paper" and that they would have to fight to make sure the agreement was enforced, but it was as if the long strike had taken the fight out of them. They were exhausted after their experience, confused by its abrupt end, and (as Denis also mentioned) their colleagues' firing had left them feeling like they had little to celebrate or be proud of.

> It was so strange, you see, because they [the fired employees] were with us the whole time, they were on the piquet every day, and they were strong. They were some of the strongest among us. They made the same sacrifices we made, so it seems unfair that they are not here now.

Although their work conditions had worsened, the reintegrated workers felt somewhat lucky to still have their jobs, thus making it harder for them to continue fighting for the implementation of their agreement.

Corinne was extremely pessimistic about the concrete results of the strike, but she did feel that it had a lasting impact on her and that she was no longer the same person. As an example, she related that she had recently confronted her neighbor about damage his dog had done to her property. She said that in the past she probably would not have done so, but now if something bothered her, she spoke up about it. She confessed that not everyone around her approved of her newfound bravado, but she now cared little about what others thought. She also said she had changed her view of work itself. She was raised to believe that a job was precious and should never be put in danger, but she said she now realized that is not true—and that everything you grow up believing is not necessarily true. "I question everything now," she said.

Victory or Defeat?

Denis, Corinne, and the other Sucré workers I spoke to all had mixed feelings about the outcome of their strike. Although they had succeeded in obtaining a contract agreement that was quite favorable for them, the bulk of the agreement was not being implemented, and their work conditions and compensation had not improved. In fact their situation had in some ways worsened. The truck drivers who used to work on commission were making less money with their new base salary and now had to take on the delivery routes of their dismissed colleagues without added remuneration. Workers on the production end also had increased duties as they scrambled to carry out the tasks of their missing coworkers, deal with tensions with the non-grèvistes, and confront a recalcitrant manager who refused to implement their negotiated agreement.

Despite these mixed results, workers still looked back on the strike with great nostalgia. "All the bad memories about the strike are in relation to the employer," said Christian, one of the drivers. "But among the grèvistes there are nothing but good memories. . . . Ah, yes, lots of good memories." When I asked him what exactly he remembered most about the strike, he explained,

> The solidarity, the relationships, the *rapprochement* [closeness]. Because before the strike there were a lot of people I didn't really know, because we never had time because, you know, in this company the drivers, we're in a different area, and the production people, they are in the lab and we don't see them unless we really go out of our way to see them, so there were people I had never spoken to. We would say *bonjour*, I knew who they were, but we had never really shared anything. And then during the strike, well, then we were together all the time! We shared so much that it brought us together. We ended up knowing each other completely, we did everything together. Lots of things—good things and bad things—things that we aren't necessarily proud of, but things that we needed to do, you know?

He chuckled mischievously but didn't elaborate on those bad things. Instead he concluded,

The fact of being together like that made us incapable of being apart, to the point where during the weekend I missed my *camarades*! Because we lived things, we shared things, things that we couldn't share with our own families. And those things changed us a bit. We don't see things the same way. But no one else understands that—only we understand it because we were there.

As Christian suggests, one of the most important aspects of the strike was the new relationships of conviviality and exchange that were forged among the striking workers. These relationships were not completely forgotten after they returned to work. For example, Corinne recounted that Denis still remained an important figure of leadership in their company. In fact she said that it was unfair in the sense that her coworkers continued to burden him with their problems.

It's ridiculous, really. We saw him the other day in the break room, and as soon as Josué saw him he started complaining that his shoulder hurt. I had worked next to Josué all day and he hadn't said anything to me. Why is it that as soon as he sees Denis he has to tell him his problems?

As Corinne suggested, the bonds built on the piquet were not easily forgotten. But once workers left their "cocoon," they were unable to maintain the same close relationships they once shared. They busied themselves with the task of cleanup at both work and home, stopped going to union meetings, and found few moments in which to bridge the production and shift divides that kept them apart. Their inability to sustain these bonds is part of why they felt such nostalgia for the strike. As Corinne suggested, the end of the strike was like the end of an affair, and she continued to mourn the loss.

Denis, too, had continued to relive the events and experiences of the strike. In fact, when I expressed my amazement that he was able to remember the exact dates of the critical turning points, he explained that this was partly because he was writing a memoir about his experiences. He said he was not in a rush to finish it and had no plans to publish it, since it might implicate his *camarades* in ways they might not appreciate. He was writing it mostly for his children, so they could know what his father had lived through. He said perhaps one day, after he and his coworkers were no longer "active," his children could publish it to set the record straight.[30]

Despite the workers' nostalgia for the strike, they all expressed great reservations about ever going on strike again. As one worker suggested, the problem with a strike is that it never ends. "A strike is like a war: it has a beginning but no end. Even if you go back to work, it is a truce, but not really an end." Most of the workers felt like they had entered the strike blindly, unaware of the toll it would take on them and their families. After their experience they were more critical of the use of strikes, less likely to go on strike impulsively, and less optimistic about the possible outcomes.

They also held a more critical stance toward the union and its methods. Denis argued that he thought the union was still doing things "à l'ancienne" (old school) and that it should eschew traditional means and turn to other forms of struggle. During our conversation he suggested that the union should focus more on legal channels and make better use of the labor courts rather than relying on these as a last resort, even if this meant less time spent on the piquet.[31] He also thought the union should carry out other types of actions. Instead of declaring another indefinite strike, he was trying to organize workers to hold a simple day of protest in order to demand implementation of their agreement or to stage some kind of collective sick-out to demand the air conditioner's repair. Corinne also agreed that they needed to do "something else." After our conversation she resolved to start carrying the contract agreement in her purse, because clearly it was not being enforced. It was unclear if this was meant to serve as a reminder or a talisman.

Although the workers were critical of the strike and its outcomes, they remained convinced of the need to organize and act collectively. They were hesitant about relaunching a strike but were eager to imagine new possibilities for struggle. They all agreed that the strike had revealed the "true nature" of their boss, his stubbornness and his refusal to make concessions, and it had shown them that unless they took significant action, their conditions would never improve. As Denis explained, "People are not ready to go on strike again, but then again, they are never ready." He said he couldn't fathom asking his colleagues to strike again. But when I asked what he would do if they asked *him* to go back on strike, he paused, looked down at his papers, and said, "Yes, I would do it. I would strike." He raised his head and nodded. Slowly a sly grin appeared, and his eyes sparkled with nostalgia as he affirmed, "Yeah, I would strike again." I caught another glimpse of that sparkle in his eyes, several years later, when I saw him, with his son gleefully bouncing atop his shoulders, marching in the general strike of 2009.

FOUR

Public Hunger

On October 4, 2004, Michel Madassamy, one of the most charismatic leaders of the UGTG, was suddenly and dramatically incarcerated. Madassamy was seized at the Place de la Victoire, the center of Pointe-à-Pitre's colonial district, where he had stopped on his way home from work to buy a bokit sandwich from one of the small food vans that surround the colonial plaza. Special police officers from the Groupe d'intervention de la gendarmerie nationale (GIGN)—France's elite counterterrorism unit—were flown in from mainland France to secure his arrest. Over a dozen special unit officers, heavily armed, in full riot gear, and sporting black ski masks under the hot tropical sun, arrested Madassamy on the plaza, handcuffed him, covered his head, and threw him into the back of a police van. They then transported him to the penitentiary at La Jaille, Baie-Mahault, to begin serving a ten-month jail sentence for the destruction of private property—charges related to his participation in recent labor demonstrations.

Immediately following his arrest, Madassamy staged a hunger strike to protest his incarceration. The UGTG in turn demanded his release and threatened to unleash large-scale strikes and spark massive unrest. The response, however, turned out to be more of a trickle than a tidal wave. Rather than setting up barricades and bringing the society to a standstill, as most expected it to do, the UGTG carried out a series of town hall meetings to inform the public of the facts of the "Madassamy affair." For the first time the union seemed to favor dialogue over action—much to the confusion of its critics. Journalists speculated and employers gloated (though nervously) that the UGTG was unable to launch a massive strike. As the weeks passed, the tension slowly mounted. Each day added to the hunger strike tally, making Madassamy's health an increasing concern. Public debate began to shift from the facts of the case to the state of Madassamy's health, with fear slowly mounting over the union's possible retaliation. How long could Madassamy hold out? How long could the union hold out? What would be Madassamy's fate?

In this chapter, I examine how the UGTG responded to Madassamy's arrest by deploying multiple, overlapping, and at times contradictory legal and political strategies. The Madassamy affair offers an example of how the union engages in syndicalism as a form of marronage by "coming and going" from the logics of French legal and labor institutions. It also marked a shift towards a greater focus on media politics. The particularity of the hunger strike as a highly mediated form of social action, combined with the rise of new media forms in Guadeloupe, led the union to engage the public in ways that would mark their tactics in the years to come. The Madassamy affair represented a moment of transition, ushering in a new era of social struggle that would be fought on the airwaves as much as on the piquet. The fact that Madassamy was part of Guadeloupe's minority Indian population also lent a particular tenor to the affair.[1] Union members were suddenly called upon to speak as particularly raced and gendered subjects of both resistance and solidarity, bringing to the fore underlying relationships of alterity and difference that are rarely the object of open debate, within the UGTG or in Guadeloupe more broadly.

Who Is Michel Madassamy?

Looking back on Madassamy's arrest, Max explained that he was imprisoned not for what he did but for what he represented. "Any other militant would have received a suspended sentence, or community service," he said, "but he was arrested for his persona." Over the years Madassamy had become an important public face for the union. In 1994 he was one of the founding members of the Union des travailleurs des produits pétroliers (UTPP), the UGTG subsidiary union for workers in the gasoline industry. Later, as secretary-general of the UTPP, he led a fight to establish safety regulations for the transportation of hazardous materials and a collective work contract for both truck drivers and gas station attendants. These victories were won through long, drawn-out strikes involving hard-line tactics that included vandalism, the disruption of gasoline distribution, and occupation of the local oil refinery.

During these struggles, Madassamy came to be known as a *tête chaud* (hothead) due to his involvement in some of the union's more aggressive actions. For example, in 2001, during stalled negotiations with the gas distribution company Société pour le transport des produits pétroliers (STPP),

Madassamy was charged with "stealing" a gas tanker that he overtook from one of the hired replacement workers, holding it hostage at the picket until the end of the strike. Later in 2002, he was part of a large group of over five hundred demonstrators that broke into the Société anonyme de raffinerie des Antilles (SARA), the central oil refinery and distribution center in Guadeloupe. During a scuffle with the gendarmes, an oil valve was released (presumably by a demonstrator, though no one claimed responsibility), leading to a large gasoline spill. This spawned rumors for years to come that the union had tried to blow up the entire island.

Along with these "hotheaded" labor actions, Madassamy also become known for his role in the battles over the commemoration of Abolition Day. For years the UGTG had organized small marches and commemorative demonstrations around abolition, but in 2001, after the ratification of the Taubira Law in France declaring slavery a crime against humanity, they decided to escalate their actions. Despite being designated as a holiday (*jour férié*) in 1983 (Loi no. 83-550), Abolition Day had not been recognized as a non-work day (*jour chômée*), which meant that many private businesses and commercial venues remained opened. In 2001 the UGTG decided to declare a general strike and called on local shop owners, described as the *petit-fils d'esclavagistes* (grandchildren of slaveholders), to release their workers, the *petit-fils d'esclaves* (grandchildren of slaves), on this important day of remembrance, in order to "respect the memory of the 'freedom fighters' and the blood shed by the millions of victims of slavery, recently recognized by the French state as a crime against humanity." The demonstrations were particularly focused on the commercial sector; as one activist explained to me, "What was slavery if not the commerce of humanity?"

During the demonstrations violent confrontations ensued. Protesters vandalized several businesses, overturning shelves, smashing cash registers, and shattering store windows. Later, after union members returned to their headquarters, young residents from the surrounding *cités* (low-income neighborhoods) followed in their wake, looting stores, vandalizing public property, destroying public phones, setting fire to trash bins and parked cars, and firing shots into the air throughout the night. These events captured both local and national attention, with the French newspaper *Le Monde* describing the scene as an "environment of civil war."[2]

Although numerous demonstrators were involved in the events, shop owners singled out Madassamy as the main perpetrator, arguing that he was the only *tête* (head) they recognized. In the days following, the police held him to await trial without official charges or bail. It was at this point that Madassamy declared his first hunger strike. This triggered a wave of demonstrations to demand his release, including a general strike among petrol workers in the UTPP that effectively shut down the entire system of gas distribution in Guadeloupe for several days. This now-infamous *grève d'essence* created a panic among local motorists, many of whom spent the night in their cars parked in line at the gas station.

During this time the UGTG produced a series of documents with titles such as "Qui est Michel Madassamy?" (Who is Michel Madassamy?), "Vivre libre ou mourir" (Live Free or Die), and "Meurtre légal" (Legalized Murder), comparing Madassamy to martyrs in Guadeloupe's past—most notably Louis Delgrés, who fought and died in protest against the reestablishment of slavery in 1802—and accusing the French state of implementing the death penalty by refusing to release him during his hunger strike. Madassamy's image took on a central importance in this campaign: his picture was featured prominently in the union's tracts, and a series of T-shirts were produced with a cropped picture of his head and long beard. In addition, implicit associations were made between his *indianité* and the spirituality and non-violent traditions of Gandhian politics. This served as a counterbalance to the otherwise hostile face of union struggle, particularly given the violent events for which he was charged.

After two weeks of candlelit vigils, public demonstrations, and labor strikes, the government finally released Madassamy to await trial. His hearing, held several months later, turned into a political circus. Supporters filled the courtroom dressed in their Madassamy T-shirts, and when the judge called the court to order, they responded with a revolutionary salute, simultaneously raising their left fists into the air. When called to testify, union members spoke in Creole—forcing the court to secure a translator. While the prosecutors attempted to argue the facts of the case, union lawyers (who were noted figures in the anticolonial movement) used the opportunity to decry the injustices of the legal system. In one of its statements the union described its defense lawyers as the "prosecutors of history" pleading a case against the injustices of the past.

In the end, one of the charges against Madassamy was suspended, but he still received a three-month sentence for destruction of private property. The union declared his trial a victory and walked out of the courtroom triumphant, perhaps assuming that the sentence would never actually be enforced. They thought the affair was behind them—until his spectacular arrest in 2004.

This cluster of events—the demonstrations over Abolition Day, Madassamy's hunger strike and solidarity campaign, the gasoline strike, and his dramatic trial—which spanned May and June of 2001, came to be known as the original Madassamy affair, with the 2004 arrest constituting the sequel. The original affair was a watershed moment due to the diversity of symbolic elements it wove together: the history of slavery and the politics of its memorialization, the disaffection of unemployed youth who descended onto the streets in the wake of the demonstrations, the problems of the legal system (which imprisoned Madassamy without due process), and the place of Guadeloupe's rarely discussed Indian population, which is often imagined to be lacking solidarity with the black majority. Moreover, during this episode Madassamy himself was consecrated as a UGTG symbol. It was precisely because of his particular persona that many believe he became the target of state repression.

Political Shifts in Guadeloupe and France

Madassamy's arrest in 2004 came unexpectedly at a time when the union was not involved in important struggles. Union membership had swelled in the early 1990s, after expansion into the lucrative hotel industry, the mammoth civil service sector, and other key areas of the economy such as communications, commerce, and the petrol industry. These efforts were aided by the political climate of the Mitterrand government (1981–95) and its decentralization policies, which provided fertile ground for both labor organizing and identitarian struggles through the revalorization of regional culture (see chapter 5). Union membership had also risen dramatically during the period of 1998 to 2000 as workers turned to the union to enforce the implementation of the new thirty-five-hour workweek. However, with the return of the political Right during Jacques Chirac's second presidential term (2002–2007), the union began to feel the effects of new anti-labor government measures.

During the 1980s and '90s, as the UGTG gained strength and continued to expand, employers banded together through employer associations, including Le Mouvement des entreprises de France (MEDEF), La Confédération générale de petites et moyennes entreprises (CGPME), L'Association des petites et moyennes industries (APMI), L'Union des entreprises de la Guadeloupe (UDE), L'Union patronale de la Guadeloupe, Les Professionnels de l'hôtellerie, and Les Professionnels du tourisme et agences de voyage. Many of these organizations were founded long before the union boom of the late 1990s, and some of them (such as MEDEF) were local chapters of French national organizations. These organizations allowed employers to share union-busting strategies and generate collaborative efforts for curtailing the UGTG's success.

The employers' anti-union campaign targeted both the media and the legal system. As the director of MEDEF, Maryse Mayeco, explained to me, their media strategy centered on generating sound bites, by using US-style "talking points," which they hoped would seep into daily discourse about the union. During our interview she boasted that many of the commonly heard anti-UGTG slogans in circulation at the time were the product of her own personal efforts—particularly the widely circulated claim that the union sought to achieve political independence by destroying the local economy. Their legal campaign consisted of pressing legal charges for acts of vandalism and imposing fines, leveling sanctions, and refusing to pay wages for days lost during a strike. Through these actions, employers—who usually complained that the labor code worked against their interests by protecting workers—increasingly sought to combat unionism by wielding the penal code instead.

This led to a significant shift in the role of both the police and the justice system in labor struggles. During the Mitterrand era, the French National Police had become less involved in labor disputes, ceding ground to local institutions and political figures. However, during the early 2000s, the gendarmes were once again deployed to break up barricades, to protect the "right to work" of the non-grévistes, and to ensure the wider population's freedom of movement.

These new tactics led labor leaders to rethink their strategy for dealing with the legal system. In April 2004, several months before Madassamy's arrest, the union produced a pamphlet describing the legal issues it was facing. The text briefly detailed several recent court cases and stated that all proceedings had been mishandled and plagued with irregularities. It went on to explain that the union would no longer engage in appeals procedures since these were consistently denied. By declaring that it would no longer seek appeals, the union implied that it would combat arrests through other means—namely collective action. It was effectively declaring a game of chicken with the legal system—fully expecting the French government to back down. Instead, the government called the union's bluff by incarcerating one of its main figures.

Spectacles of Arrest: The New Madassamy Affair

Madassamy's arrest in 2004 was marked by a particularly spectacular display of force and theatricality. Although his sentence had been issued months prior, the timing of his imprisonment came as a surprise since the period for appeals had not yet lapsed. Further, as his supporters contended, the

4.1. Cartoon depicting Madassamy's arrest in the journal *Mot Phrasé*.
Artist: Richard-Viktor Sainsily-Cayol.

conditions of his arrest were at odds with the nature of the charges against him. The use of a special counterterrorism police unit was particularly contentious. At a time when the United States was at the height of its "war on terror" in the Middle East, the theatricality and spectacle of his arrest seemed better suited for an infamous and elusive enemy of the state rather than a simple labor activist—as editorials and cartoons in local newspapers were quick to suggest.

In the satirical newspaper *Le Motphrasé*, Madassamy's arrest was parodied as Guadeloupe's version of the notorious Osama bin Laden's capture. An editorial cartoon depicted Madassamy in a union T-shirt (the standard "uniform" of Guadeloupean labor activists) being brought to the central authorities by the special unit police. The officers are boasting about the fact that they have captured him "ben" (presumably a play on *bien*, meaning that they "got him good" but also a reference to Osama *bin* Laden) and that they even managed to beat the Americans to the punch. In the caption below the drawing, Madassamy's name is rendered as Oussama Dassamy (again a play on Osama bin Laden). The officer on the other side of the desk looks surprised, and the reader is left to speculate as to whether the counter-terrorist specialists confused Madassamy with bin Laden, or if they simply felt their "catch" was equal in magnitude to the target of the international manhunt that US Special Forces were undertaking at the time.

Madassamy's arrest appeared to be a symbolic gesture on the government's part. The exact meaning of this gesture was, however, unclear. In the press, columnists described the arrest as a *piège* (trap), arguing that the state was trying to provoke the union into its usual hard-line tactics. They argued that the government expected the union to either fail to adequately respond (thus losing credibility in the eyes of its membership) or to engage in large-scale violent actions that would then allow the government to carry out further arrests. Some even speculated that the government sought to wipe out the union completely by goading it into illegal activity, so they could justify banning it.

The amount of speculation surrounding the arrest was due in part to the lack of official explanation. Despite the spectacular nature of the arrest itself, the state issued no statements, held no press conferences, and provided little clarification for its actions. Unlike the ever-vocal *patronat*, who are quick to take to the airwaves, the state—represented by the state prosecutor and the prefect—refused to engage in a publicity battle. The details of the case and the arrest thus came to light mostly through rumor, supposed witness accounts, and the statements of union leaders.

If the government's actions were the subject of much speculation, the union's reactions were even more so. Immediately after the arrest, the union threatened to paralyze Guadeloupe with massive demonstrations. Yet instead of the expected strikes, barricades, and usual disruptive actions, it instead waged a slowly escalating campaign that involved town visits, meetings with local politicians, TV appearances, and an international solidarity campaign. These efforts baffled observers who had come to expect spectacular displays of social paralysis.

In the days immediately following Madassamy's arrest, the morning radio reports, which usually provide detailed coverage of labor demonstrations and their effects on the morning commute, focused instead on the surprisingly normal traffic conditions. Programming throughout the day was sporadically interrupted, as is often the case during strikes and demonstrations; on this occasion, however, reporters would break in to simply confirm that conditions were normal and that there were few disturbances to report. Reporters seemed disappointed, or dumbfounded, by the fact that the union had not reacted in a more spectacular fashion. In print media and online news services, columnists and pundits speculated that the union had lost its popular support and was unable to launch an organized response. The same journalists who would usually accuse the union of being *jusqu'au-boutistes* (hard-line extremists) were suddenly accusing the union of pandering to public opinion. For example, on the RFO morning news, the following exchange took place:

REPORTER: There is a general sentiment that the UGTG has changed its strategy. Gone are the days when you would wake up early in the morning and find every road *bloké* [blocked], every road *baré* [barricaded]. . . . Are you trying to soften your image?

UNION REPRESENTATIVE: First of all, we have always spoken to our people. It is true that we had a period where we had a lot of strikes and a lot of barricades—that's because the situation required that we block the streets and barricade enterprises to make ourselves heard. And eventually the employers recognized that we had a right to what we were demanding. But if there is no need to block the streets, we're not going to block them—we're not idiots [*nou pa tébé*].

During these interviews journalists would goad union leaders, scoffing at their responses and forcing them to defend their positions. The underlying accusation was one of weakness, infused with a challenge to the union's usual hard-line, testosterone-driven politics. For example, in the interview below, the reporter asked skeptically if Madassamy had really been on a hunger strike for seven days.

UNION REPRESENTATIVE: Well, I don't know how many days, because we believe that it is not up to us to do that macabre form of accounting [*kontabilité macab lá-sa*]—that criminal responsibility lies with the French state.

REPORTER: You don't know how to count? [*Zot pa sav konté?*]

UNION REPRESENTATIVE: We don't know how to count, no. We feel it's not up to us to do that sort of accounting—that is their responsibility.

In addition to confronting the union leaders themselves, the media also gave ample airtime to the union's critics: the high-profile business leaders and employer association representatives. The "business community" is usually quick to take to the airwaves to decry the union's unfair actions and the harm that they inflict on the local economy. In the days following Madassamy's arrest, however, business representatives questioned the lack of hard-line tactics, suggesting that there were rifts between the union's leadership and the "base." For example, in an interview with Radio Caraïbe Internationale (RCI), Maryse Mayeco stated,

> If forced to make an assessment, I would have to say that that the call put forth by the UGTG has not resonated with the workers of the private sector. Workers have finally understood that the union is in the process of leading them down a path that is contrary to the law and that would put their jobs at risk.

Union leaders responded by defending their actions, arguing that even if the union was not out in the streets, the police were, and that was a sign of their success. As the UGTG secretary-general at the time, Raymond Gauthierot, explained,

> The French state is feeling the pressure of our actions because you will find that on every corner, on every bridge, you have a police truck, which means that they are scared of something. If you have helicopters circling the sky all day long, it's because they're scared of something. We are not in a normal situation! And yet they dare claim that our strike has had no effect.

He further argued that their actions were part of a larger strategy. Rather than launching a full attack, he said the union was escalating its efforts in a "crescendo" of action. Gauthierot argued that workers were making their own choices about when and how they wanted to express their solidarity with Madassamy, and that their actions would soon be increasing.

In their official statements (and in conversations with prying anthropologists), the union tried to paint these efforts as a coherent strategy. Any questioning of their strength, or of the systematic nature of their approach, was met with ambiguous Creole proverbs—"kok atè sé pou bat" (roosters were put on earth to struggle), "la i pann, i sek" (laundry will dry where you hang it)—which seemed to convey a blanket message of "justice will prevail" one way or another.

Whatever the actual motivations for these actions, their result was a climate of expectation and anxiety. Everyone seemed to be waiting for the proverbial other shoe to drop. The media's critical and cajoling jabs only served to heighten public interest. In the end, this climate of expectation created a sense of social crisis comparable to that produced by the usual barricades and more spectacular forms of union action.

Months later, when I spoke to Max about the initial criticisms surrounding their actions, he argued,

> The problem is that the people who comment on the social movement in Guadeloupe have their own schemas, which is to say—and again this is an issue of Eurocentrism—that it is on the basis of what they know about social movements in Europe that they describe the social movement here. The press suggests one single possible schema of action. They force you to conform to a certain *créneau* [domain of action], and as soon as you stray from that, they criticize you and say that you have no more force, no more authority, and that the people aren't following you.

The challenges faced by the union during this time are common to all social movements—collective action is often speculative, improvisational, and prefigurative. Activists throughout the world often face criticism when they arrive at crossroads that require them to shift tactics and targets. Part of what fuels these critiques is what Max describes as "Eurocentric models"—political expectations based on modernist ideas of total revolution. In the absence of alternative political forms in the present that could challenge these expectations, Max turned to the political traditions of runaway slaves. During our conversation he reconfigured this moment of improvisation and rupture as part of the union's maroon tactics of escape from the logics of prescribed social action.

> They are always trying to be the *maître de notre jeux* [the masters of our game]. But we decided that the sole authority, that the sole person, the sole power, to tell us how to operate would be *nous memes* [ourselves], and nobody knew what we should do or how we should do it. Nobody knew! Our *démarche* [project/strategy] in this movement was to say, "On verra ce que nous faisons. On ne dit pas ce qu'on fait." [It is to be seen what we will do. We do not say what we do.]

As Max's comments suggest, the union found itself at a crossroads during the Madassamy affair. It was unable to react with the same strength and speed as it had in 2001, and thus it had to regroup and develop a new strategy—one that would respond to the changing political and legal climate. This was not the first time that the union experimented with its methods, nor the first time that its contradictory tactics became the object of debate. In discussing the union's seemingly confusing plan of action, Lukas, one of the union's economic consultants, told me that over the years he had often seen the union employ strategies that appeared completely illogical and untenable—but they always seemed to work out in the end. He compared their actions to a gwoka dance. Much like gwoka, he argued, union actions have inherent chaos and syncopation at their center, and the leadership's genius lies in their ability to channel that chaos into a coherent pattern of action. For Lukas, union leaders were like gwoka dancers—carving a rhythmic dance out of the polyphonic beats of the ka drum, taming the drum with their movements, and eventually usurping the rhythm and forcing, or perhaps seducing, the *marquer* (drummer) to follow their lead.

The Deliberating Public

The UGTG's experimentation and improvisation during the Madassamy affair extended to its management of media coverage and its manipulation of rumor, gossip, and myth in the public sphere. In addition to managing the press and engaging with the commentary of employers and government officials, union activists were also forced to come to terms with the rise of a new "deliberating public" that was called into being through the new forms of interactive radio and TV programming that had come to dominate the local airwaves in Guadeloupe.[3]

During the 1980s, under the government of François Mitterrand, restrictions were lifted on radio and TV programming throughout France, fostering the proliferation of independent media outlets (many of which previously operated without a license).[4] In the *outre-mer*, these alternative forms of media began to emphasize greater programming *de proximité*, that is, local programming based on community concerns. This programming de proximité sets itself up in opposition to the state-run network, Réseaux France Outre-mer (RFO), with its centralized structure and "imported" French programming.[5] In Guadeloupe, the epitome of this alternative local media is Canal 10, a popular, privately owned TV channel that began as an illegal pirate channel and flourished following the Mitterrand government's decentralization program.

Canal 10's programming is in many ways the opposite of the sleek, expertly produced RFO lineup. Most of its programs are shot in a one-room studio with guests and hosts seated at a simple table with a pale blue curtain as their background. Sometimes the curtain is used as a "blue screen" onto which the station's logo is displayed, though this detail is most often skipped. There is no doubt that one has stumbled upon Canal 10 when one flips the channel and finds a mixed assortment of Guadeloupean social actors debating in Creole about local events (land disputes, tensions with immigrant communities, and of course labor disputes).[6] However, in case there is any doubt, the transmissions always display the station's logo in the upper right-hand corner and the station's phone number on the lower left side of the screen.

One of the staple elements of Canal 10 programming, along with its use of Creole, low production values, and unfiltered commentary, is the use of live transmissions, especially call-in shows. Some shows follow an interview format with the guests fielding calls at the end of the broadcast. Others simply feature a host taking calls from the public on the topic of the day. During these shows callers often respond to one another and some even call back a second time to offer a rebuttal.

In recent years radio stations have also created new forms of interactive programming, among them a segment called *le répondeur*. This is basically a gripe hotline: listeners call in to the radio station's *répondeur* (answering machine) and leave messages that are later transmitted in short segments throughout the day, sandwiched between the usual zouk and kompa music. Many in Guadeloupe complain about this feature because unlike the call-in shows, where participants usually identify themselves and sustain a dialogue with the hosts or guests, répondeur callers are entirely anonymous and often launch into controversial and aggressive commentary that they wouldn't usually make in public. Many argue that the répondeur is simply an excuse for people to say *n'importe quoi* (nonsense) outside the conventions of polite society.[7]

During the Madassamy affair the répondeur and other call-in shows were flooded with callers. Some praised Madassamy and pledged their support for the union. Others criticized Madassamy's actions, denounced the union in general, and declared that they should all be thrown in jail. During these shows, few would openly identify themselves as actual members or militants of the UGTG. Most would speak of the UGTG as a foreign "they" and represent themselves as members of a deliberating "we" that needed to pronounce its support or disapproval.[8]

Through this heightened mediatization and invocation of public commentary, the union became the object of much debate, but also of much speculation, or *kankan* and *vyé pawol* (malicious commentary and gossip). Rumors and speculation always circulate about the union, but during the Madassamy affair they took on a particular valence. During labor conflicts, parties on both sides of the dispute usually take to the airwaves to put their side of the story into circulation. One would normally find workers on

Canal 10 fielding calls one night and employers pleading their case the next. However, on this occasion the state was silent about both Madassamy's arrest and the unfolding of his hunger strike. Journalists complained that the state prosecutor wouldn't even take their calls. In addition, the state denied press access to Madassamy, making it impossible for journalists to assess his current state of health. As a result, rumors took over, reportedly based on long chains of association with someone who knew someone, was related to someone, had connections to Madassamy's family, or had some form of access to the prison (and later the hospital) where Madassamy was being held. Accounts supposedly based on firsthand knowledge circulated widely during this time—both through networks of gossip and through the media itself, which gave airtime to individual speculations and claims. Thus, ironically enough, at a time when the state was providing little information on Madassamy's conditions or the facts of the case, everyone seemed to feel surprisingly well informed.

Union members usually dismiss media portrayals, expressing little interest in the rumors that circulate about them. They regularly make TV and radio appearances but spend little energy trying to dispel rumors about their actions. In fact, I was told on more than one occasion that they often use rumor, myth, and disinformation to their advantage. As Max playfully explained to me, rumor and myth are all part of keeping the authorities, the employers, and even union members themselves guessing.

> It is true that we let misinformation happen, because the UGTG needs to appear mysterious—we choose to function within the realm of myth. It protects us. It is good for people to be a little scared of us, to keep their distance, to not be quite sure what they would be getting into with us. So you see, that protects us—it helps assure our liberties and our independence. The fact of not being able to fully know us or understand us helps us. And the truth is that this union is truly not understandable. That is our choice also: to not codify things too much, to not make things too rigid—you need to leave things open, you need things to be a little mystical and mysterious as well.

As Max's words suggest, the misinformation and rumor that surround the union operate to its benefit. By not making clear statements about its actions, motivations, and strategies, the union can circumvent having to justify or explain what to some might seem as failed or incongruent actions. When I asked Max what this veil of mystery protects them from, he explained,

When I say that people can't understand us completely—that protects us, that protects us from . . . from ourselves really. It protects the union from the *dérives* [drifting/moments of excess], from the *dérives* of the delegates, militants, and leaders. Since the UGTG doesn't codify and control everything there are moments that simply can't be explained, don't need to be explained.

These *dérives*—these moments of excess or of straying—are not just the product of overzealous militants, but rather part of a collective strategy of chaos, unpredictability, and purposeful opacity. Max further elaborated, "Sometimes we chose to let ourselves be a little *déréglé* [disordered/chaotic] as well . . . we let ourselves go . . . because you can't live in a world that is too *carré* [regulated/ordered]. We refuse to let the world be too *carré*." As if to further emphasize his point, Max concluded by affirming that their actions would never be fully legible: "Do you understand? You don't understand! You can't understand! And I can't explain it to you!"

As Max suggests, an integral part of union strategy is to let some actions remain misunderstood (including by me). When union leaders appear on TV and the radio, they are thus not necessarily seeking to inform the population but simply to involve them. That is, they seek to extend their disputes beyond the realm of the workplace in order to create a feeling of large-scale struggle. What the population is saying about them is rarely a concern; just getting them talking is enough. As Max explained,

> It doesn't matter what they say, it just matters that they *en parle* [talk about it]. . . . Once they start talking, well, then people have two ears—one ear which is in favor, and one which is against [*une oreille qui est pour et une oreille qui est contre*]. And so that is a part of the popular debate—of the construction of a public opinion.

Labor activists' relationship to the press is thus similar to their relationship to the law (as discussed in chapter 2). They use it to their advantage—participating as far as it suits them and retreating from its logics when it doesn't.

UGTG "Live"

To manage the public discourses being produced by the *répondeur* during the Madassamy affair, the union organized a series of *mitins*, or rallies, during which speakers made public statements, explained the details of the affair, and called for general support. Rallies are a regular part of UGTG life but they are usually held in front of the union's headquarters in Pointe-à-Pitre or at the site of a localized conflict. On this occasion, however, the union scheduled a series of events throughout both regions of Guadeloupe (Grande-Terre and Basse-Terre). The press mocked the union for packing up and taking its show on the road to plead its case. They described the rallies as the "Konvwa UGTG," *konvwa* being a Creole word for collective delegations, a kind of convoy of supporters that arrives to help in solidarity actions or *koudmen* (collective agricultural practices).[9]

The events were held in the evening at the central plaza of each community. These plazas are important gathering places, especially in small towns. Even in the larger towns that have nightclubs, restaurants, and *boîtes de nuit* (discos), the main plazas are well populated at night because they are one of the few places where both young and old can gather to socialize—particularly unemployed youth with limited funds for entertainment. During these town visits the union was thus guaranteed an audience, one that would probably not have made the trip to the union headquarters in Pointe-à-Pitre. As Max explained, this was one of the few occasions when these populations could see the UGTG "live," as opposed to the mediated versions of the union found on local airwaves.

Each event had a different lineup of speakers, including some of the more public faces of the union (such as Max), Madassamy's lawyers, and union delegates with close ties to the community in question. The rallies would generally start with the lawyers explaining the details of the three charges Madassamy was facing: the theft of a gasoline truck during the STPP conflict of 2001, the vandalizing and ransacking of a supermarket and fast-food restaurant on Abolition Day 2001, and the vandalizing of Texaco gas tankers during the oil spill in 2003.[10] Union delegates would then take to the stage. Max was the featured speaker at most of these rallies. His speeches were all performed in masterful Creole, full of folk sayings, proverbs, and pointed humor. At each rally the audience cheered him on, laughing and hooting in delight, and often chiming in with commentary of their own in an impromptu call-and-response. His speeches were so popular, in fact, that people who noticed I was recording them began asking me for copies; soon I was producing bootleg CDs of the greatest hits from the Madassamy tour.

Max's speeches would quickly depart from the legal details of the case, and even from Madassamy himself, veering off into a wider commentary about Guadeloupean society and daily life. As Max explained to me, the goal of the solidarity campaign was to put Madassamy's actions into a larger frame and to portray his hunger strike as part of a broader social movement, rather than an individual act.

> Our approach was to support his personal decision but also to widen his revolt—it would no longer be a personal revolt, but a *revolte militaire*. We understood that we had to give his personal struggle an "echo" in order to transform it from a personal struggle into a social struggle.

The bulk of the speeches were thus devoted not to details of the Madassamy case but to the wider ills of Guadeloupean society. In this way, Madassamy's actions were placed within a wider narrative of resistance to the contemporary political and social climate of Guadeloupe. Moreover, the speeches sought to enroll support not just for his individual actions but for the wider actions of the UGTG.

"An Tan ke Fanm": Women's Solidarity with Madassamy

During the Madassamy town visits, a different set of union members took to the stage to offer their *témoignage* (testimony), thus bringing a change to the usual public face of the union. For example, in the town of Morne-à-l'Eau, I was surprised to see Veronique, a woman I had come to know through various union events, address the crowd. Veronique was an active member of the UGTG and a frequent participant at rallies, demonstrations, and solidarity events. Married with three small children, she managed to artfully balance family life, unionism, and a full-time job as a civil servant, along with night school for an advanced degree. She was charismatic and engaging, poised, and always well dressed and coiffed. Even when she wore her UGTG T-shirts, she would tie them to the side or wear them with a brooch, giving them her own style and panache. Still, her elegant air should not be confused with Francophile tendencies—although she did not wear traditional dress (as did some of the other women in the union), her form of engagement and her mastery of Creole evidenced her cultural fluency. She came from a family of gwoka musicians who were very active in the local cultural scene. Although I had never seen her take the microphone, I had often seen her take command of the *léwoz*—the traditional gwoka drum circle—where she was not shy about showcasing her skills.

When Veronique took to the stage at the Madassamy rally I discovered that she was as adept a speaker as she was a dancer. She captured the audience's attention with her flair for drama and her carefully chosen words and gestures. Whereas union leaders are often said to speak an "intellectual-ized" form of Creole (creolizing terms like "neoliberalism" and "globaliza-tion"), Veronique spoke in simple Creole, peppered with proverbs and local idioms without French adaptations.

On that night she began her comments by stating, "I don't really make it a habit of speaking at rallies. I don't really like that [*an pa tèlman anmé sa*], but I think, *camarades*, that it is time for us to find our place within the struggle." By "us" she referred specifically to the women of the UGTG. Before engaging the role of women, however, she made sure to disentangle her comments from French notions of feminism, tying together the false promises of abolition with those of women's liberation. "In terms of this 'emancipation of women' that the colonizing French like to talk about," she said, "we know that the emancipation of the French was not our emancipa-tion, because we know what our society went through."

Before engaging with the details of the Madassamy affair, Veronique paused to briefly discuss the problematic role of women in the union and how they are perceived.

> There is a tendency to think that a woman who is a militant is a woman with nothing to do. It is a woman who is *hors champ* [out of the norm/out in left field], it is a woman who is looking for a man, a woman who is looking for *an bitin* [something]. And, especially, if you choose to be a *fanm-fanm* [a femi-nine woman]—in other words, a *fanm antyé* [complete woman]—we are *fanm doubout* [upstanding/ready for action women], we are *fanm ki té bèl* [beautiful women], but we are also *fanm ki té goumé* [women who struggle]. And often, when people see this they think that it is a *bon fanm* [good looking woman] who has come to *fè pòz* [strike a pose], who has come to *fè pòz* at the UGTG, to *fè pòz* at the demonstrations. Well, I am here to say, and specifically to the prefect, that the women of the UGTG—yes, we know how to *fè pòz* and we do *fè pòz*, but when the time comes to light the fire against them, we light the fire against them, and we *will* light the fire against them! [*Lé se pou limé-difé si-yo, nou ka limé-difé si-yo, et nou ke limé-difé si-yo!*]

In her comments, Veronique states that women are just as combative as men. However, she ascribes very particular roles to the women of the union.

> We who are women have a particular job to do, alongside the men of the UGTG, to be permanently alongside them, permanently behind them, per-manently with them, so the French state can be sure to know that the men of the UGTG are not stray dogs on the street whom no one cares about, and

whom they can snatch up and throw in jail without anyone asking questions! The women of the UGTG are here! The militant women are here! And we are always going to demand explanations for what is done to our men, because they have mothers, children, and sisters who will always fight for them!

Veronique's speech was met with much excitement and appreciation by the crowd. When she was done, numerous women—both militants and women in the general public—came up to congratulate her on a job well done. The men were also extremely pleased with her participation. In fact, Veronique's speech was so successful that she was quickly added to the roster of speakers at other town visits. In the end, I saw Veronique give her speech three times, the last of which was at the *grand mitin* in Pointe-à-Pitre.

Part of what was remarkable about Veronique's speech was that, although women often spoke at rallies, they rarely spoke as women per se. Thus Veronique's speech *an tan ke fanm* (as a woman) was uncommon and much appreciated. Union leaders were always eager to demonstrate that women had an important role to play within union actions; they were quick to point out the few exemplary women who were on the union board and were particularly fond of speeches in which women affirmed their place as militants. These speeches and moments of gendered affirmation served to reassure the leadership that there were no problems of gender inequality within the union—and they would often argue (as Veronique did) that feminism was a French preoccupation. Moments of female affirmation were thus welcome and easily found. However, moments of gender critique, and reflection on why there were only a few "exemplary" females in positions of leadership, were nearly absent.

One reason why this is so, as Veronique suggests in her speech, is that women indeed often *fè pòz* within the union—as do men. For both women and men the space of syndicalism often becomes a space of social (and sexual) encounter. Many union members have met and fallen in love (or simply in lust) within the context of labor struggles. In fact, political action is in many ways inherently erotic—with highly stirred passions, physical confrontations, moments of euphoria and interpersonal communion. It is thus not surprising that numerous relationships are formed (and others betrayed) within the context of union action. Max himself met and fell in love with his wife on a piquet. Once they married, she retired from political action, as is often the case. In fact, many of the women involved in unionism are single or divorced. The demands of union activism—constant availability for demonstrations, late-night meetings, predawn barricades—are hard for women to manage alongside their domestic obligations. When they do manage to participate, it takes a toll. Women become exhausted from getting up at four in the morning to prepare their families' breakfast and lunch before heading to the piquet, or running after work to pick up and feed their children before heading to an evening rally. Thus it is single or childless women who can most easily manage the demands of union life.

Ironically, the predominance of single women serves to perpetuate the stereotype that they are there to meet men. I suspect that Veronique's speech was so well-received precisely because it represented one of the few moments when these issues were openly (though subtly) addressed. As she suggests, "Yes, we know how to *fè pòz*"; that is, women know how to use their sexuality and are indeed engaged in sexually charged interactions within the sphere of unionism, but they are also capable of militant action. Veronique fails to mention that men *fè pòz* as well, and are equally implicated in the erotics of union struggle. She further fails to mention how the liminality of the piquet and the generally heated space of social struggle can become a site for sexual transgression. Indeed, her speech was in many ways a strong affirmation of heteronormativity, a celebration of the *fanm fanm*: militant but traditionally feminine women standing behind the UGTG's masculine, combative men.

Throughout her speech Veronique also emphasized the importance of women as mothers in the Madassamy campaign.[11] She urged audience members to display compassion for Madassamy as a son, as any woman's son.

> *Camarades*, we who are women don't know at what moment our children will be sleeping in jail or for what reason, especially for what reason—doctors sleep in jail, police sleep in jail, *syndikalists* sleep in jail, anyone can sleep in jail! Our children who are five, ten, fifteen, could sleep in jail tomorrow, and we women who are here, we mothers who are here, we would never stand for this, even if our child had killed fifty people, we would never let anyone say, "Let him die in jail."

Veronique concluded her speech by reminding the audience that they needed to think about Madassamy's mother and the suffering she felt as she listened to people calling radio and TV programs saying "n'importe quoi" about her own son. She went on to say that it was particularly inexcusable for mothers to take these sorts of positions.

> Right now we have people hiding behind a telephone and calling all sorts of idiotic programs [*tout kalité d'emysyon kouyon*] to say, "Let Madassamy die,

let Madassamy *ceci* [this], let Madassamy *cela* [that]." Suddenly everyone is a prosecutor, everyone is a judge, everyone is a lawyer in Guadeloupe! It is unacceptable to have women hiding behind a telephone—mothers! It is one thing for men to say those things, I think that is not as *grave* [bad], men don't make children [*nonm pa ka fe ti moun*], men don't know the suffering of having a child—but women? *Camarades*, we need to put an end to that kind of thing [*fo nou tchouye ce calité de bitin*] and we need to make sure that those women shut their mouths! [*fo fè fanm la-sa fèmé-w bouche a yo!*]

Although Veronique began by rallying women as morally superior beings endowed with greater compassion by the fact of motherhood, she ended her speech by condemning women, suggesting that they bore greater responsibility for Madassamy's defamation. When she concluded that women should remain silent about Madassamy's fate, the (mostly male) crowd cheered. And Veronique smiled, without the least bit of irony.

Needless to say, not all women in the union supported Veronique's speech. Other women who took the stage at town visits would echo some of her rhetoric about the role of mothers and sisters in the union but would quickly veer off into more gender-neutral denunciations of the state and the police. Applause for their speeches was notably less enthusiastic. Interestingly enough, Madassamy's own sister (who was an active union member and part of the union council) declined to make any speeches. Although she was present at all demonstrations, press conferences, and legal proceedings, she refused to become a spokesperson for "the women's point of view." Madassamy's mother, though often mentioned in speeches for her suffering and courage, was also absent from the spotlight, as was Madassamy's wife, from whom he was reportedly estranged. Madassamy himself was also extricated from the sentient dimensions of union struggle, portrayed not as a passionate being but as a static, lifeless symbol.

Creating a Martyr

During this time of speeches and rallies, the one voice that was never heard was that of Michel Madassamy. In some ways this was not surprising, since he had always been a man of action rather than words. The first time I met him, he was answering phones at the union headquarters. The secretary was gone for the day, and Madassamy—one of the most notorious labor leaders at the time—was anonymously fielding calls to the union's general line. During my fieldwork, I often found him taking on similar sorts of thankless tasks. At big union events, he was rarely front and center, preferring instead to stand outside the door guiding stragglers and even helping them park their cars. At fundraisers and cookouts, he was often hidden away behind the serving trays, preparing food and carefully loading up attendees' plates while others gave speeches and worked the crowd. He always struck me as someone who would never seek the spotlight. He seemed rather like the kind of person who simply figured out what needed to be done and unceremoniously took on the task.

This is not to say that he blended into the background. His tall, lanky build, his trademark long beard, and the fact that he was one of the few union leaders of Indian descent had always made him stand out. Yet, despite his seemingly charismatic persona, he was a man of few words. He rarely spoke publicly or granted interviews, and throughout the events surrounding his legal battles he remained mostly silent, preferring to let the other union leaders handle the press. When I asked if he would grant me an interview, he declined, arguing that he wished to let his actions speak for themselves. At the time, I was frustrated by his silence, but I later came to realize that it was appropriate, and perhaps even fitting, given the silent role that he played in his own "affair."

During his solidarity campaign, Madassamy was transformed into a silent icon of union struggle. At meetings, rallies, press conferences, and demonstrations held in his name, his words or thoughts were rarely mentioned. His image, however, was ever present. Large poster boards with a cropped picture of his face were seemingly mass-produced. They hung behind the presenters at different town visits and rallies, were carried by demonstrators during protests, and were strewn about everywhere union activities were held—giving the impression that Madassamy was quietly looking down on the events being carried out in his name.

To a certain extent, these kinds of representations are part of the process of "sacralization" and "purification" through which hunger strikers are often transformed from criminals into political heroes and martyrs.[12] In Madassamy's case, the mobilization of his static, lifeless image allowed him to be represented as a martyr even though he had not actually sacrificed his life for the cause. It also served to transform his image from that of a person involved in acts of vandalism and sabotage to a person of conviction, principles, and political commitment. The image that circulated of him, with his long beard and serene stare, was not that of a hotheaded activist but of a serene and spiritual *Indien*. He was often compared to Gandhi, and one of his lawyers (who was particularly prone to hyperbole) went so far as to call him the *fils de Gandhi* (son of Gandhi). In the same way that the union

4.2. Madassamy images at picket site. Photo by Dominique Chomerau-Lamotte.

would often refer to Afro-Guadeloupean workers as the sons of the nèg ma-wons, Madassamy suddenly became not just the son of indentured workers but the son of Gandhi—the ultimate figure of Indian resistance.

When I asked Max what role Madassamy's ethnicity had played in his affair, he acknowledged that it had been "fundamental," particularly in regards to the Abolition Day demonstrations. "Because if he, who had not experienced slavery, was engaged, that gave the movement another dimension—a more popular and general dimension. It became not a personal, particular struggle, but a political struggle." For Max, Madassamy's indianité served to frame the battle over the commemoration of slavery as a universalist political struggle, rather than confining it to the realm of Afro-Guadeloupean politics. But his particularity as an Indian was also key to his transformation into a political icon. As Max explained, "The physical is very important in communication, in the diffusion of information. And in any case, he [Madassamy] has a very particular head [*une tête particulière*], which makes the *ancrage* [anchoring], the *accroche* [appeal] . . . the *accroche* is of a unique sort, because of his origin but also because of his head."

As Max suggests, Madassamy's indianité carried a deep communicative value. His "particular head" and his particular relationship to Guadeloupean history allowed him to become a polyvalent symbol of struggle and resistance, at once both particular and universal. The way he was represented during the solidarity campaign was deeply marked by this tension between universality and particularity. For example, although he had written a letter "to his supporters" from prison, this letter was read only once, at one of the initial rallies in Pointe-à-Pitre, but was not incorporated into the later rallies because, as Max explained, it was too general and universal.

> What he wrote could have been written by anyone. "I am in jail, I am on a hunger strike, I am writing to you." That has less appeal, less weight than what the *chair* [flesh] can suggest. Writing is limited, because you use words, words which are recognizable by everyone, and easily assimilated by everyone, and which have particular connotations. But here you have an individual who is invested in his person [*investi dans sa personne*]. There are no words for that. From his image each person crafts their own critique and their own words, they each create their own story as well—they each construct a story and create a narrative, each person creates their own script as well. That is the role of the imagination—of myth.

In his explanation of the use of Madassamy's image, Max argues that Madassamy's letter from prison was too generic in the sense that its meaning was determined by its genre. His image, however, represented a blank canvas onto which various narratives could be projected. Although Max does not say it explicitly, it is evident that Madassamy's indianité was part of what allowed for that malleability.

Although Guadeloupe has the fourth-largest Indian community in the Caribbean, Indians have long had a "silent" place in contemporary society.[13] Contrary to parts of the English-speaking Caribbean where Indo- and Afro-Caribbean relationships have been characterized by histories of violence and antagonistic struggle over political power, the French Caribbean is thought to have relatively harmonious ethnic relationships. Some scholars have attributed this presumed harmony to the Indian community's relatively small size, significant integration through out-group marriages, and socioeconomic advancement within agriculture, commerce, and public service. Others suggest that Guadeloupe's political integration with France eliminated tensions over postcolonial rule.[14]

Within the literary canon, the Indian presence has been extolled as part of what gives the Antilles their distinctive multicultural "creolité."[15] Yet, despite these celebratory claims, the figure of the Indian in the French Antilles has for the most part been absent from public representations, and important historic dates for the Indo-Guadeloupean population—such as the extension of citizenship and voting rights to Indian immigrants and their descendants in 1923—have not become the object of public commemoration. In recent years activists from the Indo-Guadeloupean community have sought to counter these silences, influenced in part by the broader turn to the past that fueled the increased commemorations of slavery and the passing of the law defining it as a crime against humanity in 2001. However, the monuments that were erected in celebration of the Indo-Guadeloupean presence during this period did not focus on local figures and communities but on abstract themes such as "arrival," and on global icons of Indian political subjectivity and identity such as Gandhi. In Guadeloupe a statue of Gandhi was placed in Saint-François, one of the towns with the most highly visible Indian population.[16] In Martinique, a bust of Gandhi was placed in a neighborhood that was populated by the descendants of indentured workers in the 1940s.[17] These were both gifts from the Indian government, seeking to strengthen ties with its diaspora. In addition to the Gandhi statues, there was also a monument erected to commemorate the ship *Aurélie*, on which the first Indian immigrants were said to arrive. The monument was made not by a local sculptor but by an Indian-born sculptor residing in France, Indrajeet Sahadev.

The emphasis on universal themes, foreign objects, and international icons of Indian identity speaks to the constraints placed on Indo-Guadeloupean identity in the context of French republican traditions, which stipulate that racial, ethnic, and religious allegiances should take a backseat to a shared civic identity. This has resulted in an ambiguous and even vacuous definition of indianité. For example, in an interview on the occasion of the Arrival Day commemorations, Ernest Moutoussamy, the mayor of Saint-François and one of the most prominent figures of the Indo-Guadeloupean community, stated,

> Indianité is not a philosophy or an ideology. Indianité is a cultural fact, a historical fact: the Indian presence. I am of Indian origin physically, but I have no Indian practices. I don't play the music, I don't dance, I don't have the language, I don't practice religion. Thus I am an Indian without indianité.[18]

Moutoussamy argues that he is an Indian without indianité because he does not engage in cultural practices that can be traced back to the Indian subcontinent. In his comments he goes on to praise those Indo-Guadeloupeans who, unlike himself, did retain cultural practices from India, particularly culinary, musical, and religious ones.[19] However, for someone like Moutoussamy—who does not see himself as having any Indian cultural traits— indianité is reduced to physicality, an image stripped of content.

This idea of indianité as a mere physical fact was part of what allowed Madassamy's image to operate as a blank slate, a sort of floating signifier, with which everyone could identify in their own particular way. Madassamy's image, disentangled from his personal history and motivations, could thus circulate freely and be read through multiple narratives—simultaneously defiant and docile, hero and victim, revolutionary and martyr. Through this process, Madassamy became a political symbol: a story to be told, a narrative to be created, and a script to be written, but not a voice to be heard.

Bik a Mada

Directly across the street from the union offices in the popular neighborhood of L'Arrandisement, there is an empty lot that the union usually refers to as le bik a travayé. Bik is a Creole word for "gathering place," though it can also be used to refer to a goal or end. Union leaders often used the bik a travayé (or workers' gathering place) as a sort of annex to their small, cramped union offices. During the span of my fieldwork, I saw this lot transformed into a lecture hall, informal dining room, artisans market, information fair, and a dance floor. During the Madassamy affair, it was temporarily renamed the "Bik a Mada" in Madassamy's honor and became the central gathering place for those involved in the Madassamy campaign.[20]

During this time, the bik came to resemble a picket site—with people sitting around in folding chairs, passing newspapers back and forth, and discussing the latest media coverage. Like the piquet, which can become an important site of communal exchange, the Bik a Mada represented an important site for the formation of community and the development of solidarity. However, the Bik a Mada had a much more somber and tense energy than the traditional piquet grève. Workers who stopped in were genuinely worried about Madassamy's health, frustrated with the seeming deadlock of the situation, and anxious about the lack of a stronger response from the union. In contrast to the picket sites, here there were no card games, shared meals, or bottles of rum. This was camaraderie of a different kind.

When asked why they were there, many said they had come to get information, to find out about Madassamy's condition, but also to check in and see what needed to be done—anything from hanging posters to setting up barricades. They also said they didn't want to go home, they couldn't sit still, something was in the air, something was going to happen, and they wanted to be part of it. In other words, workers showed up at the bik to demonstrate their readiness for action. The bik also served as a gathering place for exchanging information on the effectiveness of the actions already undertaken. Newspapers were passed around, coverage was analyzed and debated, and new actions were planned.

During this time rumors about Madassamy's health circulated widely, and the bik was where union members could come to get confirmation on his condition. These rumors spread mostly through phone chains: someone would get a call with speculative new information and instantly call everyone they knew, who would then also follow suit. These rumor chains combined the efficacy of a chain letter with the misinformation of a child's game of telephone. The rumor chains are indicative both of how information circulates in Guadeloupe and of local mistrust of the media. Although the newspapers reported daily on Madassamy's health, these reports were quickly dismissed in the face of a cousin's or friend's account. The rumors also contributed to the general climate of tension and suspense, making it seem as if death and mayhem were just a phone call away.

Crescendo

On Monday, October 18, 2004, as Madassamy entered the third week of his hunger strike, Guadeloupeans awoke to a new wave of barricades and disruptions. Morning radio reporters excitedly relayed the news and journalists "embedded" in the barricades gave play-by-play accounts of confrontations with the police. The union's forecasted crescendo seemed to have finally arrived.

Labor strikes suddenly emerged through many of the key sectors of the economy. Some of them were merely "solidarity strikes," meaning that workers in these sections had no real demands and were simply shutting down key sectors of the economy to increase pressure for Madassamy's release. In sectors where there were already labor conflicts, the Madassamy affair triggered strikes that had already been brewing. Some of these strikes—particularly that of the dockworkers—unleashed a panic throughout the society, which braced itself for the *penuries*, or scarcities, that would surely follow.[21]

This period also marked an escalation in direct actions. Demonstrators set up barricades, overturned dumpsters, and even shattered windows at a local McDonald's. As the tension mounted, the demonstrations became more violent. Politicians eventually called for a resolution, arguing that although they did not support the union's methods, a compromise was needed to restore *la paix sociale* (social peace). As Madassamy's hunger strike entered the critical phase in terms of the dangers posed to his health, passions ran high and the conflict reached its climax.

"An La Ri-La": Taking It to the Streets

The Friday night after the barricades went up, the UGTG held a large *léwoz* at the Bik a Mada. *Léwoz* in Creole means "party," but it refers to a specific type of gwoka drumming and dancing party. Union léwoz are usually quite festive, with music, food, and dancing. Looking back on events, however, union members told me there was a different energy that night. A large number of young people from the surrounding neighborhoods attended the léwoz. Union members originally assumed the youth were there for the music but would soon realize that they were to play a decisive role in the Madassamy affair.

The following Saturday morning, union activists and supporters gathered at the bik to march from the union headquarters to the colonial center in downtown Pointe-à-Pitre—the usual route for their political marches. Organizers were surprised by the turnout, which they estimated at about five hundred (police estimated three hundred). The crowd was mostly male and mostly UGTG members, but there were also many nonunionized supporters (*militants*), members of other unions, and participants from other cultural and political organizations in Guadeloupe. They carried placards with simple slogans, such as "Lagé Mada!" (Free Mada!) and "Pa manyé syndikalis!" (Don't touch the syndicalists!), as well as the ubiquitous posters of Madassamy's head.

The energy that day differed from the excitement generated in the previous town visits and demonstrations. The tone was violent, confrontational. The usual slogans were uttered with extra force, and the voices echoed ominously through the quickly emptying streets of the colonial center: "Si yo vlé, si yo vlé pa, l'igtg an la ri-la!" (Whether they want it or not, UGTG is in the streets!) "L'igtg kay kchou a yo!" (UGTG is going to destroy them!) During most marches, demonstrators usually walk at a leisurely pace, distributing flyers to onlookers and chatting with each other between chants and songs. But on this occasion marchers walked forcibly and briskly, fists raised high in the air. It was almost as if they were going to break into the prison and free Madassamy themselves.

The following day, I discussed the march with Katrine and Nicolas, two militants who had participated in the demonstrations. They were both committed activists, involved in the nationalist movements of the 1980s, who were now *solidaire* with the UGTG. They had attended the march because they knew it would be important; they figured the UGTG had done enough talking and was ready to escalate its actions. We spoke the following day at the Bik a Mada as we leaned against some parked cars. I had spoken with them numerous times before but had never seen them so giddy and playful. They told me they'd experienced a feeling of déjà vu during the demonstrations and had been reminded of their younger years of confrontation and militancy. They couldn't stand still as they recounted the events and kept moving about, tugging and pushing each other like excited children.

Nicolas started telling the story.

> It was incredible! You could feel the energy—from the beginning I knew it was going to be *chaude* [heated]. There were so many of us! As soon as we descended onto La Pwointe [Pointe-à-Pitre], all the businesses started closing their doors—they knew better than to stay open. The streets emptied and we kept walking, gaining steam. We started turning over trash cans, creating a disorder. . . .

Katrine kept interrupting and eventually took over the narration.

> Suddenly these kids came out of nowhere. Most of them were bare-chested and had shirts or bandannas covering their heads and faces. I'm telling you, they came out of nowhere! It was like they were waiting for us . . . and they had Molotov cocktails ready to go. They started throwing them through store windows. . . . Then suddenly it was all smoke, and we were running, turning everything over, and running. . . .

At this point, Nicolas jumped back in. "It was like old times, right?" Katrine just laughed and shoved him playfully.

As Katrine and Nicolas suggested, once the violence began, union demonstrators (or at least those clearly identified with union T-shirts and placards) made their way back to the union headquarters. Many crowded into the small balcony of the union offices to watch the events unfolding below. Meanwhile, "the youth" (as the media would later refer to them), probably joined by unidentified union supporters, took over the streets, vandalizing, looting, and setting Pointe-à-Pitre ablaze. The media would later refer to these demonstrators as "uncontrollable elements." Most of them rode around on motor scooters, maneuvering easily through side streets and alleys and communicating with each other through text messages on their cell phones to avoid the police. They managed to elude the police for over eight hours, creating what the media called an "insurrectional environment" all afternoon and into the evening.

4.3. Protesters during the Madassamy affair. Photo by Dominique Chomerau-Lamotte.

Most of these young demonstrators came from the *cités* and *quartiers populaires*, the poor and working-class neighborhoods that surround Pointe-à-Pitre. These neighborhoods are filled with the low-income youth commonly referred to as *RMI-istes*—so named because they are often the beneficiaries of the French *Revenu minimum d'insertion* (RMI), a form of national welfare that allows citizens who do not qualify for unemployment benefits to be "inserted" into the economy. Given the 30 percent unemployment rate in Guadeloupe, the *RMI-iste* population is substantial. These "undesirable" or "uncontrollable" elements are the source of much anxiety—second only to the anxiety created by labor conflicts. Also referred to as *djobbers* due to their participation in the informal economy, the *RMI-istes* are generally imagined as young, uneducated men and unwed mothers. They embody the anxieties that exist in Guadeloupe over job insecurity, lack of affordable housing, inflation, and the general alienation that comes from the economic malaise underpinning the island's facade of prosperity.[22] The union is often criticized for involving these young people in its demonstrations. It is unclear, however, whether the union recruits them or whether they are simply attracted by the possibility of confrontation. As one *RMI-iste* told me at a union event, he was always eager to join union demonstrations because he liked to confront *le mamblo* (police).

These disaffected young people are quick to join union actions because these events provide them with a vehicle to express their general discontent. Much like the infamous 2005 riots of the Parisian *banlieues*, union demonstrations become ambiguous sites of protest where various forms of discontent find expression.[23] At the same time, they also represent an opportunity to engage in illicit actions. In a society that values conspicuous consumption, these moments offer an opportunity to acquire much-coveted goods. On the day of the Madassamy demonstrations, numerous stores were looted, as the young *RMI-istes* loaded up their motor scooters with desirable wares.

During these actions, radio and TV programming was interrupted to warn of the unfolding events. Radio announcers reported that young people were looting, creating barricades, and setting cars and dumpsters on fire. They cautioned residents to stay away from the area and from what they described as "a climate of insurrection." One reporter went so far as to say that Pointe-à-Pitre was the new Baghdad. Meanwhile, Canal 10 offered "live" video footage (in the sense that they shot it, then ran to the station to play it minutes later) of masked youth running in the streets. They also showed footage of heavily armed police officers in gas masks, accompanied by military tanks, walking hesitantly through the *cités* of Pointe-à-Pitre unleashing tear gas and seemingly tiptoeing toward the center of action.

Canal 10 immediately opened the phone lines for an impromptu call-in show. Reactions ranged from condemnation of the union to condemnation of the police, the local government, and the prosecutor. Some defended the union, arguing that it had tried to inform the population and to use other means but had gone unheard. Others blamed the union for stirring up the disaffected youth and for exploiting Madassamy—turning him into a martyr to conceal its past mistakes. Others argued that the union had been provoked and that the government should have known better than to imprison Madassamy. The special programming continued through the afternoon and into the night, concluding with a live broadcast titled simply *Édition Spéciale*, which featured several political figures (mostly pro-independence sympathizers) commenting on the events and taking questions from viewers.

That night, many young men in the streets of Pointe-à-Pitre were harassed and even assaulted by the police. Although ten were arrested, none were implicated in the looting and vandalism of stores. The justice system—which is notorious for its slow pace—acted quickly in this case, and the young men stood before a judge the following week. The UGTG offered to provide legal assistance to the boys, but most of the families turned it down because they were hesitant to be associated with the union. Although the defendants had no prior criminal record and were not implicated in the more violent actions that took place, they were given relatively harsh sentences. The lightest sentence—one month of jail time—was given to a nineteen-year-old who said he had nothing to do with the events and had simply stepped outside to see what was happening. He was the only one who repudiated the union during his testimony, stating that he neither supported the UGTG nor agreed with its methods. Most of the others, who disassociated themselves but did not repudiate the UGTG in their testimony, were sentenced to four months. As the sentences were given, one of the boys (apparently the youngest) and his mother began to weep; others began shouting at the judge, who abruptly ended the proceedings and vanished from the room. The audience was removed from the building, and a scuffle ensued in front of the courthouse as some of the boys' friends and relatives began shouting at the police, who quickly gathered around the courthouse creating a human barricade between the Palais de Justice and the increasingly agitated crowd.

The young boys' arrest weighed heavily on union members. The day after the hearing, I tried to address the issue with Max, but he seemed reluctant to talk about it, so I let the matter drop. At the end of the day, as we drove back to the union headquarters from one of the picket sites, I sat in the front passenger seat with two other union members squeezed into the back of Max's old Volkswagen Fox. We rolled down the windows to get some air, and Max turned on the afternoon news on the radio. He tuned in to Radio Caraïbe International (RCI), which was having a special call-in program devoted, once again, to the Madassamy affair.

Suddenly one of the callers started talking about Max, about how he was a wealthy *fonctionnaire*, a well-paid state employee who manipulated poor workers and who was now manipulating the unemployed youth for his cause. I had heard the same comments made dozens of times before, but it was surreal to hear them while sitting inches away from him. I turned to see what his reaction was, but he was inscrutable: eyes on the road, hands on the wheel, with an expressionless face. I had often tried to engage him about these sorts of discourses and rumors: that he was rich and had all the money he had blackmailed from employers tucked away in Swiss bank accounts, that he had a summer house in the south of France where he loved to go despite his supposed nationalist ideologies, and that his children all studied in expensive universities and boarding schools in the United States and Europe. Max never wanted to acknowledge these rumors. He would artfully deflect my inquiries, playfully teasing me and swiftly disarming any claims I might make to anthropological authority.

Where did you hear that? Who told you that? Who do you even know in Guadeloupe? You think you know a lot of people here? How many people do you know? How many? You think you know what Guadeloupeans think? Beh, you don't know anything!

But on that night there was no teasing. The callers on the radio show kept criticizing the union leaders for manipulating workers, putting Madassamy's life in danger, and taking advantage of the local unemployed youth, whom they were supposedly paying to participate in their struggle. One woman blasted the union for exposing so many young boys to police abuse.

When we arrived at the union headquarters, we pulled into the Bik a Mada, where workers and sympathizers had gathered to listen to the news coverage. We joined the dozen or so other cars that were parked around the bik with their headlights lighting up the small lot. The drivers and passengers sat silently in the cars, engines off, keys in the ignition, windows and doors wide open, as everybody listened simultaneously to the same radio program. As callers launched into their usual complaints and criticisms of the union's methods, the union was actually listening.

This was the first time I had seen union members monitor the media coverage in this way. Usually when I asked them about media portrayals, they would shrug and laugh it off, somehow resigned to being misunderstood and not really giving it much weight. But on this occasion, there was a solemnity and sadness in the air, perhaps because they felt misunderstood or perhaps because they felt responsible for the fate of the imprisoned youth. Once the radio program was over, the group quickly dispersed. Max went up to the union headquarters for a closed meeting, and everyone else left. The Bik a Mada was suddenly empty, with only the pictures of Madassamy's face staring out into the night.

Nothing but the Law

A month after Madassamy had begun his hunger strike, the social crescendo predicted by union leaders reached its peak. There were numerous strikes throughout Guadeloupe (including a dockworkers' strike that paralyzed the local port), television and radio programming was dominated by analysis and commentary on the affair, and the gossip and rumor mills were overrun with news of Madassamy's impending death and the union's violent revenge. Amid this climate of heightened expectation and upheaval, union leaders prepared to resolve Madassamy's "affair" through a new legal approach.

The union's legal strategy was characterized by the same improvisational stance and seemingly chaotic actions as their solidarity campaign. First they contested the charges against Madassamy, arguing that there was insufficient proof and that the case was based on unreliable witnesses. At the same time, they contested Madassamy's arrest and imprisonment, arguing that he had not received due process and that an arrest had been premature because he still had the right to an appeal. Later, near the end of his strike, they initiated a new legal procedure: a demand that Madassamy be released due to his deteriorating health. The union sustained these different legal battles simultaneously, even though they were in some ways contradictory and at odds with the union's own previous disavowal of appeals. Consistent with their usual form of "kaskod" politics, labor leaders engaged with the legal system while simultaneously fleeing from its constitutive logics.

The prosecutor contended that the union's chaotic engagement with the legal system made a mockery of the legal order. The simultaneous and incompatible tactics, along with the use of hunger strikes, labor strikes, and public demonstrations to, as the prosecutor would later suggest, "pressure the court from the streets," were characterized as an affront to the rule of law and order. With the political climate at its peak, the prefect called a press conference to condemn union actions, particularly its "instrumentalization of the local youth," arguing that "in a legally constituted state, one can only contest a court decision through litigation." The union responded by continuing its legal campaign in tandem with its actions on the street.

When Madassamy was initially imprisoned, the union and its lawyers constructed a legal defense based on the "irregularities" of both his detention and incarceration, effectively demanding that Madassamy be released on a technicality. But as the days turned into weeks and Madassamy's hunger strike began to pose a danger to his health, the union's legal team changed its strategy. Aided in part by a new human rights lawyer from Martinique, they began to rework Madassamy's case—dropping technical matters and recentering their efforts around a discourse of human rights. They filed a new motion for release based on article 720-1 of the French legal code, which states that the court can temporarily suspend the sentence of prisoners who require urgent medical care or whose medical condition does not allow them to serve out their sentence. The prosecutor responded by urging the court to ignore the claim, given that Madassamy's medical condition was self-inflicted, and requested that the court order force-feeding instead.[24] As part of this new wave of legal proceedings, court-appointed doctors examined Madassamy and testified that his health was indeed at risk and that in order to end the hunger strike, he would require medical assistance and a slow process of "réanimation" under the care of a specialized medical team.

On November 5, 2004, over a month after Madassamy began his hunger strike, the Juge d'application de peines (JAP) was deliberating over the question of releasing him for medical treatment. At the same time, a hearing was being held in criminal court concerning the original request for release on the basis of legal technicalities. As these simultaneous but incongruent legal proceedings unfolded, union leaders and militants gathered in front of the union's headquarters for a demonstration. The turnout on this occasion was considerable (newspapers estimated between fifteen hundred and two thousand participants). It seemed clear that this would be the turning point in the Madassamy affair.

The demonstrations began with a march from the union headquarters to the Centre Hospitalière Universitaire, where the JAP court was deliberating. After a small rally, demonstrators packed up and made their way toward Pointe-à-Pitre. They were expected to head directly to the Palais de Justice, where Madassamy's lawyers were pleading his case. But they instead detoured through the commercial streets of Pointe-à-Pitre, with both the press and the gendarmes anxiously following.

Once again, the energy was tense and confrontational, with what the press described as "virulent" slogans demanding Madassamy's release. In addition, marchers brandished a severed pig's head, which they placed atop a long wooden stake. The pig's head was meant to represent Patrick Vogt, the procureur de la république (prosecutor), whom many thought bore a striking resemblance to local swine. It was something easily found at any butcher's market, but its presence struck a nerve with some observers, who felt that the act of marching with Vogt's metonymic head on a stake through the streets of Pointe-à-Pitre was particularly aggressive.

For over an hour marchers walked through the colonial center's narrow streets, carefully avoiding the Palais de Justice, where Madassamy's trial was taking place. I was later told that this detour was a way of stalling, as labor leaders waited to get word of the JAP court's decision on Madassamy's release for medical treatment. Uncertain whether the JAP was going to rule in favor of Madassamy's release, they circled around Pointe-à-Pitre once again, improvising as they waited to see when and where they needed to channel their energy.

As demonstrators wove through Pointe-à-Pitre's commercial district with their virulent chants and staked pig's head, I sat in the back row of the courtroom at the Palais de Justice listening to the arguments of Madassamy's case. I had arrived at the courthouse early, on the advice of labor leaders who assured me that once the demonstrations began I would be unable to get through. However, I had spent most of the morning shivering in the overly air-conditioned courthouse, struggling to make out the whisperings of the lawyers at the front of the room over the loud hum of the massive air-conditioner. Several hours into the proceedings, as the prosecutors stated their case, a new noise began to penetrate the courtroom. Soft but unmistakable, the sounds of the ka drums started to fill the air, and powerful chants began reverberating in the room.

Lawyers struggled at first to proceed as if nothing had changed, but the chants became increasingly louder, eventually drowning out their arguments. Instead of the details of the case, all that could be heard was the chant of the demonstrators: "Li-be-ré Ma-da! Li-be-ré Ma-da!" Eventually the court declared a recess. I exited the cold hall of justice and made my way out to the balcony overlooking the small plaza facing the courthouse, which was overflowing with union supporters and leaders. They had set up a drum circle near the court steps, where they were singing popular gwoka protest songs accompanied by the sound of seashell horns. In the middle of the plaza, at the foot of a small statute to the former French admiral Gourbeyre, someone had placed the controversial pig's head, which seemed to be quietly observing the developments.

The court reconvened after a short recess, but the session came to a quick end. Rather than ruling on the Madassamy case, the court declared that another hearing was needed to consider the court's jurisdiction in the matter. Technically, Madassamy would have to remain in jail for months as this new legal episode played itself out. Meanwhile, however, the JAP court issued its ruling, declaring that Madassamy did indeed require medical assistance and that he should be released for two months to receive care. The only thing keeping Madassamy in jail at that point was the prosecutor, who could appeal the decision and drag out the affair. As the session drew to a close, the prosecutor exited the courtroom without acknowledging the presence of the demonstrators or their pig-head effigy. In a small corner of the Palais de Justice, he spoke to reporters and declared that he would not appeal the decision because he felt confident that the magistrates had reached a sound conclusion. "Magistrates don't rule to appease or to excite," he said. "They apply the law, nothing but the law, and the whole law."

Once the labor leaders heard the news, they announced it to the crowd, which erupted into a loud, roaring cheer. After a few statements from the lawyers and leaders, they sang the union's revolutionary anthem and marched back to UGTG headquarters, singing all the way, waving palm leaves in the air, dancing, and rejoicing to an impromptu song.

> Wa-yoooo! Wa-yo Wa-yo!
> Yo liberé Madassamy! [They liberated Madassamy!]
> Péyi-la changé! [The country is changing!]
> Yo liberé Mada jod-la! [They liberated Mada today!]
> Way-yoooo! Way yo-o-o!
> Yo liberé Madassamy! [They liberated Madassamy!]
> Pou péyi-la changé! [So the country can change!]
> Yo liberé Mada jod-la! [They liberated Mada today!]
> Way-yoooo! Way yo-o-o!

As the demonstrators emptied the plaza, I looked for the controversial pig's head. It had been left behind, discarded at the foot of the statue, with a celebratory cigarette dangling from its mouth.

*

After sustaining his hunger strike for thirty-two days, Madassamy was released into medical care. He slowly regained his strength and eventually made a full recovery. Since then, he has appeared before the courts on multiple occasions. The charges against him were not dropped, but he was not forced to serve his sentence. Due to his criminal record he lost his job as a truck driver, but with the help of the union he started his own business: a small animal feed store in his native town of Port-Louis. When I encountered him in 2007, three years after his hunger strike, he seemed at peace. His beard had grown and grayed, and although he still held a post in the union's Conseil Syndical, he had for the most part retreated from union life. I asked him once more if he would grant me an interview, but he simply smiled and walked away. I didn't see him again until the massive strike of 2009, where he once again remained dutifully behind the scenes, stocking water bottles in the union headquarters and silently distributing flyers to demonstrators who would glance up at him and accept his leaflets with a small nod of recognition.

FIVE

The Route of History

During my time conducting research in Guadeloupe, I was invited to participate in what was described to me as a *marche historique*—that is, a historical
walk or memory walk. The slogan in Creole used to promote these events is
"fè mémwa maché," which literally means to "make your memory walk" or
"take your memory on a walk." This phrase refers to the process of thinking
back and scanning your memory for past events. When something or someone prompts you to recall something, they are making your memory walk.
Having already participated in numerous union rallies and collective demonstrations (*manifs*), I expected the memory walk to involve a large mass of
workers with signs and banners, chanting political slogans as they blocked
busy city streets. When I arrived at the designated meeting place, however, I
found myself among a markedly smaller and quieter group. There were no
placards, banners, bullhorns, or loudspeakers—just a few dozen workers
milling about quietly with their families and friends. As I would soon discover, these memory walks differ sharply from the usual mass marches and
demonstrations organized by labor activists.

Once we set off on our journey, the busy streets of Pointe-à-Pitre slowly
faded away, and we found ourselves walking in silence through former plantation lands and overgrown sugar fields, surrounded by the pungent smell—
both sweet and sour—of ripened cane. We struggled through the unfamiliar
terrain, trudging up steep, slippery hills and marching single file through
small, tunnel-like paths that cut through the tall blades of cane. At several
stops along the way we paused to chew on freshly cut cane while an amateur historian, or someone else with close ties to the particular place, talked
to us about historic events that had once unfolded there. Slave uprisings,
labor strikes, and anticolonial struggles were all brought together along a
common path.

5.1. Memory walk, May 2008. Photo courtesy of UGTG.

As we walked, I struggled to find Max and the other labor leaders who were usually at the front of union marches yelling out directions, chanting slogans, and directing the crowd. I was surprised to find them lingering at the back of the group, walking quietly with their children. Their usual energy and aura of authority seemed overshadowed by the landscape itself: the whisper of the wind rustling through the fields, the looming presence of the tall centenarian trees with their thick, twisted trunks and overgrown roots, and the rhythmic crunch of our footsteps on the unpaved soil.

Weeks later, I discussed this event with Sabine, a young schoolteacher and fellow tenderfoot. She became excited as she reflected back on that day and explained how powerful the experience had been for her. "During that walk," she said,

> I could not help but feel connected to those who had gone before. For me, it was like being part of history. I was there, where they had been, where they had walked—it was like I could feel their presence, because I was there, in the very site where history was made!

Many of the participants I interviewed echoed Sabine's feelings of historical witnessing, particularly her sense of having "been there." They would often remark that the memory walks had provided them with a personal, direct connection to the past and as a result they claimed not just to know more about their past, but to finally understand its trajectory. In this chapter, I explore how the memory walks generate this feeling of historical intimacy and why this form of historical and archival production became salient to the work of Guadeloupean labor activism at the start of the twenty-first century.

The Problem of History

Guadeloupean activists' turn to the past was influenced by a larger commemorative wave that began taking shape in France during the 1990s and early 2000s.[1] This was sparked by a series of important anniversaries, including the Columbus quincentennial in 1992, the 50th anniversary of departmentalization in 1996, the 150th anniversary of abolition in 1998, and the 200th anniversary of the Haitian Revolution in 2004. These events spurred a wave of activism and debate regarding the place of colonialism and slavery within public memory in France, leading to mass demonstrations in 1998, the passing of a law recognizing slavery as a crime against humanity in 2001, and the 2005 designation of May 10 as an official day for commemorating "the memory of slavery" in both mainland France and the DOMs. With this surge of memorial events, the twenty-first century appeared to promise a break with the long-standing silence that has shrouded the histories of colonialism and slavery in France.[2]

These commemorative politics significantly impacted debates that were already brewing over public history in the DOMs—particularly in regard to the abolition of slavery. Since the early 1900s, most commemorations had focused on the figure of French abolitionist Victor Schoelcher, who had long been exalted as a symbol of the progressive promises of French integration. As anthropologist Marie-José Jolivet has shown, during the campaigns for assimilation in the early 1900s, the image of Schoelcher "the emancipator" was often mobilized as a foil against the conservative and exclusionary practices of the planter class.[3] Over time Schoelcher's image slowly evolved into a larger symbol of integration, becoming a "sublimated substitute for the colonizer," in the words of Édouard Glissant, displacing the crimes of slavery onto the plantocracy.[4] Schoelcher eventually morphed into a symbol of both the project of freedom and the project of inclusion, increasingly becoming metonymic of republicanism itself.[5] After departmentalization, his name and likeness was etched into the local landscape with an over-abundance of monuments, statues, towns, schools, and boulevards erected or named in his honor. In 1948 (just two years after departmentalization), when Césaire presided over the hundredth anniversary of abolition, Schoelcher remained the focus of the events, with little mention of the actions of enslaved populations.

It was not until the 1960s and 1970s—as the promise of departmentalization began to fade—that Antillean intellectuals began to question what they termed "Schoelcherisme" or the "cult of Schoelcher." During this period a new generation of historians and activists began to produce new histories of freedom that focused on the role of slave revolts in precipitating the process of abolition. It was during this time that the local dates of abolition—such as May 22 in Martinique and May 27 in Guadeloupe—became endowed with significance and political meaning, as the "cult of Schoelcher" was tackled head on.

In the case of Guadeloupe, from the 1960s to the 1980s historians, activists, and novelists began to publish accounts not just of the revolts that precipitated the 1848 abolition but also of the earlier battles against the reimposition of slavery in 1802. From these efforts a new series of local heroes emerged, notably Louis Delgrés, Joseph Ignace, and the *mulâtresse* Solitude, all of whom fought Napoleon's troops in 1802 to prevent the reestablishment of slavery. Solitude was a former slave, while Delgrés and Ignace were both free men of color who joined the military after slavery had been initially abolished. There are few traces of these figures in the archives, but through the work of activists, historians, and novelists such as André Schwarz Bart, Roland Anduse, Maryse Condé, and Daniel Maxim, these names came to hold a prominent place in the contemporary imagination.[6] When Maxim was placed in charge of the local 1998 commemorations of abolition, he spearheaded attempts to further memorialize these figures by erecting new monuments and renaming several streets and historical sites in their honor.[7]

These efforts were facilitated by the decentralization policies of the Mitterrand administration and the new emphasis it placed on the promotion of "regional culture." After Mitterrand's election in 1981 the budget for the ministry of culture was doubled and, as part of the larger decentralization policies of the Socialist administration, new regional cultural bureaus (Directions regionales des affaires culturelles, or DRAC) were created.[8] In addition, under the Mitterrand administration local councils in the DOMs were given new economic, social, and cultural authority. The regional councils were charged with "promoting development" and were handed the management of special funds including the "octroi de mer" (the tax levied on imported goods), the FIDOM (Fonds d'investissement des DOM) for public works, and the FIR (Fonds d'investissement routier) for the expansion of roads and highways. This administrative restructuring allowed local politicians to promote "regional culture" in new ways leading to a new era of *patrimonialisation*, characterized by the formation of new historical museums and monuments. This led to a "frénésie patrimoniale," with the number of museums in Martinique jumping from six to forty-two between 1986 and 2001.[9] However, these sites of government-sponsored folklore were often subjected to what Richard Price describes as the "postcarding of the past," through which "memories of oppression, inequality, and struggle are replaced by nostalgia, complicity and celebration."[10] This is most evident in the proliferation of plantation museums and resorts in the French Antilles, where former slave barracks are transformed into luxury accommodations for foreign visitors, while their underlying history is reduced to a technological account of sugar, tobacco, coffee, and rum production—with little discussion of the social and economic relations that underpinned these industries.

In Guadeloupe the "frénésie patrimoniale" also led to the proliferation of monuments atop the *rond-points*, or roundabouts, that have increasingly come to characterize Guadeloupe's French road system. As local politicians gained control of transportation funds under decentralization, these rond-point monuments became ubiquitous, to the point where now nearly every traffic circle in Guadeloupe features a tribute to local history or cultural *patrimoine*. Activists and cultural groups have tried to appropriate these sites as important realms of memory, most notably by using them as gathering points for historical marches and other commemorative events. However, unlike statues placed in public plazas and other open spaces, the rond-points have no benches, sidewalks, or other vantage points from which to contemplate the monuments. Moreover, the monuments are mostly found along segments of the national highway that have little or no foot traffic. Some suggest that their strategic placement in the middle of high-traffic avenues gives them a prominent place in the landscape; others argue that this kind of historical representation does not promote a sustained engagement with the past, encouraging one to simply "drive by" the past with little reflection.

While the rond-point monuments began dominating the commemorative landscape, and former centers of slave labor were reworked as objects of folkloric and touristic consumption, other historical sites became centers of confusion rather than commemoration. A particularly poignant example

5.2. Mulâtresse Solitude rond-point on the Boulevard of Heroes. Photo by author.

is the case of "the steps of the slaves" (*marches des esclaves*) in Petit-Canal, a haunting set of forty-nine oversized white steps—each of which bears a small wooden sign with the name of a different African ethnic group—that lead up to the town's church from a small dock on the edge of the mangrove. The historical origins and semiotic intention of the steps, and of the inscribed African names, remains unknown, and even the local mayor's office could not explain the memorial's intended meaning or offer information on the details of its construction.[11] It is a commonly held belief in Guadeloupe that the steps were either built by slaves or used by them to climb up from the nearby port. Some even claim the steps as evidence that Petit-Canal was once the main center of the slave trade in Guadeloupe. Yet historians date these steps to some time after emancipation.[12] In her discussion of the French Antilles' landscape of history, Catherine Reinhardt describes such places as "silent sites of memory," lacking the referential context necessary for their appreciation. "The past is there, before the viewer," she writes, "but does not have a direct bearing on the historical consciousness he/she brings to the scene."[13]

One could argue that the importance of collective histories does not lie in their accuracy or even veracity, and in fact all historical narratives are also inherently "bundles of silences."[14] But in the Antilles these sites of muted

5.3. Steps of the Slaves in Petit-Canal. Photo by author.

and confused history, together with the absence of local history in the education system (due to the imposed French national curriculum) and the
overpowering presence of a triumphant French national history, lead to
what anthropologist Christine Chivallon describes as "a lack of stable narratives about the past."[15]

Throughout the Caribbean, postcolonial writers and scholars have long
been concerned with the problem of historical memory, and particularly
with how to reconcile the traumatic history of slavery with a narrative of collective destiny. Authors such as Derek Walcott and Orlando Patterson have
at times suggested that the trauma of slavery has led to a kind of New World
historical amnesia.[16] Édouard Glissant shared this preoccupation, but he
argued that it was not a question of collective amnesia, or mere *oubli* (forget-
ting/oversight). Glissant argues that in the Antilles the past is "obsessively
present" but it constitutes a form of "non-history," in the sense that it lacks
the organizing telos and triumphant narratives of Western history, resulting
in a fractured and disorganized form of historicity.[17] For Glissant, new forms
of historical production in these contexts should thus not simply aim to
reanimate obscured moments of historical action but, rather, to forge new
inventive and "prophetic" visions of the past.

Glissant's views on nationalism would shift over time, but when these critiques appeared in *Discours Antillais* in 1981 he was writing from within the problem-space of postcolonial nationalism and thus concerned with the relationship between non-history and non-sovereignty. Although he recognized that History "with a capital H" was a "functional fantasy of the West," he also understood that the production of national histories was integral to the postcolonial project. That is, he recognized that national histories were, as others have noted, "a sign of the modern," and that their absence posed a challenge to the development of a national project.[18]

Glissant, Chamoiseau, and a host of other writers have argued that the traditional forms and methods of Western history are "insufficient" in the Antilles, and as a result, alternative approaches to both archival sources and narrative forms are necessary. As I show below, the project developed by the UGTG-affiliated cultural organization NONM speaks directly to these challenges. Through the production of memory walks, these activists seek to craft new forms of historical memory and new ways of routing the past outside of the telos of the nation.

Making Memory Walk

The historical project of the memory walks emerged in tandem with the original Madassamy affair (discussed in the previous chapter), particularly the struggles over the commemoration of Abolition Day and the solidarity campaign for Madassamy's hunger strike. During this time, historical politics became central to the UGTG. Whereas in previous years the union had rallied around the slogan "Gwadloup pé ké konstwi san travay, ni san travayé" (Guadeloupe cannot be built without work or workers), in 2002 the slogan was expanded to "Gwadloup pé ké konstwi san mémwa, san travay, ni san travayé" (Guadeloupe cannot be built without *memory*, work, or workers).[19]

To better develop their historical efforts, UGTG leaders decided to foster the creation of a new organization or cultural arm charged exclusively with issues of historical memory and cultural identity. In collaboration with a handful of politically engaged historians and university professors, they launched an organization called NONM, which was charged with expanding the struggles of the UGTG beyond the sphere of labor disputes.[20] The group's name is the Creole word for man/humanity, and its stated goal is to further the union's attempts at "making new men" (*fè nonm*).[21] Within the domain of union struggles this idea is often invoked in relationship to the development of an increased political consciousness. Labor strikes are thought to *fè nonm* on the piquet through the creation of new social relationships among workers and new attitudes towards employers and the wider society. Within the context of the NONM organization, to *fè nonm* speaks to the creation of a new historical consciousness through an engagement with local histories of resistance and collective struggle. The memory walks represent one of the key practices through which the organization seeks to *fè nonm* by engaging workers in an active, purposeful form of historical praxis, which they describe as "fe mémwa maché, pou fè konsyans vansé" (making memory walk in order to make consciousness advance).

One of the main engineers of these events is Raymond Gama.[22] Gama holds a doctorate in history from the Université de Lille and taught at a local middle school until his retirement in 2009, but has always been more interested in serving as a public intellectual than an academic instructor. He hosted his own history show in Creole called *Istwa an Nou* (Our History) on the TV station L'Une, frequently speaks at public events and historical commemorations, and maintains a sleek website (with the help of his tech-savvy nephews), where he posts recent writings, sells self-published books, and uploads videos of his presentations.[23] A self-described "patriot" activist, he sees his vocation as political rather than academic, arguing that his aim is to be a Guadeloupean historian, rather than merely a historian of Guadeloupe.[24] Gama views history as an important political tool, but when I asked if he could be accused of "presentism," he explained,

> I do not regard history through the eyes of the present, no. I simply offer a new reading of the past. Every historian creates meaning, creates facts. Historical facts are not lying around in an archive, waiting to be plucked out and pasted onto the pages of history. We *make* facts. The historian is inherently a maker of facts. He relies on documentation to build facts, but each person who approaches a document produces facts in their own way. Historical facts are not immutable. It is we who produce them.

Gama views historical narratives as scholarly arguments, open to new interpretation; he recognizes the narrative power of the historian as a maker of facts and a granter of meaning. His sentiments echo historiographical theories that see the production of history as an act of power asserted throughout various forms of silencing, plotting, and particular readings of the archive.[25]

Gama was also acutely aware of the particular challenges of history-making in the postcolonial context. "We are confronted with a particular duty," he explained, "to find ourselves within the culture of the other." He asked: "How can you find yourself in documents that have not bothered to archive you, that have actually sought to eliminate you? How do you find yourself there?" Gama is clearly aware of how silences enter into the process of historical production.[26] He understands that the repertoire of stories that are said to matter, the events deemed worthy of commemoration, and the places that are chosen for preservation, are all products of and testaments to the relations of power that condition their moment of production.

In Search of a Useful History

The first memory walk organized by NONM was held in May 2002, inspired by the bicentennial of the antislavery insurrection of May 1802. During this walk, participants attempted to follow, in real time, the path of the rebel insurgents to Fort Matouba. They walked for three days, building campsites along their route and reflecting each night on their experiences. After this initial walk, however, organizers lost interest in historical reenactment and became focused on rerouting, rather than reenacting, the past.[27]

The NONM organization currently leads several memory walks each year, many of them concentrated around the month of May, which labor activists declared a "month of memory" due to its many commemorative dates (discussed below). The group of participants is usually small—around two dozen—but some of the larger events draw crowds numbering over a hundred participants. Participation in the walks reaches well beyond the usual rank and file of the union membership. In fact, one of the goals of creating the NONM organization was to reach out to students, housewives, unemployed youth, and other nonunionized sectors of the population. Unlike piquets and barricades, which are considered potentially dangerous sites of violent confrontation, the memory walks represent a family-friendly activity that can appeal to a wide spectrum of participants.

For each walk, participants gather early in the morning at a designated meeting place where they park their cars and board buses to the starting point for the route. From there, walkers are led on foot through a series of historical locations. At each site a small historical reflection, or *témoignage* (testimony), is offered by a designated expert, often someone with a personal connection to the events that unfolded in that place. At the end of each walk there is a collective celebration and meal consisting of highly symbolic local foods, such as *mori* (salt fish), *pòyò* (green bananas), and *rasin* (root vegetables), accompanied by freshly prepared juice from local fruits. Some of the more seasoned participants bring their own plates, fashioned out of hollowed-out coconuts or gourds, so they can eat "like the ancestors." These meals stand in sharp contrast to the diet of many Guadeloupeans, which is increasingly dominated by imported and prepackaged French foods.[28] For many participants, these dishes bring back powerful memories of childhood, especially the local fruits and vegetables that are not always available at the large supermarket chains where Guadeloupeans increasingly do their shopping.

In addition, the act of walking itself represents a radical departure from the daily routine of the French Antilles, which is characterized by an over-abundance of cars and permanently congested roads.[29] Walking is associated, not with quotidian life, but with the exceptional rituals of carnival, particular the *déboulés* during which carnival participants "descend" onto the streets in mass parades.[30] On some occasions, memory walk participants have met at midnight, in order to march throughout the night while carrying torches. Other marches have lasted several days, with participants building campsites along their route.

Such long walks require a good deal of stamina, especially since the terrain covered is sometimes quite difficult to navigate, consisting of abandoned cane fields, brush-covered hills, and ruins of old sugar mills currently overrun with vegetation. Routes also cut through highways, shopping malls, schools, and even the old airport landing strip, which was built on the site of a former plantation. Through these pathways, the modern landscape is forced to reveal the historical residues of the past, demonstrating both the transformations and the continuities of the area's history of colonial extraction: here cane fields turn into airports the same way sugar production has given way to tourism, and the former sites of plantation agriculture lead into new centers of unbridled consumption in a landscape increasingly dominated by French discount stores and American fast-food outlets.

Unlike the "freedom trails" or "heritage routes" that have become popular forms of public history in other parts of the world, these events have no accompanying markers, guidebooks, or other lasting explicative texts. They are usually advertised by simple flyers that mark the starting point for the walk but do not indicate the route itself.[31] In addition, the routes are never cemented as official pathways of remembrance. Rather, for each memory walk a new route is drawn to narrate a history that speaks to the conflicts of the current moment.

For example, following the Madassamy affair in 2001, there was much discussion on call-in radio and TV shows about the role of an *Indien* in the battles over the commemoration of slavery, the argument being that Indians did not experience the cruelty of the slave trade and thus had no claims to that history. In response, the union, along with NONM, organized a historical march. But instead of focusing on the arrival of indentured workers to the Caribbean—the traditional focus of celebrations of indianité in Guadeloupe, as discussed in the previous chapter—they commemorated a labor strike that took place in Petit-Canal in 1925. This strike, they argued, marked the first instance in which Indo-Guadeloupean workers had fought and lost their lives alongside black workers on the piquet. The organizers felt that this was a strike of great historical importance because it represented the genesis of Afro- and Indo-Guadeloupean solidarity against repressive French forces. They argued that it was precisely because moments like this had been forgotten that people could continue to question the role of an Indian in the battle over the commemoration of slavery.

Gama explained on a local TV segment that in preparation for this walk, they had searched the historical record for a relevant event with which to "think through" the Madassamy affair and rethink the place of Indians in Guadeloupe. "We decided," he said, "that we needed our history to respond to us in an original way, in a very particular way."[32] Gama's words hint at the kind of historical vision guiding the event. Unlike history books, which are constrained by a canonized series of events, historical marches are redrawn and reworked each time depending on the current context and social climate. In this case, the organizers decided that the official narrative of "Indian arrival" did not provide the necessary context for understanding the Madassamy affair and that an alternative narrative that would speak more directly to the struggles of the present was needed. As this case shows, during these events the landscape becomes both a site of textual production through pedestrian "speech acts" and a historical text itself, open to multiple interpretations.[33]

Nature as an Archive of Traces

During the memory walks, participants are encouraged to develop new relationships with the landscape and to rework the ways in which they imagine and experience nature and its fruits. The walks usually include several pauses for refreshment, during which participants can snack on raw sugar stalks and drink from freshly chopped coconuts deftly prepared by the organizers. These practices reclaim the landscape as a source of nourishment and nurturing. Cane fields and former plantations, which are traditionally seen as sites of backwardness or the settings of dark and violent histories, are thus reimagined as sites of resistance, strength, and sustenance.[34]

Participants in the walks regularly stated that their relationship to the natural environment was transformed during these events and that, as a result, they now viewed and experienced nature differently. Adeline, a middle-aged cafeteria worker and a passionate participant in the memory walks, described this transformation as follows:

> Before, I simply consumed my environment. I consumed my country cultur-
> ally, politically, whatever—before I just lived, I didn't valorize my environ-
> ment. I lived without any awareness of the value of what was around me. I did
> things without realizing what I was doing. Now I live differently. For example,
> I used to always go to the river with my family, but I never thought about why.
> But now I understand the importance of the river in our past, how it served as
> a gathering place, where people came to wash their clothes, to bathe, to fish—
> the river used to be so important! But today we just go and play in the water,
> with no attention to the importance and value of that place!

For Adeline the memory walks generated a new awareness of the natural environment as an important element of history. Nature no longer consti-tuted a backdrop for mindless activity. Instead, it was transformed into an agent and ally of social action. Rivers, trees, and other parts of the natural landscape were recast as integral elements in the unfolding of history by providing shelter, refuge, and nourishment. This became evident as Adeline explained how she had changed her relationship to the local breadfruit.

> I eat differently now—I realize now that it's not just about how things taste,
> that there are other things besides taste that come into play—there is respect
> also. For example, the breadfruit—I have so much respect for the breadfruit!
> Did you know that every year I have a party for the breadfruit?

When I asked her why she had decided to hold an annual *fête* for the *fouyapen*, she recounted the following story:

> Once I was walking in the forest with a historian. And he told me: "Voilà,
> maroons lived here at some point." I asked him how he knew this and he
> said, "It's not complicated. Look around you—what do you see here?" I told
> him, "I don't know, I don't see anything." He said, "Come, I'll show you. Look
> at the breadfruit here, look at the breadfruit there, look at the breadfruit over
> there. . . ." You see, breadfruit doesn't just grow in the middle of the forest like
> that. If there is a breadfruit tree, it's because someone planted it a long time
> ago. It is a trace.[35]

In Adeline's narratives of the river and the breadfruit we can see how the natural landscape is reconfigured as both site and source of historical evidence. Here breadfruit trees provide evidence for otherwise silenced maroon communities, while rivers stand as testaments to forgotten forms of social organization.

Through this process, the memory walks' organizers assert "archival power" by assembling the natural landscape into a catalog of historical traces. As others have noted, archives condition what counts as historical evidence, imparting the qualia of authenticity, validity, soundness, and truth by conditioning the epistemological "rules of credibility" for historical discourses.[36] In this instance, the natural archive produces a particular kind of evidentiary authority. Unlike the words of a historian or the pages of a textbook, trees, rivers, and valleys are saturated with an animate materiality that privileges proximity and sensuous experience over and above narration. Historical knowledge in the wilderness is thus not acquired through textual or discursive engagement alone, but through material and sensorial experience. History is not simply read or written; it is perceived, witnessed, consumed, lived, and felt. What makes history convincing in this instance is thus not simply its evidentiary authority, but its emotional impact.

Feeling History

The importance of emotional and sensorial experiences to this form of historical production became evident during an interview I conducted with Jean Michel, a young grocery cashier. Jean Michel was a seasoned participant in the memory walks and an active member of NONM. But during our conversation he referred to the memory walks with the same level of wonder and emotion as the more neophyte walkers. As he described the events he had participated in, he often shivered and rubbed the goose bumps that appeared on his arms. He became particularly animated when he recounted his experiences during the inaugural memory walk, which was organized in 2002 to commemorate the 1802 insurrection against the reimposition of slavery:

> It was during that walk that I really came to understand Guadeloupean history, because we went to the different sites. There—where the struggles actually happened—where the traces still remained: the old cannons, and the trees, the tree where slaves were hung. . . . There, with those traces, I felt it. You would get these shivers, you would tremble. . . . The trees, you see, they . . . they speak. There's a spirit there that makes you feel. . . . It's not the same as in a classroom. When someone tells you about history in a classroom, well, I would listen, I would hear it, but I didn't have that feeling, that feeling of

shivering, as it passes through you. . . . It's not the same in a lecture hall. When you're in a lecture hall, you listen, but maybe you doubt. You have doubts about the history that they're telling you. But when you're there, when you're at the site, you see it, and you have no more doubts. You can't doubt it; it's there, running through you. There's something that runs through you and that tells you—voilà, it's true. And you have no more doubts, because now you know it, you were there, you lived it—you don't just know it, you lived it because you were there.

Underlying Jean Michel's words is the idea that the physical landscape can provide a unique testimony to history. The animate materiality of nature generates a particular feeling of truth and credibility.[37] In Jean Michel's account, the tree "where slaves were hung" is invoked as both evidence and irrefutable witness to the past. Further, the materiality of the tree as a historical source conditions not only its evidentiary status but also its form of (sensorial) transmission. What Jean Michel remembers most from his experience are the shivers than ran through him, rather than the words spoken by his guides; here history becomes something to be felt, witnessed, experienced, and lived—rather than simply learned.

As Jean Michel suggests, this form of historical praxis creates a feeling of firsthand knowledge about the past. Participants do not feel as if they simply learned about the past; they feel as if they lived it, as if "they were there" and are now its witnesses. For Jean Michel this intimate form of knowing is best understood as the constitutive difference between *savoir* and *connaissance*, which he explained as follows:

> *Savoir* is when someone else tells you that slavery was abolished in 1848—that's what I was told in school—that's what I knew [*c'est ça que j'ai su*]. But why did slavery exist? I didn't know. What was slavery like? I didn't know. Why was it abolished in 1848? I didn't really know it! In my opinion, by just being told history in a lecture hall, I wouldn't have known or understood or been able to explain that history to others. But by participating in the memory walks, I feel like I lived through those events, I was there, I was in it—that's how I feel about it. It's as if I was present in that past—well, it's not like I was present, but I was somehow . . . there. Now I know it [*je le connais*] and I believe it [*je le crois*].

The memory walks thus did not simply help Jean Michel discover a past he was unaware of, but rather they helped organize and channel a knowledge he already possessed. The sensorial emotions provoked by the walk made the narrative more concrete and believable. This helps participants such as Jean Michel move from a detached and disorganized from of knowledge (*savoir*) to an intimate, firsthand knowledge (*connaissance*). As a result, the past is no longer just something they know *about*, but something they know *intimately*, something they experienced directly, something they lived and *felt*.

Routing History

In addition to creating a feeling of historical intimacy, the memory walks also help participants bridge the gaps of their historical knowledge by establishing links between historical events. However, unlike the timelines of official commemorations, in which historical events are placed in a linear relationship that lengthens the distance between the "faraway past" and the immediate present, this form of historical presentation collapses temporal distance and presents history as a series of overlapping moments within a shared space. Here the banner of history does not unfurl in a linear chronology of events stretching out and away from the present. Instead, history is experienced as a spiral of events, spinning around a shared space and place, encompassing the landscape and saturating it with the weight of what came before. What matters is not the sequence of events—what happened when—but the spatiality of history—what happened here. As a result, the past is ordered, not through a chronology of events, but through a thematic spiral that spins through the past, present, and future of a shared space.

This is most clearly seen during the month of May, which labor activists have increasingly come to identify as the "month of memory." Officially the French government recognizes only two historical dates in May: International Workers Day on May 1 and the 1848 abolition of slavery on May 27. However, in Guadeloupe, May also carries the commemorative weight of two of the most violent and repressive moments in the island's history: the reimposition of slavery in May 1802 and the more recent events of May 1967, when French forces opened fire on political demonstrators during a construction workers' strike in downtown Pointe-à-Pitre. This was followed by two days of police violence in which eighty-seven Guadeloupean civilians were killed and numerous anticolonial activists were arrested and forced into exile.[38]

That these events all took place in May seemed to pass unnoticed (or at least unremarked) by local residents until recently. Each year journalists would pick a different moment to memorialize, focusing one year on 1967, another year on 1802, and at another time on 1848. These events were treated as discrete incidents rather than as part of a common history of colonialism, exploitation, and repression. But when I sat down to talk about the memory walks with Didier, an employee of the local cable company, he carefully navigated through each of these events, describing them as part of a larger struggle for autonomy and independence. As he described their importance, he interlaced his explanation with references to the more recent Madassamy affair in 2001, when the police arrested several notable labor activists for protesting local businesses that remained open on Abolition Day (discussed in the previous chapter). When we spoke on the veranda of his modest home in Baie Mahault, Didier leaned forward and looked at me intensely as he emphatically stated,

> The war of 1802 was a political war. It's true that there was also the issue of slavery—of people being enslaved—but there was also a political side to that struggle. What is the political side? It was a seizing of power, a Guadeloupean seizing of power [*la prise de pouvoir des guadeloupéens*]. Guadeloupeans wanted to be emancipated, they wanted to rule their own country. In 1802 they fought to rule their country. In 1967 again it was a seizing of power. Guadeloupeans wanted to be emancipated, to take power, to chase out the French *carrément* [in no uncertain terms]. And in 2001 again it's the same thing. There is always that desire for power—for political power, for liberty, for emancipation. And it's precisely by studying the history of 1802 and the reactions of the colonial state in 1802. . . . And when you look at the history of 1967—it's more or less the same thing. It's practically the same reaction and practically the same demands for liberty and emancipation. In 2001 it's the same thing! It's the same reaction of the colonial state after seeing that Guadeloupeans were demanding their liberty.

In Didier's narrative these different moments of Guadeloupean history come together into a collective story of repression and resistance: the massacre of 1802 is made to signify not the reimposition of slavery but the refusal to be reenslaved; 1967 is portrayed not as state-sanctioned violence but as a colonialist reaction to a nationalist will. Both these moments, which in official histories are narrated through a discourse of failure (1802 being represented as collective suicide and 1967 as a senseless massacre), are rescued as expressions of resistance and refusal. The events of May 2001 are then read as yet another chapter in this history. The history that is constructed is thus not one of victimhood, trauma, and subjugation, but of resistance, perseverance, and bravery. French slaves become proto-Guadeloupean insurgents as the history of slave rebellions is folded into a telos of collective destiny that defines today's striking workers as the heirs of an epic struggle for emancipation.

Numerous participants in the memory walks insisted that the most powerful aspect of these commemorations was precisely how different moments of historical action were brought into relationship. For example, one of the participants remarked that the walks had helped her understand not just the events of the past, but the links between historical moments. She described this as "l'acheminement de l'histoire." In common French parlance, *acheminer* means "to route" something, to send it on its way (in the case of a package) or to place it on its correct path (in the case of a train). However, *acheminer* also implies a progression toward an intended result or outcome.[39] Thus, understanding the *acheminement* of history implies understanding both its trajectory and its goal. It means knowing not just where the past has been but also where it is headed. Through this form of historical production, history is recovered as an agentive process—not simply "one damn thing after another" but a purposeful series of events. As Édouard Glissant might argue, history finally becomes ordered into a narrative that can "stretch into our past and calmly take us into tomorrow."[40] In fact, Didier stressed that the biggest lesson he got from the memory walks was not about the details of the past but about the possibilities of the future.

> Whether they want it or not, men will always fight for their liberty. . . . Man was born to be free, free in his thinking, free to think in order to construct himself, and to construct his future. That means that even if the UGTG loses the struggle today, there will be another *quelconque* [unspecified] generation that will rise up for their liberty. As long as Guadeloupe is not decolonized, as long as it is not free, there will always be Guadeloupeans who will rise up and demand their liberty.

For Didier, and many of the other participants, the memory walks provide both clarity about the past and a newfound faith in the political efficacy of the present. During these events participants are remade as both subjects and agents of history. History spirals around them, shivers through them, and leaves them with the distinct feeling that they "were there." This certainty about the past in turn fuels their hope in the possibility of a new collective future.

SIX

Hope and Disappointment

In the early months of 2009, UGTG activists forged a coalition with forty-eight other organizations to wage a campaign against the high cost of living (*la vie chère*) in the French Antilles. This effort built on the union's previous attempts to reach beyond the realm of labor politics by collaborating with historians, cultural associations, and other political groups. The 2009 movement was distinctive, however, in that although it was driven by the UGTG, it eventually surpassed the union, appearing to become, for a moment at least, Guadeloupe's version of a "national" uprising.

For forty-four days, most Guadeloupean residents experienced the temporal suspension of life on the piquet. All schools and universities were closed, commerce was suspended, government services were discontinued, public transportation came to a halt, barricades blocked major roadways, and gasoline distribution was interrupted throughout the island for over a month and a half. As a result, Guadeloupeans found themselves engaged in different social relationships and practices. Rather than rushing off to school and work, they remained at home, debating the strike's means and ends with their families and neighbors. With supermarket chains and department stores inaccessible, residents turned to local fishermen, small-scale farmers, impromptu fruit vendors, and their own "creole gardens" to supplement their meals. They found themselves consuming more fruits and vegetables and making do without French imports. When propane gas distribution came to a halt, some residents turned to previous cooking practices, relighting their long-extinguished wood and charcoal stoves and rediscovering traditional culinary practices.

Every aspect of this social revolution was documented in both traditional media outlets (newspapers, magazines, television, and radio) and

6.1. LKP demonstration, Pointe-à-Pitre, January 2009.
Photo by Dominique Chomerau-Lamotte.

in a new spate of blogs and websites that quickly emerged, offering news and commentaries on the strike. Negotiating sessions with government officials were live-streamed on the Internet, and social networking and video-sharing sites were flooded with clips from demonstrations, interviews with participants, and other forms of digital ephemera that quickly went viral among Guadeloupean netizens. Even the French president at the time, Nicolas Sarkozy, participated "virtually" in the strike by offering a televised and live-streamed speech to his overseas compatriots. The heightened media coverage in turn fueled massive participation, with nearly a quarter of the population marching in the streets, camping outside negotiating sessions, setting up makeshift barricades, and echoing everywhere the popular song that became the slogan of the movement: "Guadeloupe is ours! Guadeloupe is not theirs! They cannot do as they please in our country!"

The 2009 strike was undoubtedly the UGTG's most successful movement to date. In the end the coalition managed to bring to the bargaining table all of Guadeloupe's most prominent employers, local elected officials, and even the French state—represented by the prefect and the secretary of the Overseas Ministry, who flew in from Paris for the negotiations. They ultimately reached an agreement on over one hundred different points of reform, including a two-hundred-euro monthly salary increase for minimum-wage workers, fixed prices on basic food items, reduced public transportation costs, a rent freeze for public housing, and a review of public utility rates, among other gains. Yet, at the end of 2009, when I spoke with Élie Domota, secretary-general of the UGTG at the time of the strike and the main spokesperson for the movement, he did not characterize the strike as a success. With neither melancholy nor anger, he stated plainly, "We failed." While steadily holding my gaze, he said matter-of-factly, "Anywhere else, this type of movement would have led to a new government, but we weren't ready. We failed."

In this chapter, I examine the hopes and disappointments that the 2009 strike generated. As I show, these protests did not aim to topple the government, to change the political status of Guadeloupe, or to transform its existing forms of governance. This was a non-nationalist movement of a different kind—one that sought societal change without seeking state power.[1] In the absence of a conceptual framework for this kind of non-sovereign politics, however, the 2009 strike was read and measured against the standards of a national revolution. As a result, many of those who participated in the strike—including its leaders—felt understandably disappointed when at the end of the strike, after the agreements had been signed, the placards put away, and the barricades lifted, Guadeloupe did not appear radically transformed. Yet, I contend, the disappointment felt was rooted less in the "failures" of the movement than in the expectations produced by the strike itself.

The 2009 strike was a political opening. It provided privileged insight into the contemporary political, economic, and social landscape of the French DOMs. Moreover, it was a moment of prefigurative politics through which alternative forms of social and political organization could be both invoked and rehearsed.[2] At a time when previous political scripts had become foreclosed, when concepts such as political independence had become taboo, but new political programs were difficult to imagine, the 2009 strike offered a glimpse, however fleeting, of an alternative political project. As a result the strike was doubly disappointing because it failed to live up to either the preexisting norms of nationalist revolution or the new expectations it itself had generated. Yet, despite Domota's claims, I contend that the disappointment produced by the strike should not be read as a sign of failure.[3] After all, disappointment—as a political and affective stance—is distinct from regret. Disappointment suggests the success of a new vision, the existence of a new model against which expectations of what is possible have become recalibrated. Although the 2009 movement did not radically transform Guadeloupe, it created a new template of political possibility and stirred the hope, however uncertain, in an alternative non-sovereign future.

LKP: A New Poetic Formation

The 2009 strike grew out of a conflict over gas prices, which had soared in Guadeloupe to $1.47 a liter, or roughly $90 for a full tank of gas.[4] The high prices reflected a global rise in the cost of crude oil, but when crude prices dropped (from $147 a barrel to under $40), gas prices remained steady in the DOMs—even as they declined in mainland France and most other parts of the world. Small business owners, notably those in the transportation industry, protested, and the local government responded by offering a thirty-cent price decrease. It accomplished this, however, by redirecting public funds to the local oil refining company, SARA (Société anonyme de la raffinerie des Antilles). In short, local taxpayers were to subsidize the decrease—a solution that activists deemed unacceptable.

On December 16, 2008, a delegation representing thirty organizations led by the UGTG attempted to meet with the prefect to discuss the gas issue, but was refused an audience.[5] In response, the group called for a general strike to be launched in January 2009. By then, the still-nameless coalition had grown to include forty-eight political, economic, cultural, and labor organizations, including a wide assortment of trade unions, political parties (such as the Communist Party and the Green Party), and pro-independence activists. It also contained groups from the wider civil society, including environmental groups, consumer rights organizations, advocates for disability rights, fair housing proponents, and several cultural groups—particularly those promoting gwoka music and dance.

As the coalition's membership grew, so did their platform, eventually swelling into a list of 120 demands that included reducing not just the price of gas but also that of food, basic necessities, housing, transportation, telecommunications, banking services, and many other goods and services that Guadeloupeans consume on a daily basis—all of which are more expensive in the DOMs than in mainland France. The platform also called for greater employment opportunities and proposed that the subsidy for the oil company be redirected toward job training, industrial development, and greater support for local fishing and agricultural initiatives.[6] This broad range of issues was brought together under the banner of opposition to "pwofitasyon"—a Creole concept that evokes both exploitation and profiteering—and the collective itself became known as the Liyannaj kont

They don't compromise or change within their own domain. They contribute that individuality to the larger whole of the LKP.

Raymond Gama, who became one of the main spokespersons of the LKP, compared the liyannaj not to the social networks of the digital era, but to the twisted roots of the Caribbean mangrove. He argued that the alliances forged among the various organizations resembled the complex entwinements of the Caribbean landscape, where plants grow together symbiotically, drawing strength and sustenance from each other, as they become an entangled whole. Each element retains its individuality, but together they produce a new ecology.

Initially the LKP was criticized for lacking a more overt political agenda, for rallying *against* something (pwofitasyon) rather than *for* something. However, in many ways the creation and theorization of this new kind of coalition—of an entangled non-sovereign community—was itself a positive goal. Liyannaj represented a new vision of social and political organization, a model of unity that did not require the erasure of difference. However, as Glissant suggested, being *en liyannaj* did not result from a single unifying gesture. Rather, it required a careful process of tying and retying. That is, being liyannaj was not a product, but a practice.

It took a while for the media to recognize the LKP as an entity. Initial reports referred to it as "the coalition for the defense of Guadeloupean purchasing power," but slowly the press and the greater population came to see the LKP as more than the sum of its parts. What started as an action campaign slowly took on the shape of a new political project. And soon, it became clear that the LKP was a new social movement with its own vocabulary, sound, aesthetic, and mode of action.

Jantiman: The Politics of Nonviolence

As discussed in previous chapters, labor activists (particularly the UGTG) are often criticized for their hardline methods, which include barricading major intersections, paralyzing traffic, harassing employers, and ransacking businesses that stay open during labor strikes. In 2009, by contrast, even though Guadeloupe was experiencing the largest social and economic disruptions in its history, observers praised the LKP for eschewing violent tactics and carrying out peaceful protest. This shift in public opinion was partly due to the movement's political platform, which was seen as beneficial to the society as a whole rather than to just one group of workers. However, it was also due to the fact that for the first time labor activists overtly described their actions as peaceful. Rather than issuing their usual threats of barricades and social strife, the 2009 activists claimed to be acting *jantiman*—a Creole term that means gently or politely.

During the 2009 strike, LKP leaders did not "demand" that businesses close; instead they requested solidarity for their movement, politely asking both workers and consumers to stay home. During demonstrations, when militants arrived at businesses that had chosen to remain open, they would not overturn shelves and cause physical damage. Instead, a leader in the group would ask the crowd, "Ki jan nou vin isidan?" (How do we arrive here?), to which the group would respond, "Jantiman!" If the manager was reluctant to close his business, the leader would ask the group, "Si nou wou-vin, ki jan nou ké vin?" (If we come back, how will we arrive?), to which the crowd would respond, "Méchaman!" (in a mean or unkindly manner).[9]

The term *jantiman* became closely associated with the figure of Ruddy Tessier, a member of the Confédération générale de travailleurs de Guadeloupe (General Confederation of Guadeloupean Workers, CGTG). Tessier functioned as an *animateur*, or emcee, at the LKP rallies, introducing the speakers and offering directives to the audience. Tessier was young and charismatic, with a broad smile and a warm friendly air. The local newspapers described him as *souriante* (cheerful) and credited him with impeccable crowd control. During rallies he would yell to the audience, "How are we going to proceed?" then point the microphone in their direction and smile broadly as he heard the roar of the collective response: "JANTIMAN!" This term became so popular that the singer Dominik Coco eventually released a single with the same title.[10] The song features a call-and-response, akin to the one Tessier was known for, between Coco and the backup singers:

> Nou ka samblé [we will gather]—Jantiman!
> Nou ka maché [we will march]—Jantiman!
> Nou ka revendiké [we will make our demands]—Jantiman!
> Pep-la an la ri-la! [the people are in the streets!]—Jantiman!

When I asked Tessier what exactly *jantiman* meant, he said it referred to being organized, being measured, being *"correcte"*—which in French means both "appropriate" and "reasonable." As a further example of the LKP's "correct methods," he pointed out that the liyannaj had its own security force because they wanted to ensure that people felt safe at meetings and rallies.

Many suggested that the LKPs nonviolent tone was part of what allowed the movement to take on a popular dimension, appealing to segments of the population that were usually reluctant to participate in "violent" labor strikes. For some, this difference in method was simply a matter of semantics, but the fact is that that the jantiman approach was a significant departure from the UGTG's usual hard-line declarations of "Si yo vlé, si yo vlé pa" (Whether they want it or not) and their assertions that "L'igtg kay kchou a yo!" (the UGTG will destroy them). The popular embrace of the slogan and the joy with which large segments of the population shouted it at marches and rallies suggest a profound desire for a form of politics rooted in nonviolence.

However, when participants were prompted, or more precisely urged, to "proceed *jantiman*," they were also being reminded that they were capable of acting otherwise. Tessier argued that ultimately, acting *jantiman* only served to demonstrate that being gentle did not work. Reflecting on the strike in hindsight, he argued that when people saw that acting *jantiman* did not obtain results, they became willing to support other modes of action—as would eventually be the case.

Sé Tan Nou: Beyond "Us" and "Them"

Although the term *jantiman* became a powerful symbol for the movement, the strike's true anthem was a song that was chanted and played repeatedly during demonstrations and rallies: "Guadeloupe is Ours." The song's lyrics are attributed to Jacky Richard, a local bank worker and LKP supporter. Initially the song emerged as a simple slogan, echoed during rallies and marches, but eventually it was set to music by the groups Akyo and Vokum and released as a single.[11] Although the song has several verses, it was the chorus that was repeated again and again.

> La Gwadloup sé tan nou (Guadeloupe, it is ours)
> La Gwadloup sé pa ta yo (Guadeloupe, it is not theirs)
> Yo pé ké fè sa yo vlé (They cannot do as they please)
> Adan péyi an nou! (in our country!)[12]

During the strike, these lyrics seemed to echo from every corner of Guadeloupe: they were shouted by thousands of demonstrators during mass rallies, sung by children on the playground, blasted out of cars and open windows, and emblazoned on thousands upon thousands of T-shirts sold by roadside vendors. The slogan's ambiguity might explain its popularity, for it is unclear what exactly is being claimed or asserted in this moment of enunciation.

Despite the lack of any explicit racial reference, many white émigrés from France, local white béké elites, and light-skinned residents of mixed descent felt that the slogan carried a message of racial exclusion and intolerance. They argued that the seemingly unmarked "nou" (us) referred exclusively to the Afro- and Indo-Guadeloupean population. But activists involved in the movement argued that the "nou" represented those who fought for Guadeloupe, those who loved her, regardless of their racial background or national origins. Ownership and belonging, according to them, did not depend on decreed citizenship but on political praxis. There were, in fact, several white *métros* who participated and marched with the LKP (particularly schoolteachers associated with the educators union), and even the French-appointed prefect at a certain point claimed that he was part of the "nou" because he was working for a better Guadeloupe.[13]

If the defining criteria for membership in the "nou" was fuzzy, the "yo" or "them" was even more so. At first blush, "Guadeloupe is ours / Guadeloupe is not theirs" might seem like an anticolonial, anti-imperial slogan of a colonized "us" versus a colonizing "them." But the *pwofitan* or *pwofiteurs* had no nationality or political ascription: they were defined simply as those who reaped abusive profits. Although the figure of the *pwofitan* is posed as the enemy of a "true" Guadeloupean people, this rhetoric does not place the burden of the Antilles' contemporary malaise on the colonial relationship with France.

The battle against pwofitasyon represents a move toward a wider analysis of the winners and losers in the relationships of colonialism, globalization, and neoliberalism. That is, it is not just a matter of who established the colonial relationship but of who profits from it today. Moreover, the slogan suggests that the target of struggle is not just the *pwofiteurs* but all those who have allowed them to "fè sa yo vlé" (do as they please)—which includes the French state as well as local elected officials.[14] Indeed, local politicians felt greatly threatened by the 2009 movement. The strike happened to unfold at a time when the political Right was in power in France, under Sarkozy, while both governmental bodies in Guadeloupe, the General Council and the Regional Council, were headed by politicians from the Left—Jacques Gillot and Victorin Lurel, respectively. This led to particular tensions between *l'état* (the French state) and *les élus* (local elected officials) over their roles in resolving the conflict.[15]

Early on in the strike, Jacques Gillot entered into a heated debate on the radio with Felix Flémin, the head of the Communist Party and a member of the LKP, about the role of local politicians in the negotiations. When the LKP launched its strike, local politicians urged the delegation to meet with them to discuss their demands, but the LKP leaders insisted that they did not want to meet with the different parties separately; they wanted to negotiate with everyone implicated in their platform. This included *les élus*, *l'état*, and *le patronat* (the employers, represented by their respective associations). During the radio broadcast Gillot argued that even though the LKP's demands exceeded the local councils' authority, the LKP nonetheless should allow the politicians to play a role in resolving the strike. "Everyone complains that politicians don't do anything in Guadeloupe," he lamented, "but when we try to do something, they won't let us!" Flémin retorted that the LKP would negotiate only with those who had the authority to make decisions. Alluding to the feeble power of local politicians, he stated that Gillot didn't have the authority to address the demands put forth in the platform. Gillot responded in Creole by chiding Flémin for not wanting to negotiate without "Papa Blanc."

The exchange between Gillot and Flémin demonstrates the difficult position that the local politicians found themselves in during the LKP strike. On the one hand, they didn't want to appear powerless because they needed to court votes and show that they could offer solutions to local problems in Guadeloupe. On the other hand, they didn't want to be lumped in with the French state as part of the "yo" or "them." Throughout the negotiating sessions they would repeatedly intervene in Creole, trying to distance themselves from the French-appointed bureaucrats. (Indeed, at one point during the negotiations the prefect complained openly that he was being left out of the conversation.) *Les élus* repeatedly sought to assert themselves as the democratically-elected representatives of the people and urged the LKP to bring its problems to them so they could take the issues up with the French state. To which the LKP delegates would retort that they *were* "the people," and as such they needed no intermediaries.

This debate speaks to the difficulties that local politicians face when attempting to assert their political authority in the Antilles. In the past, whenever politicians have tried to obtain greater competency and autonomy, the electorate has shut them down, repeatedly rejecting any proposal that would expand their powers. For example, in 2003 elected officials ran a collective campaign to unify the two governing bodies in Guadeloupe, the Regional and General Councils; this was portrayed as an effort to trim a bloated government bureaucracy and create a leaner, more efficient system. Local residents voted massively against the reform, in what was read by local analysts as a fear of centralized power.

During the LKP conflict, elected officials tried once again to assert their role and claim greater autonomy by seeking to shift the focus of the negotiations away from the French state. They refused to attend the negotiating sessions organized at the prefecture, calling instead for separate meetings in the Regional Council or at City Hall. This tactic quickly proved unpopular as the public began to perceive them as hindering rather than contributing to the strike's resolution. Eventually the politicians agreed to participate in collective negotiations in a "neutral place." This set the stage for the public negotiations that were held over the course of three days at the Pointe-à-Pitre World Trade Center (WTC). Unbeknownst to the LKP members, the elected officials also invited the local press, which broadcast the negotiations live on television and over the Internet. Presumably, the politicians invited the press in an effort to showcase their role as mediators. But, unable to broker an agreement, they ultimately demonstrated the limits of their power. They also inadvertently created a new political hero by thrusting the LKP spokesperson, Élie Domota, into the spotlight.

Le Feuilleton Guadeloupéen

Whenever I asked Guadeloupean residents what distinguished the 2009 strike from previous labor struggles in Guadeloupe, without exception respondents would point to the particular role of the media in the conflict—and specifically to the broadcast of the WTC negotiations. In a place with little local programming, where most shows on television are either French national productions or dubbed American series, the negotiations became known as the *feuilleton guadeloupéen*—the local soap opera.

As noted in previous chapters, labor strikes are regularly given ample coverage in the local press, but on this occasion the coverage took on a different dimension. Rather than a simple "news event," the LKP strike became what some scholars describe as a "media event."[16] As a television genre, media events share certain features. They tend to be "monopolistic," taking over not just one television channel but the entire dial, and are usually transmitted live. The fact that the events are unfolding in real time means that they are unpredictable, thus creating a particular kind of narrative tension—viewers are not just watching history being documented, but rather history unfolding unpredictably before their eyes. In addition, the immediacy of the broadcast creates a sense of community and participation in the event. In this case, the negotiations were transmitted live on television and radio, and were also streamed on the Internet—which meant that Guadeloupeans were participating even beyond the territorial bounds of the island. The negotiations were also televised in Martinique, where just a few weeks later a parallel strike would emerge, inspired by the LKP.

During the negotiations, Guadeloupeans—who were almost all home from work and school because of the strike—found themselves glued to their television sets, sending each other text messages discussing the day's events, and reminding each other to stay tuned for the next episode of the political *feuilleton*. Excerpts from the broadcasts were posted on the Internet and became the subject of numerous debates on- and offline. In these spaces, as well as in traditional print, television, and radio outlets, a new collective public—the Guadeloupean "nou"—was both imagined and brought into being.

The protagonist of the three-day *feuilleton* ended up being the LKP, and Élie Domota in particular. Domota had assumed leadership of the UGTG in April 2008, less than a year before the launch of the general strike. Born in 1967 (a symbolic year of political upheavals, as discussed in chapter 1), he had been raised by a single mother who worked in a school cafeteria in Basse-Terre—she was the epitome of the kind of worker the union had sought to mobilize as it expanded into the civil service sector during the 1980s. As a teenager, Domota had been involved in the Catholic youth groups organized by the Père Céleste. He later went on to obtain multiple degrees in French universities, including the equivalent of an MBA and an advanced degree in urban studies. After completing his education he obtained a high-ranking position in the civil service as the joint director of the Agence nationale pour l'emploi (ANPE), the government agency that focuses on assistance for the unemployed.

Domota was not the first *fonctionnaire* to lead the UGTG. As discussed in chapter 4, the union is often faulted for having "elite" workers in its leadership positions. These workers are considered elites in the sense that they have secure, well-paying jobs, but they are still viewed as relatively uneducated and a bit "sauvage" (untamed or unrefined). Domota was the first secretary-general of the UGTG who was not only a *fonctionnaire* but a *cadre*—that is, he held the kind of high-ranking executive position that is usually reserved for French *métros*. Although he was a longtime militant in Guadeloupean labor movements, up until the strike of 2009 he had received little attention from the press. Now, suddenly thrust into the spotlight, he brought a new, more sophisticated image to the UGTG.

Lukas insisted that this was a significant change.

You have to understand, Domota is the assistant director of the ANPE— a national institution. That means that he has an advanced degree. Yet he is the leader of a union that is supposedly composed of ignorant people—of janitors, chambermaids, security guards, gas station attendants, people who don't speak French properly, folks who talk in Creole all the time. These are supposed to be the folks who didn't make the grade. "Everyone who flunked got together and formed a union": that was the image of the UGTG for a lot of people. And now suddenly they see Domota and they discover that within the UGTG there are intellectuals, there are directors of the *grande administration française*—no one expected that!

Aside from his age and education, Domota was also remarkable for his racial background: he was lighter skinned than previous union leaders— what many in Guadeloupe would describe as a *chabin*. Lukas confided that before the LKP strike, he used to joke with Domota about his racial background, teasing him and going as far as to call him "le blanc." But after the movement began, that sort of teasing stopped.

> I realized that kind of joke was no longer appropriate. The fact is that he is no longer *ni chabin, ni mulâtre*. Now he embodies everything [*il incarne tout ca*]. People don't even see anymore that he isn't black. They don't see him as a *chabin*, like [Victorin] Lurel. Now he is seen as a *mulâtre*.

As the head of the Regional Council, Lurel was one of the most important politicians in Guadeloupe at the time of the strike and would become a key player in the negotiations. When Lukas described Lurel as a *chabin*, he was referencing not just Lurel's phenotype but also his way of dress (suit and tie), manner of speaking (proper French), and his political discourse, which is often peppered with references to French republican principles. Domota by contrast is described as shifting from *chabin* to *mulâtre*— a darker category—through his political action. Interestingly, in pictorial representations of Domota during the strike—in newspaper illustrations, cartoons, and Internet memes—his skin was increasingly darkened and his Afro-Caribbean features were accentuated as the strike intensified. Initially, the local newspaper *France Antilles* described him as a "chabin à l'air presque poupin" (a light-skinned doll-like figure) and ran a full-page interview with pictures of him looking dashing. As the events intensified, however, the representations changed. Although tall and lanky, he was increasingly drawn as short and chubby, his skin was darkened, the size of his Afro was exaggerated, and his lips accentuated. "That is the genius of the Caribbean," Lukas remarked. "You can transcend your color by affirming your freedom."

6.3. Élie Domota (*center*) with LKP negotiators at the WTC.
Photo by Dominique Chomerau-Lamotte.

During the strike, Domota became a local celebrity. Children would shout his name as he passed, crowds would cheer wildly when he took the stage at union events, and he was constantly sought out for autographs and photos. In mainland France he became well known for his numerous appearances on the local news, and he even had a marionette made to represent him on the famous sketch comedy show *Les Guignols de l'info*. In Guadeloupe, however, what cemented his popularity was his role in the three-day public negotiations.

During the negotiating sessions, Domota delivered a powerful *j'accuse* performance, directly confronting the representatives of the French state for their lack of oversight, publicly airing the corrupt practices and outrageous profits of the local employers, and deftly exposing the fiscal policies of the elected officials and their misuse of public funds. The viewers I interviewed described the televised event less as a negotiation and more as a public trial, with Domota acting as the people's prosecutor, unmasking the relations of inequality that prevail in Guadeloupe.

Many suggested that Domota caught the attention of the public not just for the content of his interventions but also for the way he presented his case, his vast technical knowledge, and the ease he projected while discussing economic affairs. As one LKP supporter explained, "It was like listening to a head of state. . . . Although he [Domota] didn't have the means, he clearly had the knowledge and the will [volonté] to carry out political change." Others argued that it was Domota's tone and his manner that impressed them the most. They insisted that his way of addressing the prefect and the békés, even his body language—his gesticulations, his carriage—demonstrated a remarkable confidence in confronting figures of authority. Jean, a local middle school teacher, explained,

> You have to understand, this is a society where the white man is still imagined to be superior. They hold all the power—both economic and political—so, to see un petit fils d'esclaves [grandson of slaves] talk to the prefect like that, to argue with him, to stand up to him, that is really something in this place!

Jean further insisted that part of what was striking about Domota's performance was not just that he spoke to the authorities as an equal, but that he actually seemed superior to them. Jean, and many others who had watched the televised event, insisted that Domota was clearly better informed, better prepared, and more knowledgeable about the workings of the local economy than either the prefect or the local officials. The LKP delegates, and Domota in particular, projected a particular kind of administrative experience and familiarity with the local context that the French-appointed bureaucrats couldn't match. In addition, the LKP delegates demonstrated a degree of political initiative that local elected officials seemed to lack. Whereas local elected officials are often seen as mere administrators of French-dictated policies, the LKP leaders were viewed as visionaries, unrestrained by the limits of French policy.

The LKP delegation was basically a negotiating "dream team," a group of forty-eight political, economic, and civic leaders, each of whom had mastered the technical language and legal intricacies of their particular area of expertise. They arrived at the WTC negotiations armed with stacks of colorful portfolios brimming with legal texts, government reports, feasibility studies, economic statistics, development plans, and detailed analyses of the Guadeloupean economy's inner workings. Over the course of the discussions they strategically brandished evidence from their portfolios documenting corruption, mismanagement, and inefficient government policies. By contrast, the politicians, bureaucrats, and entrepreneurs who lined the other sides of the negotiating table sat with their arms folded across a sparse tabletop, with little more than the LKP platform placed in front of them, completely unprepared for what would become a public hearing. When pressed on their political choices, policies, or the basis for the prices and taxes paid by Guadeloupean consumers, the prefect and the elected officials had few answers. At the end of the first negotiating session, Lurel told reporters that he had intentionally remained silent simply to demonstrate that the Regional Council was not "le facteur bloquant" (an obstacle to the strike's resolution).[17]

For the viewers at home, the negotiations offered a crash course on Guadeloupean politics. For many, this was the first time they had witnessed the opaque nature of power and authority in the DOMs publicly discussed and dissected. Those who phoned in to live radio and television programs to comment on the negotiations repeatedly remarked upon how much they learned over the course of the broadcast. Many stated that they had never quite understood the role of the different councils and the prefect, how taxes were set, how government funds were allocated, and why prices were so much higher in Guadeloupe than in mainland France. In the Antilles it had long been common to blame the high price of goods on the basic fact of transportation costs. For example, I was once with a friend at a local shop when she asked the owner why the products (mostly body lotions and soaps) were so expensive. The shopkeeper grabbed the bottle of lotion my friend was holding, lifted it up, and exclaimed, "Madame, you have to remember, this product has *traveled* [*ce produit a voyagé*]!" In other words, the assumption was that high prices were necessary if one wished to consume cosmopolitan goods.

Over the course of the LKP negotiations, however, it was revealed that transportation costs did not fully explain the high prices in the DOMs. Indeed, many of the products sold in Guadeloupe (particularly fresh food) come from surrounding Caribbean islands—not faraway France. Most of the surcharges imposed on them are not due to transportation costs but to local taxes—taxes that are then used to fill the coffers of the local governmental bodies. Although elected officials were long thought to be securing money from France, it now seemed that local consumers were the ones financing a significant part of their budget.

The LKP delegation also made public the wholesale cost of many imported items before taxes. The figures showed that high transportation costs and local taxes alone were not enough to explain why certain goods were on average 30 percent more expensive than in mainland France—with some goods being as much as 155 percent more expensive. The LKP delegates maintained that the high prices were enabled by the carefully controlled monopolies held by béké merchants, who could impose high prices in the DOMs due to lack of competition. They further argued that these monopolies were kept in place by the French state thanks to heavy lobbying on the part of béké representatives in the metropole through organizations such as MEDEF. The fact that Guadeloupeans imported the great majority of their consumable goods—including food that could easily be farmed locally—was in turn blamed on faulty governmental planning, which has consistently redirected funds toward developing tourism and commerce rather than promoting local agriculture, fishing, and small-scale industry. During the negotiations the complex workings of the *pwofiteurs*, and those who allowed them to "do as they please," were slowly revealed.

The Fugitive State

After two and a half days of what had essentially become a public hearing, the prefect arrived at the WTC with a prepared statement from the secretary of state for the Ministry of Overseas France, Yves Jégo, announcing that the "general assembly" was over and that negotiations were to begin in small, unmediatized working groups under the guidance of "specialists." After reading the statement, the prefect and his advisers—all the French *métropolitains* present at the session—stood up and abruptly walked out. Only the head of the labor department, Urbain Martial Arconte, the sole state bureaucrat who was Guadeloupean, stayed defiantly at the table. "*C'est pas facile* [it's not easy], is it, Arconte?" remarked Domota.

The local politicians seized upon the prefect's departure to try to retake control of the negotiations. Without missing a beat, Lurel took hold of the microphone and declared almost with relief, "Well, now we are *entre guadeloupéens.*" The LKP ignored his remark and stormed out of the WTC, blasting the prefect for "fleeing." The politicians then followed suit and proceeded to express their outrage at the prefect's departure, with Lurel calling on all local officials to join him in a protest the following day dressed in their *écharpe tricolore* (the sash worn by mayors at civic functions) in order to demand that the state respect Guadeloupeans and return to the negotiating table.

The prefect's departure outraged most local residents and led to even greater support for the LKP. This result stood in contrast to what usually happens when negotiations are suspended in workplace strikes: the blame for failing to reach a resolution usually falls on the striking workers, who are publicly urged to settle their claims, quit being intransigent, and return to work. On this occasion, however, the public's inside view of the dynamics of the negotiation room conditioned its reaction. As one viewer explained to me, "People saw everything with their own eyes. They saw what the prefect did—the disrespect he showed. It was an insult to all of us." Indeed, many viewers insisted that the negotiations left a lasting impression. "Guadeloupe is different because of everything we have learned—we see the béké differently, and the state differently; we even see the LKP differently," said another viewer.

The LKP refused to participate in the proposed working groups, insisting that the negotiations should proceed with all the interested parties at the same table. With tensions escalating, and after two weeks of sustained strike activity, Secretary Jégo himself suddenly arrived in Guadeloupe to, in his words, "solve the conflict." Jégo declared that he was ready to establish his headquarters in Guadeloupe for as long as necessary to broker a solution. During his time in Guadeloupe he attempted to play the role of a disinterested (and wildly uninformed) third party just arriving on the scene, unaware of the stakes of the dispute. He made a spectacle of touring the island and approaching "the people" to hear their concerns, repeatedly expressing great outrage at what he claimed was just now being revealed to him. In one press conference that was much commented on, he detailed the utter shock he experienced when he discovered that a toothbrush that cost two euros in France sold for seven euros in Guadeloupe. Jégo blamed the economic situation on what he described as the "ancestral" practices of the local "colons," who he said were reaping unjust profits—seemingly without the knowledge of the French state. He assured the population that these practices ran counter to the ideals of the republic and would not be tolerated.

Playing the populist card—and driven, according to many, by an interest in furthering his political career—Jégo sought to relaunch the negotiations but this time insisted on conducting them behind closed doors. Politicians, employers, and LKP leaders agreed to meet with Jégo at the prefecture in Basse-Terre to resume negotiations. LKP supporters rallied outside the building, setting up drum circles around the clock. The music of the drums spilled into the negotiation room, where the LKP representatives carefully detailed the economic situation of the overseas departments for the seemingly naive French minister.

Three days later, after a twenty-hour negotiating session that ended at seven in the morning, the group arrived at an agreement for a two-hundred-euro monthly wage increase to be subsidized by the French state. Curiously, despite having publicly denounced the local *colons*, Jégo agreed to continue subsidizing the békés by providing state financing for the wage increase. The different parties left the prefecture early in the morning and agreed to meet later that day to sign a finalized agreement. However, that afternoon, as LKP representatives and local elected officials were on their way back to the prefecture, they learned that Jégo had boarded a plane back to Paris. Canal 10 broke the news and was the only one to reach Jégo on his cell phone for comment. He assured viewers that he was off to Paris to defend their agreement. But the prime minister, François Fillon, soon declared that Jégo didn't have the authority to broker such a deal and that the French state would not be picking up the tab for local employers.

Crescendo

Following Jégo's departure, tensions in Guadeloupe reached an all-time high as Guadeloupeans witnessed a second representative of the French state abandon the negotiating table. Lurel again expressed outrage, declaring on the airwaves of RFO that all public offices should remain closed to demand respect for the Guadeloupean people. Meanwhile in France, *Le Monde* published a report detailing corruption and mismanagement at the Guadeloupean oil refinery, backing many of the LKP's claims. In addition, the financial magazine *Votre Argent* reported that banks in the Antilles had the highest service fees in all of France, yet again confirming the claims of the LKP. At the same time, the popular French TV channel Canal Plus aired a documentary about the békés titled *Les derniers maîtres de la Martinique* (The Last Masters of Martinique), featuring candid, racist commentary by Antillean elites; this further aggravated racial tensions, particularly in Martinique, where a parallel strike was also underway.

With tensions running high, the LKP organized a memory walk in the town of Le Moule to commemorate the fallen victims of a labor strike that took place on February 14, 1952, which had resulted in four deaths (including that of a pregnant woman) and fourteen injuries. The walk ended up being the largest LKP demonstration to date, with as many as one hundred thousand participants—a quarter of the population—according to some reports. Among those in attendance was the Guianese deputy Christiane Taubira, a beloved figure in the DOMs given her role as author of the law mandating that the French government recognize slavery as a crime against humanity.

The march concluded with a large rally, where Domota proclaimed that the LKP had "walked enough." The message was clear: the movement was now going to change methods—no more *jantiman*. The following morning, barricades sprang up across the territory, blocking all major thoroughfares, and for the week of February16–21, Guadeloupe came to a halt. The *barrages* were assembled mostly out of debris: fallen palm branches, old tires, abandoned cars, overturned trash dumpsters, and surplus construction materials. More importantly, the barricades consisted of people. In fact, life on the barricades did not differ radically from life on the piquet. Residents would spend their day "securing the barricade," that is, not letting people pass (except emergency vehicles or people who were attending a movement meeting) but also just holding down the fort, passing time with their neighbors, talking politics, getting information about new developments, and laughing over the latest events. The prefect and the French minister, in particular, were the target of heavy mockery, with many poking fun at the French state for having been "scared away" by the LKP.

Along with the LKP-organized barricades, there emerged a number of "barrages sauvages" ("wildcat" barricades). These were organized not by LKP supporters but by young people from the surrounding *cités*. At the *barrages sauvages* the mood was different; motorists would often be charged to pass through, and the barricades were accompanied by acts of looting and arson. The UGTG is often criticized for using "dangerous elements" to escalate actions during labor strikes (see chapter 4). But according to Christien, a young union delegate who participated in the barricades at Gosier, matters were more complex.

> People blame the union for stirring up these young people, but they don't realize the anger that's within them. These kids are completely abandoned. There's no place for them, no projects for them here. . . . And what does a burned-out car mean in the face of so many broken young souls? So they break things, they loot, and they set fire—well, now you noticed them.

As the violence at the barricades escalated, Guadeloupe was inundated with military police sent from mainland France. French gendarmes began rounding up demonstrators in violent confrontations. Both professional and amateur journalists closely documented these clashes, and their pictures of heavily armed French troops confronting unarmed local protesters further stoked the fires. Around the world images circulated of fiery barricades, young people with ski masks throwing rocks through clouds of tear gas, and gendarmes approaching demonstrators waving the Guadeloupean flag. Suddenly, the strike began to look like a national insurrection. In an interview with the *Nouvel Obs*, Lurel declared that Guadeloupe was "on the verge of sedition."[18]

6.4. Demonstrator waving the nationalist flag at an LKP barricade.
Photo by Dominique Chomerau-Lamotte.

On the night of February 17, the violence reached a new level when
Jacques Bino, an LKP supporter and union militant, was killed. Bino was
on his way home from an LKP meeting when he found himself heading toward a flaming barricade. As he began to turn his car around, he was fatally
shot in the chest. According to the authorities, the shot came from young
protesters on the barricades who mistook him for a police officer. But many
in Guadeloupe question this official story and suspect foul play. Some say
Bino was murdered to weaken or discredit the movement. Others think he
was killed because, as a customs officer, he had privileged knowledge of the
mismanagement of funds. Still others argue that he was simply the victim
of mistaken identity, taking sniper fire meant for Domota or another of the
more prominent LKP delegates.

The investigation into his death was inconclusive, and most feel that the
truth will never be known. As one LKP supporter explained, "This is our
Kennedy assassination." In the end, his death rallied even more supporters.
His funeral turned into a massive demonstration when some twenty-five
thousand mourners crowded into the small town of Petit-Canal to pay him
tribute—with the entire event live-streamed. The death made national head-
lines, and this time even Sarkozy took notice. The day after Bino's death,

the president publicly addressed the Antillean population on RFO, vowing to resolve the crisis and asserting that France needed to rethink its relationship with its overseas departments. In Guadeloupe most remained skeptical and dissatisfied with Sarkozy's statement; just the fact that it was transmitted on the overseas network, and not on the mainland, was taken as a sign that the Antilles and their problems remained marginal to the nation.

Soon after Sarkozy's address, LKP leaders returned to the negotiating table with a new set of mediators newly arrived from mainland France. Initially the local employers, represented by the MEDEF, refused to reach an agreement. This changed, however, when a new employer organization emerged: the Union des chefs d'entreprise gwadloupéyens (Union of Guadeloupean Business Leaders, UCEG), which represented smaller, local Guadeloupean business owners, many of whom had long struggled against the economic monopoly of the békés. Along with local elected officials, these small business owners reached an "interprofessional agreement" that would grant the two-hundred-euro monthly wage increase—to be subsidized initially by the local councils and later passed on to the employers. The agreement was named the Bino Accord, in memory of the fallen LKP delegate.

On February 26, after signing the Bino Accord, the prefect declared the general strike over, but LKP leaders insisted that they still had over one hundred more points to discuss. Negotiations thus continued at the Port-Autonome in Pointe-à-Pitre, where drum circles were held around the clock with activists camped out in support. With a feeling that the major hurdles had been cleared, supporters flooded into town to witness the historic end of the strike. In the final days the space outside the negotiation became a site of celebration and reminiscence. It was as if nostalgia for the piquet was already setting in.

With the barricades lifted and gasoline flowing a bit more regularly, groups came from across the island to gather and share memories. Many said they relished the final days of the strike and joked that they were a bit sad to see it all come to an end. As one woman commented, "I'm going to miss this little life [*petite vie*]!" She said she had enjoyed the break from her job and her commute and had grown fond of her daily routine of visiting neighbors, purchasing food from local merchants, and trading stories on the barricade. Many of the people I spoke with were excited to share the new culinary skills they had developed during the shortages. "I'm never buying yogurt from [béké magnate] Monsieur Hayot again!" insisted one ardent LKP supporter. She later mumbled that she would purchase one, but just one. (Apparently her yogurt recipe required one yogurt to get the yeast going.) "Only one, though!" she proclaimed, smiling proudly. "And I'll buy it at the *ti lolo* [the corner store], not at Destrelland [the mall]!"

Like Nothing Before

After forty-four days of the general strike, labor activists, business leaders, elected officials, and the local prefect reached a 165-point agreement, and the strike was lifted. Schools and businesses reopened and Guadeloupeans slowly returned to their quotidian routines of life and work. The agreements included a two-hundred-euro monthly salary increase for minimum-wage workers (subsidized by the local government councils), a reduction in gas prices, fixed prices on basic food items, reduced public transportation costs, rent control for public housing, and a review of public utility rates, among other gains. Many of these concessions have, however, proved difficult to implement. Prices have dropped on some foods but spiked on others, and promised development projects have failed to materialize. LKP leaders seem to have foreseen this outcome when, at the end of the final negotiations, they asserted that the strike had been "suspended" rather than concluded. Likewise, slogans on T-shirts and banners in Guadeloupe after the strike did not proclaim victory but offered instead yet another ambiguous slogan: "Nothing will/can ever be like before" (ayen pé ké kon avan).

On the political front, most of the protagonists of the *feuilleton guadeloupéen* subsequently lost their mandates. In June 2009, Yves Jégo was asked to step down from the Overseas Ministry. He retained his position as mayor of the town of Montereau in central France, where, since 2012, he has been busily promoting the development of a Napoleon-themed amusement park. Jégo was replaced by Marie-Luce Penchard, the first Antillean to ever head the Overseas Ministry. In October 2009 the prefect of Guadeloupe, Nicolas Desforges, was transferred to the prefecture of Oise, a department in northern France. In 2012, Sarkozy was defeated by the Socialist candidate François Hollande. Under Hollande's administration, Victorin Lurel replaced Penchard as the minister of overseas France and, for the first time in history, an *antillaise*, Marcelle Pierrot, was appointed prefect of Guadeloupe. Hollande also appointed Christiane Taubira of French Guiana as minister of justice, marking the first time a politician from a DOM has held an appointment of such stature. Élie Domota continued on as secretary-general of the UGTG, and in 2014 the union celebrated its fortieth anniversary. The LKP did not disband but lost several organizational members, after it failed to build on the momentum of 2009.

In the strike's immediate aftermath, many hoped that the LKP would evolve into a larger political movement, perhaps even becoming a political party. Indeed, there was a popular hope that Domota would become the new head of the Regional Council, or perhaps . . . something more. The problem was that there was no script for what the LKP could become. Although the 2009 movement managed to forge new political categories—including pwofitasyon as a new target of struggle and liyannaj as a new model of collectivity—many in Guadeloupe fell back upon exhausted scripts when it came time to measure the success, and plot the future, of their movement. Even Domota himself, who has made it clear that he has no interest in electoral politics, had little to say other than, "We failed."

It would be easy to read these disappointments as signs of political failure, extinguished dreams, and exhausted options—yet further evidence of a contemporary political "dead-end." But I would like to suggest otherwise. For disappointment is always intimately bound with hope; disappointment proves that apathy has not settled in. Even if Antilleans have become disillusioned with the projects of the postcolonial era, they still have faith in the possibilities of collective action and in their own individual abilities to transform their daily lives. Their political projects might not resemble the nationalist struggles of a previous era, and indeed they may be harder to quantify, measure, assess, and even recognize—since they do not involve grand gestures of state overthrow or the large-scale projects of social engineering associated with modernist statecraft.[19] Yet, as Deborah Thomas cautions, if we continue to keep our gaze fixed on the supposedly empty horizon of nationalist revolution, we are sure to miss the many "unspectacular" transformations that abound in the daily re-creations of ordinary life.[20]

Since 2009 ordinary life in Guadeloupe is subtly different: there are more farmers' markets available, greater interest in artisanal products, increased support for small enterprises, and renewed interest in the use of local gardens and medicinal plants. Guadeloupeans increasingly assert the need to manjé local (to consume local products), and are paying greater attention to how their political entanglements impact their food, their land, their health, and their reproductive lives.[21] Few of these initiatives are radical or even pronounced, many were already brewing before the LKP, and most reflect a larger global reassessment of how centuries of pwofitasyon have impacted bodies, lands, plants, food, water, and air. Yet, these changes reflect precisely the kind of subtle transformations possible in an era of non-sovereign politics: delicate shifts in the ways and forms of everyday life that challenge, even as they are unable to fully escape, the political and economic binds of modern life.

Like the *Sucré* workers described in chapter 3, participants in the 2009 strike look back on their experience with both disappointment and nostalgia. Their involvement in the movement fostered feelings of empowerment, exposed them to the pleasures of collective action, stirred their desire for alternative models of community and political action, and emboldened their search for small-scale forms of ordinary change. Yet, it also cemented their skepticism in the traditional means and ends of modern politics. As a result, in the contemporary Antilles hope for social change is met with studied cynicism—but it is entertained nonetheless.

Transcripts of the Future?

And yet it may be said that Europe has been successful, in as much as everything that she has attempted has succeeded.

—Frantz Fanon, *The Wretched of the Earth*

I arrived in Guadeloupe at a moment of political transition. From the 1970s to the 1990s the labor movement in the Antilles had grown steadily; by the turn of the century Guadeloupe had reached a level of union density unimaginable in other parts of the world, where labor rights had been slowly whittled down to the mere "right to work." During this period, labor activists managed to bring together workers from across a broad spectrum of society—cane cutters, chambermaids, civil servants, gas station attendants, and even *fonctionnaires*—all of whom felt shut out of Guadeloupe's post-departmentalization economy. With Jacques Chirac's second presidential term (2002–7) and the election of Nicolas Sarkozy in 2007, however, France began to undertake a project of neoliberal reform that significantly constrained the activity of unions.

Simultaneously, throughout the world a new era of political disenchantment was setting in—the iconic wall had fallen, but no new projects had arisen to replace it. In the absence of new political models, the labor movement turned increasingly to the transcripts of the past. References to slavery had long been common among Antillean activists, but at the dawn of the new millennium the Antilles experienced a "memory boom," as narratives of slave resistance were revisited and reshaped to address the concerns of the present. The entry into historical politics gave labor activism new breadth: struggles began extending further and further away from the piquet, spilling across the landscape and airways.

In 2009 the union's efforts expanded even further with the creation of the LKP. During the 2009 strike, new concepts of struggle and visions of community emerged offering the hope of an alternative future. Yet these categories eventually reached their limits when confronted with the lingering expectations of political modernity. Thus, despite the massive success of the LKP, once it became clear that it would not produce a revolutionary transformation, disappointment ensued.

Those of us who study social movements are frequently called upon to shed light on the ambiguity that political actors leave in their wake. *Decryptage* is the word my colleagues in Guadeloupe use to describe this act, wherein we are asked to decode and interpret what has just been witnessed and to evaluate its success. The truth, however, is that it is difficult to truly judge the lasting impact of a social movement. Most measures of political success focus on tangible outcomes, such as the acquisition of material gains, the enactment of new governmental policy, or other similarly measureable markers of change. Yet these markers are deceptive: policy is often not applied, gains in one arena are canceled out by losses in another, and in the end it is hard to say with any certainty what, materially, has changed in the lives of participants. Qualitative measures are only slightly less ambiguous. The political actors I interviewed for this book repeatedly expressed disappointment with the outcomes of their struggles; despite these disappointments, however, they relished their memories of the experience: the feelings of solidarity, the pleasure of creative activity, and above all the feeling of being a historical actor—the awakened sense of "being there," of not having missed one's rendezvous with history.

In addition to producing these subjective experiences, the events described in this book also opened up new conceptual space from which to imagine an alternative non-sovereign future. Before the strike of 2009 few could have imagined that anything like the LKP was possible: that such a diversity of actors could come together behind a common agenda, that such a large segment of the population would join them, or that the French government would engage in direct negotiations over their demands. This was not just *du jamais vu*, it was *de l'impensé*—both unseen and unimaginable.

I am unable to say whether *liyannaj* and *pwofitasyon* will become part of what Raymond Gama, in the statement I quote in this book's introduction, describes as the "transcript of the future." These terms provided a temporary clearing from which to imagine new political forms, but I cannot predict whether they will become the watchwords of a future generation, or whether they will fall by the wayside—like Césaire's search for "equalization," which eventually ceded ground to the norm of independence. This book, thus, ends with uncertainty. Indeed, it ends but it does not conclude. I cannot judge whether the LKP was successful, or even if the movement launched in 2009 has actually ended. For, as the Sucré strikers in chapter 5 remarked, what may appear to be an end might simply be a moment of truce.

At the close of the 2009 strike the slogan that appeared across banners and T-shirts in Guadeloupe did not proclaim victory, instead it merely stated, "Ayen pé ké kon avan" (nothing will/can ever be like before). Perhaps this can serve as an example for how to think about the political impact of social movements in a way that breaks with modernist models of sweeping revolutionary success. For even movements that fail at eradicating the injustices they seek to overcome can still manage to have transformative consequences. Indeed, one could argue that they can effectively change the world by radically altering the possibilities imaginable for it.

At present, the native categories forged in 2009 continue to circulate and animate political life in the French Antilles. *Pwofitasyon* has become the label for an otherwise diffuse target of struggle—one which neither "postcolonialism" nor "neoliberalism" could fully define—while *liyannaj* evokes a new model of community and collective possibility outside of the traditional categories of citizenship and nation. Meanwhile, the acronym LKP invokes not merely a particular group of individuals but a particular moment in time—a milestone of possibility. These concepts have become the new markers of what is currently reasonable to imagine and desire. As signposts, they point to a world that has not arrived, and indeed may never arrive, but of which many are now able to dream.

ACKNOWLEDGMENTS

The writer's craft is notoriously lonely. And yet, researching and writing this book has filled my life with a stunning array of generous, inspiring, and gifted individuals.

This project began at the University of Chicago, and I remain indebted to the mentors and peers I found there. My greatest debt is to Michel-Rolph Trouillot, who dared me to break with Caribbean insularity and inspired me in more ways than I can list here. Jean Comaroff, Stephan Palmié, and Jennifer Cole were careful readers of my dissertation and continue to routinely grace me with sound advice and generous encouragement. I am also grateful to José Lopez, the chancellor of my other intellectual community in Chicago, my favorite instigator, and (according to him) my conscience.

Mayanthi Fernando provided extensive commentary on multiple chapters—I am indebted to her critical editorial eye and overall intellectual fierceness. Greg Beckett has commented on nearly every word I've written since graduate school with quiet generosity and brilliance. Jonathan Rosa has been a valued sounding board for both the theoretical and the ethical concerns that guide this project; I could not ask for better fictive kin. Michael Ralph offered incisive commentary on the entire first draft and indulged many an argument about it. Lisa Outar contributed greatly to my thinking about indianité and has been a kindred spirit along this journey. True to form, Harvey Neptune arrived late to the project but managed to leave an indelible mark, providing pointed commentary on both the substance and form of the entire manuscript.

Throughout the years I have also benefitted from support, advice, feedback, and encouragement from a large cadre of informal mentors including Lynn Bolles, Vincent Brown, J. Michael Dash, Laurent Dubois, Arlene Dávila, Jorge Duany, Les Field, Carla Freeman, Isar Godreau, Aisha Khan,

Sidney Mintz, Gina Perez, Richard Price, David Scott, Faith Smith, Connie Sutton, Deborah Thomas, and Gary Wilder.

In Guadeloupe I was aided, inspired, and uplifted by more folks than I could possibly list here. Among these: Gaby Clavier, Élie Domota, Rosan Mounien, Raymond Gama, Pierre Gervain, Serge Apatout, Jean-Luc Bigard, Harry Thomias, Reedan Nadir, Sarah Mozar, Julien Mérion, and Fred Reno. While in Guadeloupe I was housed, cared for, scolded, nurtured, and guided by Hélène Delannay, Ari Oujagir, and Claire Telchid, while Marie France (a.k.a. Marie Gwadeloup) helped me circumvent French governmental bureaucracy with brazen generosity. Writing about the French Antilles has placed me within a tiny but very solidarious network of colleagues who generously shared their thoughts, writings, and personal archives; this includes Vanessa Agard-Jones, Jerome Camal, Andrew Daily, and Kathe Managan.

At the University of Virginia I found a nurturing environment in which to begin developing this manuscript. Hector Amaya, Stephanie Bérard, Ellen Contini-Morova, Robert Fatton, Richard Handler, Claudrena Harold, Cynthia Hoehler-Fatton, Deborah McDowell, Susan McKinnon, George Mentore, Geeta Patel, Pamela Pecchio, Jennifer Peterson, Simone Polillo, and Kath Weston made life in Charlottesville happy and productive.

At Rutgers University I stumbled into fortune with a cadre of amazing Caribbeanists. Nelson Maldonado-Torres, Yolanda Martinez San-Miguel, and Michelle Stephens read and commented on the entire first draft of the manuscript, and my students and colleagues in both Anthropology and Latino/Caribbean Studies have made Rutgers an inspiring place to think, teach, and write. (I am particularly thankful to the participants in my Fall 2012 graduate seminar, who signed up for a course on the anthropology of sovereignty but happily withstood a semester of thinking about non-sovereignty instead.)

Final revisions were completed at the Schomburg Center for Research in Black Culture at the New York Public Library. I am indebted to the 2013–14 cohort of scholars who read and commented on numerous drafts, particularly Marisa Fuentes, Belinda Emondson, and Rafe Daello, who offered astute commentary and pivotal recommendations. My deepest thanks go to Farah Griffin, for making the scholars seminars a space of true conviviality, camaraderie, and passionate debate on all matters big and small. I am thankful also to the Schomburg's director, Khalil Gibran Muhammad, for periodically gracing our scholar's lunch with inspiring conversations, and to the center's librarians, archivists, and staff, particularly Maira Liriano, who never once questioned why I needed to check out over 150 books from the research collection. Lastly, I must thank the building maintenance and security personnel for indulging my late night presence in the scholar's center and for making the Schomburg feel like a pan-Caribbean home.

This book benefitted from a great amount of skilled assistance. At the University of Virginia, Stephanie Jean-Charles, Claudelle Gehy, and Rhode Baptiste deftly transcribed my interviews in French and Creole. During their serendipitous *séjour* in Charlottesville, Landon and Jonna Yarrington helped me prepare the first draft of the manuscript, providing early feedback and suggestions that were key to the project. At Rutgers, Catalina Martínez-Sarmiento brought light, energy, and enthusiasm to this project—as she does to all things. Adam "Max" Hantel found, checked, fixed, answered, and solved everything I threw at him and was unflappable, insightful, and indispensable. Francesca Portier provided assistance with French translations and in securing photo permissions. Nancy Gerth patiently guided me through the indexing process, and Pablo Morales offered friendly and astute editorial assistance, helping to clarify my occasional moments of opacity.

At the University of Chicago Press, I am happily indebted to David Brent for being an irreverent, patient, and kind-hearted supporter. I am thankful also to Priya Nelson, Ellen Kladky, Ryo Yamaguchi, Erik Carlson, and Curtis Black for their expert assistance during the production process and to the anonymous readers who offered careful and detailed suggestions for revision that spurred new lines of thinking.

Lastly, deep thanks go to my family, particularly to Abigail Ramos Fuentes, *mi cómplice*, and Monserrate Fuentes Gerena, the real anthropologist in the family. I am also grateful to Hector Ramos Fuentes and Rosa Esther Fuentes Solla for lending me an idyllic beachfront balcony in Dorado, Puerto Rico, where I was able to unravel many of these thoughts.

The Wenner Gren Foundation, Chateaubriand Foundation, University of Chicago, University of Virginia, and Rutgers University all funded research for this book. Writing was enabled by the Carter G. Woodson Institute at the University of Virginia and the Schomburg Center for Research in Black Culture at the New York Public Library.

Parts of chapter 4 were published in "Between Terror and Transcendence: Global Narratives of Islam and the Political Scripts of Guadeloupe's *Indianité*," in *Islam and the Americas*, edited by Aisha Khan (Gainesville: University Press of Florida, 2015). An earlier version of chapter 5 was published as "The Past Is Made by Walking: Labor Activism and Historical Production in Guadeloupe," in *Cultural Anthropology* (vol. 26, no. 3). And parts of chapter 6 appeared in "Gwadloup sé tan nou! (Guadalupe es nuestra): El impacto de la huelga general en el imaginario político de las Antillas Francesas," in *Caribbean Studies* (vol. 40, no. 1); "Guadeloupe Is Ours:

The Prefigurative Politics of the Mass Strike in the French Antilles," in *Interventions: International Journal of Postcolonial Studies* (vol. 12); and "Non-Sovereign Futures: French Caribbean Politics in the Wake of Disenchantment," in *Caribbean Sovereignty, Democracy and Development in an Age of Globalization,* edited by Linden Lewis (New York: Routledge, 2012).

NOTES

PREFACE

1. On native categories as "the language of routine," see Michel-Rolph Trouillot, *Peasants and Capital: Dominica in the World Economy* (Baltimore: Johns Hopkins University Press, 1988), 231.

2. For a more sustained discussion of this political moment, see Frances Negrón-Muntaner and Ramón Grosfoguel, eds., *Puerto Rican Jam: Rethinking Colonialism and Nationalism* (Minneapolis: University of Minnesota Press, 1997).

3. David Scott, "The Sovereignty of the Imagination: An Interview with George Lamming," *Small Axe* 6, no. 2 (2002): 72–200.

4. I call these electoral performances "opinion polls" rather than plebiscites because they have never been associated with an actual bill, which would require the prior approval of the US Congress. For more, see *Report by the President's Task Force on Puerto Rico's Status*, March 2011, available at http://www.whitehouse.gov/administration/eop/iga/puerto-rico.

5. This phrasing comes from a controversial series of Supreme Court decisions that established the legality of the United States' relationship to its unincorporated territories in the aftermath of the Spanish-American War. For more, see Cristina Duffy Burnett and Burke Marshall, eds., *Foreign in a Domestic Sense: Puerto Rico, American Expansion, and the Constitution* (Durham, NC: Duke University Press, 2001) and Bartholomew H. Sparrow, *The Insular Cases and the Emergence of American Empire* (Lawrence: University Press of Kansas, 2006).

6. On the relationship between sovereignty and notions of political and cultural "distinctiveness," see Jessica R. Cattelino, *High Stakes: Florida Seminole Gaming and Sovereignty* (Durham, NC: Duke University Press, 2008). On cultural nationalism in Puerto Rico, see Silvia Alvarez-Curbelo and María Elena Rodríguez-Castro, *Del nacionalismo al populismo: Cultura y política en Puerto Rico* (Río Piedras: Universidad de Puerto Rico, 1993); Arlene Dávila, *Sponsored Identities: Cultural Politics in Puerto Rico* (Philadelphia: Temple University Press, 1997); Negrón-Muntaner and Grosfoguel, *Puerto Rican Jam*; Jorge Duany, *The Puerto Rican Nation on the Move: Identities on the Island and in the United States* (Chapel Hill: University of North Carolina Press, 2002); and Isar Godreau, *Scripts of Blackness: Race, Cultural Nationalism and US Colonialism in Puerto Rico* (Urbana: University of Illinois Press, 2014).

7. Reinhart Koselleck, *Futures Past: On the Semantics of Historical Time* (Cambridge, MA: MIT Press, 1985); David Scott, *Conscripts of Modernity: The Tragedy of Colonial Enlightenment* (Durham, NC: Duke University Press, 2004).
8. Michel-Rolph Trouillot, *Global Transformations: Anthropology and the Modern World* (New York: Palgrave Macmillan, 2003).
9. For a review that addresses some of these issues see Emilio Pantojas-García, "The Puerto Rican Paradox: Colonialism Revisited," *Latin American Research Review* 40, no. 3 (2005): 163–76. For a view of Puerto Rico as "anomalous," "indeterminate," and "enigmatic," see Ramón E. Soto-Crespo, *Mainland Passage: The Cultural Anomaly of Puerto Rico* (Minneapolis: University of Minnesota Press, 2009).
10. The overseas departments were created in 1946. The ELA was established in Puerto Rico in 1952, but Puerto Ricans had been able to elect their own governor since 1947. Similarly, the move to autonomy emerged in the Dutch Antilles around the same time with the founding of the National People's Party (Partido nashonal di pueblo) in 1948.
11. In Puerto Rico, self-deprecating narratives by local intellectuals can be found as early as 1912 with Antonio S. Pedreira's essay "Insularismo," though it is perhaps Rene Marqués who most famously articulated this vision in his 1960 essay, "El puertorriqueño dócil." In the French Antilles, Édouard Glissant has often lamented the "alienation" of his Antillean compatriots; see for example *Le discours antillais* (Paris: Seuil, 1981). However, it is the contemporary *creolité* writers, and particularly Raphaël Confiant, who are best known for launching vitriol at their compatriots. See, for example, Confiant's open letter following the 2010 vote against autonomy: "Péyi-a sé ta nou, sé pa ta yo! Clamaient-ils en février 2009 . . . ," *Potomitan*, January 11, 2010, http://www.potomitan.info/confiant/peyi.php

    Among foreign analysts, William Miles and Richard Burton (from whom I borrow the phrase "self-advancement by self-negation") are perhaps the most explicit in their categorization of the French Antilles as a paradoxical and pathogenic site of exception. See William Miles, *Elections and Ethnicity in French Martinique: A Paradox in Paradise* (New York: Praeger, 1986); William Miles, "Schizophrenic Island, Fifty Years after Fanon: Martinique, the Pent-Up Paradise," *International Journal of Francophone Studies* 15, no. 1 (2012): 9–33; Richard D. E. Burton, *Assimilation or Independence? Prospects for Martinique* (Montreal: Centre for Developing-Area Studies, McGill University, 1978); Richard D. E. Burton, "The French West Indies à l'Heure de l'Europe: An Overview," in *French and West Indian: Martinique, Guadeloupe, and French Guiana Today*, ed. Richard D. E. Burton and Fred Réno (Charlottesville: University of Virginia Press, 1995).
12. "C. L. R. James (West Indian Writer and Activist)," YouTube video, posted by Afrikanliberation, July 22, 2009, http://youtu.be/viwYx3uIYiU.
13. For a more celebratory view, see Katherine Browne, *Creole Economics: Caribbean Cunning under the French Flag* (Austin: University of Texas Press, 2004); and Crespo, *Mainland Passage*.
14. For a review of Puerto Ricans in the US military, see Raymond Carr, *Puerto Rico: A Colonial Experiment* (New York: New York University Press, 1984). For a more general discussion of the militarization of Latino populations, see the work of Hector Amaya, including "Latino Immigrants in the American Discourses of Citizenship and Nationalism during the Iraqi War," *Critical Discourse Studies* 4, no. 3 (2007): 237–56; and "Dying American, or the Violence of Citizenship: Latinos in Iraq," *Latino Studies* 5, no. 1 (2007): 3–24; and the work of Gina M. Pérez, including "Hispanic

Values, Military Values: Gender, Culture, and the Militarization of Latina/o Youth," in *Beyond El Barrio: Everyday Life in Latina/o America*, ed. Gina M. Pérez, Frank Andre Curidy, and Adrian Burgos (New York: New York University Press, 2010). For a history of military bases in Puerto Rico and the Caribbean more broadly, see John Lindsay-Poland, "U.S. Military Bases in Latin America and the Caribbean," in *The Bases of Empire: The Global Struggle against U.S. Military Posts*, ed. Catherine Lutz (New York: New York University Press, 2009). On military participation in the modern French Caribbean context, see Richard S. Fogarty, *Race and War in France: Colonial Subjects in the French Army, 1914–1918* (Baltimore: Johns Hopkins University Press, 2008). On the toxic legacy of the US Navy in Puerto Rico, see Katherine T. McCaffrey, "The Struggle for Environmental Justice in Vieques, Puerto Rico," in *Environmental Justice in Latin America: Problems, Promise and Practice*, ed. David V. Carruthers (Cambridge, MA: MIT Press, 2008). On the use of chlordecone, a toxic pesticide that endangered local populations in Martinique and Guadeloupe and polluted the environment for two decades, leading to disproportionately high cancer rates, see Louis Boutrin and Raphaël Confiant, *Chronique d'un empoisonnement annoncé: Le scandale du chlordécone aux Antilles françaises, 1972–2002* (Paris: Editions L'Harmattan, 2007); Alfred Wong and Roxanne Gomes, "Problèmes socio-économiques insolubles de la Martinique," *Études Caribéennes* 21 (2013), http://etudescaribeennes.revues.org/5795; and Vanessa Agard-Jones, "Spray," *Somatosphere*, May 27, 2014, http://somatosphere.net/2014/05/spray.html. On the use of Puerto Rico as a laboratory for repressive surveillance techniques, see Ramón Bosque Pérez and José Javier Colón Morera, *Las carpetas: Persecución política y derechos civiles en Puerto Rico; Ensayos y documentos* (Rio Piedras: Centro para la Investigación y Promoción de los Derechos Civiles, 1997). This extensive study of how Puerto Rican nationalists were targeted during COINTELPRO suggests that US intelligence agencies were perfecting techniques that would later be applied on the mainland, especially against the Black Panthers. For a broader discussion, see René Francisco Poitevin, "Political Surveillance, State Repression, and Class Resistance: The Puerto Rican Experience," *Social Justice* 27, no. 3 (2000): 89–100. More broadly, Laura Briggs argues that an examination of Puerto Rican history reveals how US imperialism in the nineteenth and twentieth centuries operated through shifting discourses of sexuality, motherhood, and national reproduction; see *Reproducing Empire: Race, Sex, Science, and U.S. Imperialism in Puerto Rico* (Berkeley: University of California Press, 2002). On the Caribbean as an emerging site of "digital off-shoring" see: Adam Hofman, "Dominica to be the First Bitcoin Nation," *Bitcoin Magazine*, August 28, 2014, http://bitcoinmagazine.com/15986 /dominica-first-bitcoin-nation/; "Apple Working on New Data Center on Curacao," *Among Tech* (blog), August 16, 2014, http://www.amongtech.com/apple-working -on-new-data-center-on-curacao/; "Google May Already Be Launching Floating Data Centers off U.S. Coasts," *Al Día Curaçao*, October 25, 2013, http://www .aldiacuracao.com/technology/google-may-already-be-launching-floating-data -centers-off-u-s-coasts/ (I am grateful to Louis Philippe Römer for bringing this to my attention).

15. On the idea of our contemporary moment as a political dead end, see the work of David Scott, esp. *Refashioning Futures: Criticism after Postcoloniality* (Princeton, NJ: Princeton University Press, 1999); *Conscripts of Modernity*; and *Omens of Adversity: Tragedy, Time, Memory, Justice* (Durham, NC: Duke University Press, 2014).

16. As I argue elsewhere, a full exploration of non-sovereign politics would encompass how these acts challenge not just our understandings of political community,

but also of personhood, materiality, and being. See Yarimar Bonilla, "Sovereign On-
tologies," paper presented at the Annual Meeting of the American Anthropological
Association, Washington, DC, December 2014.

17. This is an example of how, as Elizabeth Povinelli suggests, immanent critique and
negative dialectics can become positive acts by shifting normative models "from a
horizonal to a background perspective." That is, they can become something to move
away from, rather than toward. See Elizabeth Povinelli, *Economies of Abandonment:
Social Belonging and Endurance in Late Liberalism* (Durham, NC: Duke University
Press, 2011), 187–91.

18. I first arrived in Guadeloupe as a graduate student in the summer of 2001 for language study and a summer research project. I returned for formal fieldwork and lived
without interruption in the island's economic capital of Pointe-à-Pitre for eighteen
months between 2002 and 2004. This was followed by near-yearly visits from 2006
to 2013.

19. Trouillot, *Global Transformations*, 132.

20. Laura Bohannan, "Shakespeare in the Bush," *Natural History*, August/September
1966.

21. Jason Antrosio, "Shakespeare in the Bush–Laura Bohannan, Hamlet, and the Tiv,"
Living Anthropologically (blog), http://www.livinganthropologically.com/shakespeare
-in-the-bush-powerpoint-living-anthropologically. The use of an extreme etic perspective in Miner's Nacirema article also raises the question of native competency
discussed below.

22. Kerim Friedman, "Anthro Classics Online: Shakespeare in the Bush," *Savage Minds*
(blog), May 22, 2006, http://savageminds.org/2006/05/22/anthro-classics-online
-shakespeare-in-the-bush/.

23. One could argue that perhaps a lesson on cultural relativism is more important for
the intended readers of the story, who are presumably situated in a part of the world
where ethnocentrism is significantly less "charming." Indeed, I suspect that the Tiv
were more aware of this than the author herself lets on, given that the narrated conversation ends with them urging her to relate their interpretations of *Hamlet* back to
the elders of her society. "Tell them you were among those who taught you wisdom,"
they implore her. By endowing her subjects with a solely referential function, however, the author suggests that their conversation was only ever about *Hamlet*. She
fails to recognize what other things they might have been doing with their words.
How, perhaps, in talking to her about *Hamlet* they too were talking about cultural
difference—about the hierarchies that orient their worlds, the forces that condition
the anthropologist's ability to be among them, her interest in their lifeworld, and
the things that would be done with their words for years to come in textbooks and
classrooms.

24. Trouillot, *Global Transformations*, 133.

25. Michel-Rolph Trouillot, "The Caribbean Region: An Open Frontier in Anthropological
Theory," *Annual Review of Anthropology* 21 (1992): 19–42, at 25.

26. For more on the difference between narrated and narrative frames, see Mikhail
Bakhtin, "Discourse and the Novel," in *The Dialogic Imagination: Four Essays* (Austin:
University of Texas Press, 1981).

27. Trouillot, *Global Transformations*, 132.

28. See Trouillot, *Global Transformations*, 129–33.

29. Clifford Geertz, *The Interpretation of Cultures* (New York: Basic Books, 1973), 448.

30. Although I claim to "cite" my informants, I am not always able to give them full attribution. Throughout the text I use the real names of many labor leaders and other public figures, but for workers who do not hold positions of leadership—what some might call the "rank and file"—I have chosen to use pseudonyms. These workers often shared personal stories and ideological orientations that they did not necessarily want to be made public; moreover, exposing their names could put their jobs at risk. There is one leader whose name I have also chosen to mask, although he is a well-known public figure. I debated with him at great length about whether or not to use a pseudonym. At times he agreed that I should use his real name, but other times he claimed discomfort with the kind of "protagonism" this could produce. In the end, I have chosen to refer to him throughout the text as "Max" in deference to his ambivalence but also in recognition that the narrative form of ethnography ultimately renders him a character within a story that is more mine than his.

31. Trouillot, *Global Transformations*, 133.

32. Caroline Brettell, *When They Read What We Write: The Politics of Ethnography* (Westport, CT: Bergin & Garvey, 1993); see also Nancy Scheper-Hughes, "Ire in Ireland," *Ethnography* 1, no. 1 (2000): 117.

33. For more on some of the problems of "giving a voice," see Audra Simpson, "On Ethnographic Refusal: Indigeneity, 'Voice' and Colonial Citizenship," *Junctures* 9 (2007): 67–80; and Mayanthi Fernando, "Ethnography and the Politics of Silence," *Cultural Dynamics* 26, no. 2 (2014): 235–44.

34. Trouillot mentions the issue of non-native anthropologists in only one single, though provocative, footnote (*Global Transformations*, 144n30).

35. See, for example, Brackette F. Williams, "Skinfolk, Not Kinfolk: Comparative Reflections on the Identity of Participant-Observation in Two Field Situations," in *Feminist Dilemmas in Fieldwork*, ed. Diane Wolf (Boulder, CO: Westview Press, 1996), 72–95; Lila Abu-Lughod, "Writing against Culture," in *Recapturing Anthropology*, ed. Robin G. Fox (Santa Fe, NM: School of American Research Press, 1991); Kirin Narayan. "How Native Is a Native Anthropologist?" *American Anthropologist* 95, no. 3 (1993): 671–86; Sonia Ryang, "Native Anthropology and Other Problems," *Dialectical Anthropology* 22, no. 1 (1997): 23–49; Karla Slocum, "Negotiating Identity and Black Feminist Politics in Caribbean Research," in *Black Feminist Anthropology: Theory, Politics, Praxis, and Poetics*, ed. Irma McClaurin (New Brunswick, NJ: Rutgers University Press, 2001), 126–49.

36. Some have already begun to explore this; see for example Gustavo Ribeiro Lins and Arturo Escobar, *World Anthropologies: Disciplinary Transformations within Systems of Power* (New York: Berg, 2006).

37. For other examples of how to challenge this position, see Mayanthi Fernando, *The Republic Unsettled: Muslim French and the Contradictions of Secularism* (Durham, NC: Duke University Press, 2014), 26–28; Joseph Hankins, *Working Skin: Making Leather, Making a Multicultural Japan* (Berkeley: University of California Press, 2014), xiii–xvii; and Greg Beckett, "Thinking with Others: Savage Thoughts about Anthropology and the West," *Small Axe* 17, no. 3 (2013): 166–81.

INTRODUCTION

1. Some might contest this claim. However, other general strikes in French history—notably those of 1899, 1936, 1968, 1995, and 2010—evolved out of broader social movements and were not strictly labor movements. These strikes lasted anywhere

from two full weeks (as in 1968) to a handful of strike days (as in 1995 and 2010), compared with the forty-four days of the 2009 general strike in Guadeloupe (January 20 to March 4). On French strikes, see Edward Shorter and Charles Tilly, *Strikes in France, 1830–1968* (Cambridge: Cambridge University Press, 1974); Josette Trat, "Autumn 1995: A Social Storm Blows over France," *Social Politics* 3, no. 2–3 (1996): 223–36; Michael Torigian, *Every Factory a Fortress: The French Labor Movement in the Age of Ford and Hitler* (Athens: Ohio University Press, 1999). For a detailed chronology of the Guadeloupe movement, see Frédéric Gircour and Nicolas Rey, *LKP, Guadeloupe: Le mouvement des 44 jours* (Paris: Editions Syllepse, 2010).

2. The exact number of protesters is debated, but a phone survey conducted by the agency Qualistat shortly after the strike found that 94 percent of the population felt the movement was justified, and 75 percent actively supported it. See Qualistat, *Les Guadeloupéens et la grève générale du LKP*, March 2009. I use the figure of one hundred thousand because this number has itself become a symbol of the movement and is widely cited by activists and supporters.

3. For more on the strikes in the banlieues, see Charles Tshimanga, Didier Gondola, and Peter J. Bloom, eds., *Frenchness and the African Diaspora: Identity and Uprising in Contemporary France* (Bloomington: Indiana University Press, 2009); and Graham Murray, "France: The Riots and the Republic," *Race and Class* 47, no. 4 (2006): 26–45.

4. These territories are referred to as the *vieilles colonies* (old colonies) because they were acquired during the monarchical age of imperial expansion in the seventeenth century, not the republican colonial ventures of the nineteenth century. They are usually left out of the narrative of French colonialism, because they preceded the "civilizing mission" of the French colonial project, and they contradict the telos of postcolonial history by not having followed the path of independence.

   The category of *outre-mer* was first established in 1946, when France ratified the Constitution of the Fourth Republic and passed the law (Loi no. 46-451) which transformed Martinique, Guadeloupe, Guiana, and Réunion into new political and administrative units of France known as DOMs (*départements d'outre-mer*). The new constitution also recognized a series of TOMs (*territoires d'outre-mer*), which were considered part of the republic but not fully assimilated into French law, with French legislation being applied only by special mention or decree. Over the years these formulas have continued to evolve. In 2003 the category of TOM was replaced by the category of COM (*collectivité d'outre-mer*). These territories are part of the French Republic but not of the European Union. They hold local control over certain aspects of their governance, such as trade and social security administration, but are subsumed under the French military defense system. As for the DOMs, they are now also ROMs (*regions d'outre-mer*) and part of the *ultra périphérie* (outermost territories) of the European Union. Mayotte voted in March 2011 to become a new DOM, French Polynesia recently became a POM (*pays d'outre-mer*), and New Caledonia is currently a *collectivité sui generis*, though it is slated to hold a plebiscite before 2018 to decide its future status.

5. The complete platform has been published (symbolically enough) in the form of a little red book: Liyannaj kont pwofitasyon, *Guadeloupe et Martinique en grève générale contre la vie chère et l'exploitation outrancière: Les 120 propositions du collectif* (Fort-de-France: Desnel, 2009).

6. Activists in Martinique came together as the Collectif du 5 février (C5F), in Réunion they launched a strike under the banner of COSPAR (Collectif des organisations syndicales, politiques, et associatives de la Réunion), and in French Guiana they created

a new collective named Mayouri kont lesplatasyon (MKL), in direct reference to the Guadeloupean LKP (Liyannaj kont pwofitasyon). Each of these movements took shape in response to the particular social and political context in which they were embedded. They were in contact with each other but did not strategize or negotiate collectively. However, this is the first time that activists in the overseas departments have engaged in simultaneous action since their integration as departments. During the 1960s, there were connections among nationalist groups in the different departments but these never developed into mass movements on the scale of the 2009 strikes.

7. "Dans la merde" is a colloquialism that suggests that one is in trouble, i.e., "in deep shit."

8. As I discuss in chapter 1, this "politics of assimilation" would later be disparaged by cultural nationalists as a conservative reformist project resulting from an alienated colonial subjectivity. Placed in its historical context, however, the search for assimilation can be understood as an Antillean "civil rights movement" comparable to the struggles of African Americans in the United States, a movement wherein the nation's unequal citizens demanded full political and civic rights.

9. See Gary Wilder, *The French Imperial Nation-State: Negritude and Colonial Humanism between the Two World Wars* (Chicago: University of Chicago Press, 2005); Frederick Cooper, "Alternatives to Empire: France and Africa after World War II," in *The State of Sovereignty: Territories, Laws, Populations,* ed. Douglas Howland and Luise White (Bloomington: Indiana University Press, 2009).

10. See Todd Shepard, *The Invention of Decolonization: The Algerian War and the Remaking of France* (Ithaca, NY: Cornell University Press, 2008).

11. For a powerful meditation on how the end of the 1980s marked a shift in the revolutionary political imagination after the fall of the Grenadian Revolution, see David Scott, *Omens of Adversity: Tragedy, Time, Memory, Justice* (Durham, NC: Duke University Press, 2014).

12. This labor movement is not just limited to Guadeloupe but is actually part of a larger wave of nationalist unions that developed throughout the former French colonies, including not just the DOMs but also places like New Caledonia and Corsica. For more, see Dominique Andolfatto, "Le syndicalisme outre-mer et les tensions sociales," *Les Etudes Sociales et Syndicales* (November 19, 2004), http://istravail .com/article219.html; Philippe Auvergnon, "Conflictualité et dialogue social à la Martinique," *Travail et emploi* 98 (2004): 109–23.

13. For more on the notion of prefigurative politics within contemporary social movements, see David Graeber, *Possibilities: Essays on Hierarchy, Rebellion, and Desire* (Oakland, CA: AK Press, 2007); Francesca Polletta, *Freedom Is an Endless Meeting: Democracy in American Social Movements* (Chicago: University of Chicago Press, 2002); Jeffrey S. Juris, *Networking Futures: The Movements against Corporate Globalization* (Durham, NC: Duke University Press, 2008).

14. Raymond Williams, *Marxism and Literature* (Oxford: Oxford University Press, 1977).

15. My approach is influenced by the anthropological scholarship on social movements, particularly that of anthropologists working in Latin America who have examined political action not as a simple means to an end but as an important realm of symbolic practice in and of itself. See, for example, Arturo Escobar and Sonia E. Alvarez, eds., *The Making of Social Movements in Latin America: Identity, Strategy, and Democracy* (Boulder, CO: Westview Press, 1992); Richard Fox and Orin Starn, eds., *Between Resistance and Revolution: Cultural Politics and Social Protest* (New Brunswick,

NJ: Rutgers University Press, 1997); Sonia E. Alvarez, Evelina Dagnino, and Arturo Escobar, eds., *Cultures of Politics/Politics of Cultures: Re-Visioning Latin American Social Movements* (Boulder, CO: Westview Press, 1998); and Orin Starn, *Nightwatch: The Making of a Movement in the Peruvian Andes* (Durham, NC: Duke University Press, 1999).

16. For an overview of Caribbean anthropological traditions that directly addresses the importance of history and historicity, see Michel-Rolph Trouillot, "The Caribbean Region: An Open Frontier in Anthropological Theory," *Annual Review of Anthropology* 21 (1992): 19–42. See also Richard Price, *Ethnographic History, Caribbean Pasts* (College Park: University of Maryland, 1990); and David Scott, "Modernity That Predated the Modern: Sidney Mintz's Caribbean," *History Workshop Journal* 58 (2004): 191–210. For examples of the kind of historically grounded Caribbean ethnographies that inform my approach, see Sidney Mintz, *Worker in the Cane: A Puerto Rican Life History* (New York: Norton, 1974); Richard Price, *First-Time: The Historical Vision of an Afro-American People* (Baltimore: Johns Hopkins University Press, 1983); Michel-Rolph Trouillot, *Peasants and Capital: Dominica in the World Economy* (Baltimore: Johns Hopkins University Press, 1988); Brackette Williams, *Stains on My Name, War in My Veins: Guyana and the Politics of Cultural Struggle* (Durham, NC: Duke University Press, 1991); Richard Price, *The Convict and the Colonel* (Boston: Beacon Press, 1998); Viranjini Munasinghe, *Callaloo or Tossed Salad? East Indians and the Cultural Politics of Identity in Trinidad* (Ithaca, NY: Cornell University Press, 2001); Stephan Palmié, *Wizards and Scientists: Explorations in Afro-Cuban Modernity and Tradition* (Durham, NC: Duke University Press, 2002); Aisha Khan, *Callaloo Nation: Metaphors of Race and Religious Identity among South Asians in Trinidad* (Durham, NC: Duke University Press, 2004); and Deborah A. Thomas, *Modern Blackness: Nationalism, Globalization, and the Politics of Culture in Jamaica* (Durham, NC: Duke University Press, 2004).

17. Interview with Bernadette Pierrot-Cassin, *InterEnterprise: Le Magazine Economique*, no. 21 (April–May 2004).

18. I borrow my phrasing and my approach from Michel-Rolph Trouillot, *Silencing the Past: Power and the Production of History* (Boston: Beacon Press, 1995).

19. For more, see the preface.

20. For more, see Peter Clegg and David Killingray, eds., *The Non-Independent Territories of the Caribbean and Pacific: Continuity and Change* (London: Institute of Commonwealth Studies, 2012); Peter Clegg and Emilio Pantojas-García, eds., *Governance in the Non-Independent Caribbean: Challenges and Opportunities in the Twenty-First Century* (Kingston: Ian Randle, 2009); Lammert De Jong and Dirk Kruijt, eds., *Extended Statehood in the Caribbean: Paradoxes of Quasi Colonialism, Local Autonomy, and Extended Statehood in the USA, French, Dutch, and British Caribbean* (Amsterdam: Rozenberg, 2005); Aarón Gamaliel Ramos and Angel Israel Rivera Ortiz, eds., *Islands at the Crossroads: Politics in the Non-Independent Caribbean* (Kingston: Ian Randle Publishers, 2001); Gert Oostindie, *Paradise Overseas: The Dutch Caribbean; Colonialism and Its Transatlantic Legacies* (Oxford: Macmillan Caribbean, 2005); and Gert Oostindie and Klinkers Inge, *Decolonising the Caribbean: Dutch Policies in a Comparative Perspective* (Amsterdam: Amsterdam University Press, 2004).

21. For more, see Godfrey Baldacchino, *Island Enclaves: Offshoring Strategies, Creative Governance, and Subnational Island Jurisdictions* (Montreal: McGill-Queen's University Press, 2010); Bill Maurer, "Islands in the Net: Rewiring Technological and Financial Circuits in the 'Offshore' Caribbean," *Comparative Studies in Society and History* 43,

no. 3 (2001): 467–501; Tami Navarro, "'Offshore' Banking within the Nation: Economic Development in the United States Virgin Islands," *Global South* 4, no. 2 (2010): 9 28; Mimi Sheller, "Natural Hedonism: The Invention of Caribbean Islands as Tropical Playgrounds," in *Tourism in the Caribbean: Trends, Development, Prospects,* ed. David Timothy Duval (London: Routledge, 2004); Mimi Sheller, "Virtual Islands: Mobilities, Connectivity, and the New Caribbean Spatialities," *Small Axe* 11, no. 3 (2007): 16–33; Peter Redfield, *Space in the Tropics: From Convicts to Rockets in French Guiana* (Berkeley: University of California Press, 2000). On Caribbean data "offshoring," see Adam Hofman, "Dominica to Be the First Bitcoin Nation," *Bitcoin Magazine,* August 28, 2014, http://bitcoinmagazine.com/15986/dominica-first -bitcoin-nation/; "Apple Working on New Data Center on Curacao," *Among Tech* (blog), August 16, 2014, http://www.amongtech.com/apple-working-on-new-data -center-on-curacao/; "Google May Already Be Launching Floating Data Centers off U.S. Coasts," *Al Día Curaçao,* October 25, 2013, http://www.aldiacuracao.com /technology/google-may-already-be-launching-floating-data-centers-off-u-s-coasts/ (I am grateful to Louis Philippe Römer for bringing this to my attention).

22. Antonio Benìtez-Rojo, *The Repeating Island: The Caribbean and the Postmodern Perspective* (Durham, NC: Duke University Press, 1996), 2.

23. For an extended version of this argument, see Yarimar Bonilla, "Ordinary Sovereignty," *Small Axe* 17, no. 3 (2013): 152–65.

24. Dipesh Chakrabarty, *Provincializing Europe* (Princeton, NJ: Princeton University Press, 2000), 27.

25. Michel-Rolph Trouillot, "North Atlantic Universals: Analytical Fictions, 1942–1945," *South Atlantic Quarterly* 101, no. 4 (2002): 839–58, at 848.

26. Talal Asad, *Formations of the Secular* (Stanford, CA: Stanford University Press, 2003), 14.

27. On "graduated sovereignty," see Aihwa Ong, *Neoliberalism as Exception: Mutations in Citizenship and Sovereignty* (Durham, NC: Duke University Press, 2006), 7. For a call to reincorporate the United States into New World Studies, see Harvey Neptune, "The Lost New World of Caribbean Studies: Recalling an Un-American Puerto Rico Project," *Small Axe* 17, no. 2 (2013): 172–85.

28. For more, see Cristina Duffy Burnett and Burke Marshall, *Foreign in a Domestic Sense: Puerto Rico, American Expansion, and the Constitution* (Durham, NC: Duke University Press, 2001); Andrew Hebard, *The Poetics of Sovereignty in American Literature, 1885– 1910* (Cambridge: Cambridge University Press, 2012); Mark Rifkin, *Manifesting America: The Imperial Construction of US National Space* (Oxford: Oxford University Press, 2009).

29. Trouillot, *Silencing the Past,* 103.

30. Touissaint could have just as easily allied with the British. His commitment, despite what others have argued, was therefore not to the French Republic or to particular forms of French universalism, but rather to a broader political project that could have been carried out in alliance with other imperial powers. For more on Touissaint's project, see Lorelle D. Semley, "To Live and Die, Free and French: Toussaint Louverture's 1801 Constitution and the Original Challenge of Black Citizenship," *Radical History Review,* no. 115 (2013): 65–90; John Patrick Walsh, *Free and French in the Caribbean: Toussaint Louverture, Aimé Césaire, and Narratives of Loyal Opposition* (Bloomington: Indiana University Press, 2013); Gary Wilder, "Untimely Vision: Aimé Césaire, Decolonization, Utopia," *Public Culture* 21, no. 1 (2009): 101–40.

31. For more, see Laurent Dubois, *Haiti and the Aftershocks of History* (New York: Metropolitan Books, 2012); and Greg Beckett, "The Ontology of Freedom: The Unthinkable Miracle of Haiti," *Journal of Haitian Studies* 19, no. 2 (2013).

32. Thomas Holt, *The Problem of Freedom: Race, Labor, and Politics in Jamaica and Britain, 1832–1938* (Baltimore: Johns Hopkins University Press, 1992), xix.

33. Saidiya Hartman, *Scenes of Subjection: Terror, Slavery, and Self-Making in Nineteenth-Century America* (Oxford: Oxford University Press, 1997), 6.

34. Other important works that have examined the problem of freedom in the Caribbean include the following: Rebecca J. Scott, *Slave Emancipation in Cuba: The Transition to Free Labor, 1860–1899* (Princeton, NJ: Princeton University Press, 1985); Rebecca J. Scott, *Degrees of Freedom: Louisiana and Cuba after Slavery* (Cambridge, MA: Harvard University Press, 2009); Frederick Cooper, Thomas C. Holt, and Rebecca J. Scott, *Beyond Slavery: Explorations of Race, Labor, and Citizenship in Postemancipation Societies* (Chapel Hill: University of North Carolina Press, 2000); Bridget Brereton and Kevin A. Yelvington, *The Colonial Caribbean in Transition: Essays on Post-Emancipation Social and Cultural History* (Gainesville: University Press of Florida, 1999).

35. See, for example, Sidney Mintz, "The Origins of Reconstituted Peasantries," in *Caribbean Transformations* (Chicago: Aldine Publishers, 1974).

36. Hartman, *Scenes of Subjection,* 115–124.

37. This was exclusive to Guadeloupe, given that Martinique was under British jurisdiction at the time. In Guadeloupe slavery was thus abolished twice. The first abolition, in 1794, which I refer to here, was short-lived. Slavery was reimposed in 1802 until its definitive abolition in 1848.

38. As Laurent Dubois shows, under the regime of Victor Hughes slaves were forced to remain on the plantation and were promised wages that never came. See Laurent Dubois, *A Colony of Citizens: Revolution and Slave Emancipation in the French Caribbean, 1787–1804* (Chapel Hill: University of North Carolina Press, 2004); on "colonial universalism," see p. 4.

39. Ibid. See also Laurent Dubois, "An Atlantic Revolution," *French Historical Studies* 32, no. 4 (2009): 655–61.

40. For more see Wilder, *French Imperial Nation-State.*

CHAPTER ONE

1. See, for example, Patrick Chamoiseau, "Césaire: Ma liberté," *Le Nouvel Observateur,* March 23, 2008; and Chamoiseau, "Nous sommes ses fils rebelles," *Le Journal du Dimanche,* April 20, 2008.

2. See, for example, A. James Arnold, "Césaire Is Dead: Long Live Césaire! Recuperations and Reparations," *French Politics, Culture & Society* 27, no. 3 (2009): 9–18; Justin Daniel, "Aimé Césaire et les Antilles francaises: Une histoire inachevée?" *French Politics, Culture & Society* 27, no. 3 (2009): 24–33; J. Michael Dash, "Aimé Césaire: The Bearable Lightness of Becoming," *PMLA* 125, no. 3 (2010): 737–42; Édouard Glissant, "Aimé Césaire: The Poet's Passion," *Small Axe* 12, no. 3 (2008): 118–23; Fred Reno, "Aimé Césaire ou l'ambivalence feconde," *French Politics, Culture & Society* 27, no. 3 (2009):19–23; Françoise Vergès, "Aimé Césaire et la lutte inachevée," *Alea: Estudos Neolatinos* 11, no. 1 (2009): 24–34.

3. Indeed, many have described it in precisely this manner. See, for example, William Miles, "Fifty Years of Assimilation: Assessing France's Experience of Caribbean De-colonisation through Administrative Reform," in *Islands at the Crossroads: Politics in*

the Non-independent Caribbean, ed. Aarón Gamaliel Ramos and Angel Israel Rivera Ortiz (Kingston: Ian Randle Publishers, 2001).

4. See Jean Claude William, "Les origines de la loi de départementalisation," in L'historial Antillais, ed. Roland Suvélor, vol. 6 (Pointe-à-Pitre: Dajani Editions, 1981), 50–61; Josette Fallope, "La politique d'assimilation et ses résistances," in La Guadeloupe 1875–1914: Les soubresauts d'une société pluriethnique ou les ambiguities de l'assimilation, ed. Henriette Levillain (Paris: Autrement, 1994); Fred Constant and Justin Daniel, eds., 1946–1996: Cinquante ans de départementalisation outre-mer (Paris: L'Harmattan, 1997).

5. Gary Wilder, The French Imperial Nation-State: Negritude and Colonial Humanism between the Two World Wars (Chicago: The University of Chicago Press, 2005).

6. Elizabeth Heath, "Creating Rural Citizens in Guadeloupe in the Early Third French Republic," Slavery & Abolition 32, no. 2 (2011): 289–307.

7. For a more sustained discussion of the political corruption of this era, which included significant acts of fraud, vote rigging, and violence toward Antillean workers who sought to assert their civic rights, see Richard Price, The Convict and the Colonel (Boston: Beacon Press, 1998).

8. Fred Constant, "French Republicanism under Challenge: White Minority (Béké) Power in Martinique and Guadeloupe," in The White Minority in the Caribbean, ed. Howard Johnson and Karl Watson (Kingston: Ian Randle, 1998); Justin Daniel, "The Construction of Dependency: Economy and Politics in the French Antilles," in Islands at the Crossroads: Politics in the Non-independent Caribbean, ed. Ramos Aaron Gamaliel and Rivera Angel Israel (Kingston: Ian Randle Press, 2001).

9. For more on how contemporary békés talk about "escaping" the French Revolution, see Emily Vogt, "The Ghosts of the Plantation: Historical Representations and Cultural Difference among Martinique's White Elite" (PhD diss., University of Chicago, 2005).

10. See Laurent Dubois, A Colony of Citizens: Revolution and Slave Emancipation in the French Caribbean, 1787–1804 (Chapel Hill: University of North Carolina Press, 2004).

11. See Kristen Stromberg Childers, "The Second World War as a Watershed in the French Caribbean," Atlantic Studies 9, no. 4 (2012): 409–30. As Childers notes, the United States planned to invade Martinique in 1940 but refrained after reaching a "gentleman's agreement" and establishing a US consulate on the island. At the time the United States was setting up "base colonies" throughout the Caribbean and building its strength by acquiring and occupying numerous Caribbean territories. For more, see Harvey R. Neptune, Caliban and the Yankees: Trinidad and the United States Occupation (Chapel Hill: University of North Carolina Press, 2007); Louis A. Pérez, Cuba in the American Imagination: Metaphor and the Imperial Ethos (Chapel Hill: University of North Carolina Press, 2008); Mary A. Renda, Taking Haiti: Military Occupation and the Culture of U.S. Imperialism, 1915–1940 (Chapel Hill: University of North Carolina Press, 2001).

12. Tony Chafer, The End of Empire in French West Africa: France's Successful Decolonization? (Oxford: Berg, 2002); Frederick Cooper, "Alternatives to Empire: France and Africa after World War II," in The State of Sovereignty: Territories, Laws, Populations, ed. Douglas Howland and Louise White (Bloomington: Indiana University Press, 2009).

13. Gary Wilder, "Untimely Vision: Aimé Césaire, Decolonization, Utopia," Public Culture 21, no. 1 (2009): 101–40.

14. For more on this period in French history, see Michael Kelly, *The Cultural and Intellectual Rebuilding of France after the Second World War* (London: Palgrave Macmillan, 2004); Richard Kuisel, *Capitalism and the State in Modern France: Renovation and Economic Management in the Twentieth Century* (Cambridge: Cambridge University Press, 1981); Michel Margairaz, *L'État, les finances et l'économie: Histoire d'une conversion, 1932–1952* (Paris: Le Comité pour l'histoire économique et financière de la France, 1991); Andrew Shennan, *Rethinking France: Plans for Renewal, 1940–1946* (Oxford: Oxford University Press, 1989).

15. Aimé Césaire, *Rapport au nom de la commission des territoires d'outre mer*, 25 February 1946; http://www.assemblee-nationale.fr/histoire/images/rapport-520.pdf.

16. Such arguments date back to the era of the French Revolution, when opponents of abolition and universal suffrage maintained that because of distance from the mainland, distinctive climate, and population differences, the colonies required a local constitution. See Dubois, *Colony of Citizens*.

17. For more on how Césaire continuously engaged in a practice of "radical literalism" through which he reread French republican traditions against themselves, subverting French political theory much as he had subverted the French language, see the work of Gary Wilder, including *Freedom Time: Negritude, Decolonization, and the Future of the World* (Durham, NC: Duke University Press, 2015); and "Thinking with Aimé Césaire," in the online forum on "Legacies of Césaire," 2013, http://cesairelegacies.cdrs.columbia.edu/political-legacy/thinking-with-aime-cesaire/.

18. Michel Giraud, "Sur l'assimilation: Les paradoxes d'un objet brouillé," in *Entre assimilation et émancipation: L'outremer français dans l'impasse?*, ed. Thierry Michalon (Paris, Perséides, 2006)

19. For more on Césaire's relationship to the French language, see chapter 2.

20. Patrice Louis, *Conversation avec Aimé Césaire* (Paris: Arléa, 2007), 55 (my translation).

21. Robert Aldrich and John Connell, *France's Overseas Frontier* (Cambridge: Cambridge University Press, 2006), 77.

22. Over the decades, there were various attempts to address power struggles among departmental authorities. In 1960, a law was passed mandating that local councils be consulted on new legislation affecting the DOMs, yet this consultation was "non-obligatory," and any opinion voiced by the councils would be nonbinding (see Aldrich and Connell, *France's Overseas Frontier*, 78). In 1972 the French president, Georges Pompidou, created new regional councils, which in mainland France were formed by uniting several departments into groups that corresponded more or less to the provinces of the ancien régime. In the DOMs, the new regional units coincided with departmental boundaries, fragmenting power even further between the prefect and now two councils. Local officials objected to the creation of another elected body, which they thought would further erode their decision-making power.

    The Mitterrand government tried to fuse the two councils into a unitary assembly (*assemblée unique*) as a way of giving local politicians more authority and autonomy, but this was ruled unconstitutional because it would create a different legislative system for the DOMs. Mitterrand then enacted a decentralization policy in 1982, giving the regional councils some of the prefects' previous authority, including the right to propose economic, social, and cultural policies to the prime minister. It also charged the general councils with allocating money for public works and administering public services; gave the prefects the auxiliary title of Comissaire de la républic, and passed some functions over to the general councils' presidents, who became the new elected departmental chief executives; and devolved certain fiscal and administrative powers to the councils. Despite these tweaks over the years, the DOMs' elected officials have consistently complained that their authority is too restricted. They have often pressed for the *assemblée unique* to be created; in 2003 it was proposed once again, but the local electorate voted it down in a referendum. In Guadeloupe, the "no" vote received a whopping 75 percent, whereas in Martinique it received 51.5 percent, suggesting slightly greater trust in local politicians in the neighboring island.

23. Until 1996 the local SMIC (*salaire minimum interprofessionnel de croissance*, or minimum wage) operating in the DOMs was substantially lower than the national SMIC. The RMI (*revenu minimum d'insertion*, income support or welfare) was not made equivalent to that of mainland France until the year 2000.

24. Aldrich and Connell, *France's Overseas Frontier*, 77.

25. These issues were at the center of the general strike in 2009 (as discussed in chapter 6); however, numerous "exposés" of the high cost of food and other imported goods can be found in local journals and magazines by the early 1980s.

26. Aimé Césaire, prologue to *Les Antilles décolonisées*, by Daniel Guerin (Paris: Présence Africaine, 1956). These statements were made, not coincidentally, at the precise time that Frantz Fanon began proposing total revolution as the answer to colonialism.

27. Ibid., 13.

28. Frantz Fanon, *Black Skins, White Masks*, trans. Richard Philcox (New York: Grove Press, 1967). A less discussed account of this period is found in Fanon's essay "West Indians and Africans," in *Toward the African Revolution*, where he writes, "After the West Indian was obliged, under the pressure of European racists, to abandon positions which were essentially fragile, because they were absurd, because they were incorrect, because they were alienating, a new generation came into being. The West Indian of 1945 is a Negro." Fanon, *Toward the African Revolution: Political Essays*, trans. Haakon Chevalier (New York: Grove Press, 1988), 26.

29. Jean-Luc Jamard, "Les békés sont des judokas," *Les Temps Modernes*, no. 441–42 (1983): 1872–93.

30. In his award-winning novel *Texaco*, Patrick Chamoiseau refers to the era following departmentalization as *le temps betón*, or the "age of concrete." Chamoiseau uses this term to highlight the massive transformations of local surroundings during this period through the rapid construction of public roads, government buildings, megastores, and other concrete testimonies to the French presence in the Antilles. Patrick Chamoiseau, *Texaco: A Novel*, trans. Rose-Myriam Réjouis and Val Vinokurov (New York: Pantheon Books, 1997).

31. Louis-Georges Placide, *Les émeutes de décembre 1959 en Martinique: Un repère historique* (Paris: L'Harmattan, 2009); Laurent Jalabert, "Les mouvements sociaux en Martinique dans les années 1960 et la réaction des pouvoirs publics," *Études Caribéennes*, December 17, 2010.

32. Raymond Gama and Jean-Pierre Sainton, *Me 67 . . . Memoire d'un evenement* (Pointe-à-Pitre: Societé guadeloupéenne d'edition et de diffusion, 1985); Georges Baden, *Le procès des Guadeloupéens, 18 patriotes devant la cour de sûreté de l'état français* (Paris: L'Harmattan, 1981); Laurent Farrugia, *Le fait national guadeloupéen* (Paris: Camus & Cie, 1968).

33. Stephanie Condon and P. E. Ogden, "Emigration from the French Caribbean: The Origins of an Organized Migration," *International Journal of Urban and Regional Research* 15, no. 4 (1991): 505–23; Stephanie Condon, "Les migrants antillais en métropole: Un espace de vie transatlantique," *Espace, Populations, Societes*, no. 2–3 (1996): 513–20; Fred Constant, *La politique française de l'immigration antillaise de*

1946–1987 (Poitiers: Université de Poitiers, 1987); Kristen Stromberg Childers, "Departmentalization, Migration, and the Politics of the Family in the Post-war French Caribbean," *The History of the Family* 14, no. 2 (2009): 177–90; Monique Milia, "Histoire d'une politique d'émigration organisée pour les départements d'outre-mer: 1952–1963," *Pouvoirs dans la Caraïbe: Revue du CRPLC* (January 1997): 141–56.

34. For more, see the personal testimonies featured in recent documentaries about the BUMIDOM generation, including: Antoine Léonard-Maestrati, *L'avenir est ailleurs* (Paris: Doriane Films, 2006); and Jackie Bastide, *BUMIDOM, des français venus d'outremer* (Paris: France 2 Infrarouge, Temps noir Productions, 2010). See also Marc Tardieu, *Les Antillais à Paris: D'hier à aujourd'hui* (Monaco: Rocher, 2005); Anny D. Curtius, "Utopies du BUMIDOM: Construire l'avenir dans un 'là-bas' postcontact," *French Forum* 35, no. 2–3 (2011): 135–55; and Renée Larrier, "'Sont-ils encore gens de Guadeloupe?': Departmentalization, Migration, and Family Dynamics," *International Journal of Francophone Studies* 11, no. 1–2 (2008): 171–87.

35. This history is intimately entwined with that of African immigrants at the time. See, for example, Paul Silverstein and Chantal Tetreault, "Postcolonial Urban Apartheid," in the online forum on "Riots in France," Social Science Research Council, June 11, 2006, http://riotsfrance.ssrc.org.

36. Confédération française démocratique du travail, *Les travailleurs antillais, guyanais, réunionnais en lutte: Contre le colonialisme et le racisme, pour le droit à la différence et l'unité des travailleurs* (Paris: Éditions Caribéennes, 1980).

37. The 40-percent wage increase, known as the *prime colonial*, was a holdover from the colonial era. In 1953 it was renamed the *indemnité d'éloignement* (compensation for distance). Aldrich, *France's Overseas Frontier*, 77.

38. For more on the importance of the Catholic youth movement and how it was protected from state surveillance, see Andrew Daily, "Staying French: Martiniquans and Guadeloupeans between Empire and Independence, 1946–1973" (PhD diss., Rutgers University, 2011), 220–56.

39. On the idea of the revolutionary survey, see Kristin Ross, *May '68 and Its Afterlives* (Chicago: University of Chicago Press, 2002), 109–13. For a personal account of this period, see Christiane Taubira, *Une campagne de folie: Comment j'en suis arrivée là* (Paris: First éditions, 2002).

40. Julien Valère Loza and Daniel Boukman, *Les étudiants martiniquais en France: Histoire de leur organisation et de leurs luttes*, vol. 1, *Des origines à l'affaire de l'OJAM* (Fort-de-France: Editions 2M, 2003); Gesner Mencé, *L'affaire de l'O.J.A.M. (Organisation de la Jeunesse Anticolonialiste de la Martinique) ou "le complot du Mardi-gras"* (Lamentin: Désormeaux, 2001).

41. The exact number of deaths is unknown; at the time the National Guard acknowledged only eight deaths, but in the 1980s the Mitterrand government recognized that at least eighty-five were killed and hundreds more injured in the three-day massacre.

42. Laurent Farrugia, *Le fait national guadeloupéen* (Camus & Cie, 1968); Comité guadeloupéen d'aide et de soutien aux détenus, *Le procès des Guadeloupeens: Dix-huit patriotes devant la cour de l'état francais* (Paris: L'Harmattan, 1969).

43. Louis Théodore, "Interview exclusive: Bilan et perspectives de 30 ans de luttes pour l'indépendance et la révolution," *Études Guadeloupéennes*, no. 4 (1991): 26–81; Union populaire pour la libération de la Guadeloupe, "La situation politique en Guadeloupe depuis le 10 mai," *Les Temps Modernes* 39, no. 441–42 (1983): 1961–73; Rosan Mounien, *UGTG 1973–1993: 20 lanné konba* (Pointe-à-Pitre: CREO, 1994).

44. In 1984, the SGEG merged with the Syndicat des instituteurs, professeurs, et agents de la Guadeloupe (SIPAG) and formed the Syndicat des personnels de l'éducation en Guadeloupe (SPEG), which, although leftist in orientation, is broadly concerned with the problem of education in Guadeloupe.

45. The UGTG's right to engage in collective bargaining is still often questioned because it is not affiliated with any of the five national trade union federations recognized by the French state as negotiating partners.

46. In many ways these efforts are comparable to those of middle-class nationalist activists in other societies who have sought to package subaltern folk practices as national culture. See Robin Moore, *Nationalizing Blackness: Afrocubanismo and Artistic Revolution in Havana, 1920–1940* (Pittsburgh: University of Pittsburgh Press, 1997); Deborah A. Thomas, *Modern Blackness: Nationalism, Globalization, and the Politics of Culture in Jamaica* (Durham, NC: Duke University Press, 2004); Michael D. Largey, *Vodou Nation: Haitian Art, Music and Cultural Nationalism* (Chicago: University of Chicago Press, 2006); Neptune, *Caliban and the Yankees*; Shannon Dudley, *Music from behind the Bridge: Steelband Spirit and Politics in Trinidad and Tobago* (New York: Oxford University Press, 2008).

47. For more, see Ellen Schnepel, *In Search of a National Identity: Creole and Politics in Guadeloupe* (Hamburg: Helmut Buske Verlag, 2004); Jerome Camal, "From Gwoka Modènn to Jazz Ka: Music, Nationalism, and Creolization in Guadeloupe" (PhD diss., Washington University, 2011); Marie-Helena Laumuno, *Gwoka et politique en Guadeloupe, 1960–2003: 40 ans de construction du "pays"* (Paris: L'Harmattan, 2011).

48. For more on Dany Bébel-Gisler's efforts see her own writings, including, with Laënnec Hurbon, *Cultures et pouvoir dans la Caraïbe: Langue créole, vaudou, sectes religieuses en Guadeloupe et en Haïti* (Paris: Librairie-Éditions l'Harmattan, 1975); and by Bébel-Gisler, *Kèk prinsip pou ékri kréyòl* (Paris: L'Harmattan, 1975); *La langue créole, force jugulée: Étude socio-linguistique des rapports de force entre le créole et le français aux Antilles* (Paris: L'Harmattan, 1976); "Corps, langage, pouvoir: Lieux et enjeux dans les luttes de libération nationale en Guadeloupe," *Langage et Société* 26 (1983): 27–49; *Le défi culturel guadeloupéen: Devenir ce que nous sommes* (Paris: Editions caribéennes, 1989); and *Leonora: The Buried Story of Guadeloupe* (Charlottesville: University of Virginia, 1994).

49. As Ellen Schnepel documents, after departmentalization, Creole was banned in schools over concern that its use would corrupt French diction. Schnepel, *In Search of a National Identity*, 70.

50. This was partly because many at the time argued that Creole impeded educational success, given that formal instruction was conducted in French. For more on the politics of Creole and the controversies that ensued when nationalist teachers began using it in local schools, see Schnepel, *In Search of a National Identity*; and Sarah Moon McDermott Thompson, "Creole Citizens of France: The Trans-Atlantic Politics of Antillean Education and the Creole Movement since 1945" (PhD diss., University of Michigan, 2012).

51. For more on the multiple, overlapping, and at times contradictory variants within the Creole movement, see Ellen Schnepel, "The Creole Movement in Guadeloupe," *International Journal of the Sociology of Language* 102 (1993): 117–34.

52. Gerard Lockel, *Traite de gwo-ka modén initiation a la musique de la Guadeloupe* (Pointe-à-Pitre: Realisation Atelier Intégral, 1981).

53. For a close analysis of Lockel's contributions, see Camal, "From Gwoka Modènn to Jazz Ka."

54. Gérard Lockel, "Chanté a Lendépandans." For lyrics and audio, see http://ugtg.org /article_69.html.
55. The focus on Catholic religion might also be related to the complex relationship between the Antilles and Haiti. In *Cultures et pouvoir dans la Caraibe*, Dany Bébel-Gisler and the Haitian anthropologist Laënnec Hurbon express their concern over the Duvalier government's "demagogic uses" of Vodou while also acknowledging the complex xenophobic discourses among Antilleans toward Haitians, who were often brought in to break up strikes in the sugar fields. The text suggests that Guadeloupean agricultural workers often expressed fear of Haitian Vodou priests, imagining them to be more powerful than the Guadeloupean *quimboiseurs*.
56. "Entretien avec Chérubin Céleste," *Les Temps Modernes* 39, no. 441–42 (1983): 1946–60, at 1956.
57. Bébel-Gisler, *Le defi culturel*, 131.
58. RFO TV had a Creole news program in Martinique but not in Guadeloupe. Some argued that this was because Creole was still deemed too subversive in Guadeloupe; others argued that it was the result of the entrance of pro-independence politicians into mainstream politics in Martinique. For more on the role of Creole in the contemporary public sphere, see the work of Kathe Managan, including "Péyi an nou: Conceptualizing Language, Place, Race and Identity in Guadeloupe," *Sargasso* (2010–2011), 147–61; and "Koud Zyé: A Glimpse into Kréyòl-Language Programming on Guadeloupean State-Financed TV," *Journal of Sociolinguistics* 15, no. 3 (2011): 299–322.
59. As Jerome Camal argues in "From Gwoka Modènn" (at 301), gwoka runs the risk of succumbing to the kind of folklorization and "postcarding" that authors like Richard Price have described, with dancers often outfitted in madras skirts and straw hats, invoking a nostalgia for a foregone *antan lontan*.
60. This was the path followed in Martinique, where pro-independence politicians eventually gained control of the Regional Council.
61. For more, see Francois-Xavier Guillerm, *(In)dépendance créole: Brève histoire récente du nationalisme antillais* (Pointe-à-Pitre: Editions Jasor, 2007).
62. It is important to keep in mind that political generations are not reducible to biological ones. For more, see David I. Kertzer, "Generation as a Sociological Problem," *Annual Review of Sociology* (1983): 125–49; and David Scott, "The Temporality of Generations: Dialogue, Tradition, Criticism," *New Literary History* 45, no. 2 (2014): 157–81.
63. "Manifeste de l'Alliance revolutionnaire caribéenne, organisation politico-militaire," in *Magwa: Magazine Gwadloupeyen Anticolonialiste*, special edition (May 1987): 3–17.
64. Maryse Condé, "Pan-Africanism, Feminism and Culture," in *Imagining Home: Class, Culture, and Nationalism in the African Diaspora*, ed. Sidney Lemelle and Robin D. G. Kelley (New York: Verso, 1994), 56.
65. One could see the Zapatista movement in Chiapas (armed mostly with toy guns and "words" as their weapons) as the final transition from this era of armed struggle. I would argue that in many ways the Zapatistas represent a hinge movement between a previous era of armed struggle and a new form of politics carried out mostly on the terrain of the imagination. For more, see Juana Ponce de Leon, ed., *Our Word Is Our Weapon: Selected Writings of Subcomandante Insurgente Marcos* (New York: Seven Stories Press, 2001).
66. For more, see Katherine Browne, *Creole Economics: Caribbean Cunning under the French Flag* (Austin: University of Texas Press, 2004) esp. chapter 2.
67. Bébel-Gisler, *Le defi culturel*, 180n3.

68. This discrepancy is often attributed to a greater perceived need for labor unions in Guadeloupe, given local employers' reluctance to apply basic labor legislation, such as the thirty-five-hour workweek. Indeed, a study conducted by the local labor department found that the majority of labor conflicts were carried out to demand the application of existing labor legislation.

69. "Le syndicalisme demeure très vivace" *France Antilles*, April 12, 2003; Direction du travail, de l'emploi et de la formation professionnelle de la Guadeloupe, *Les conflits collectifs en 2003*.

70. The Conseil de prud'hommes is a specialized labor court composed of representatives from both trade unions and employer associations; the latter include organizations like the Mouvement des entreprises de France (MEDEF) and the Confédération générale du patronat des petites et moyennes entreprises (CGPME).

71. "L'île-chaudron: Chômage, conflits sociaux et insécurité en font une zone explosive," *L'Express*, April 18, 2002, http://www.lexpress.fr/tendances/voyage/l-ile-chaudron_458142.html. This surge of national attention was due in part to the importance of the 2001 "Madassamy affair," discussed in chapter 4.

72. One of the most vocal critics of the union is the philosophy teacher and writer Jacky Dahomay, who has repeatedly denounced the UGTG for engaging in violent practices that he has variously described as "fascist," "antidemocratic," forms of "terrorism," and "macoutisme." The latter term caused much controversy for its association with the Tontons Macoutes in Haiti, but Dahomay insists that *macoutisme* has a broader connotation, referring to the abuse of power in postplantation societies. For more, see Dahomay, "Dénonciation des actes de violences de l'UGTG, syndicat indépendantiste guadeloupéen," *Creoleways*, June 5, 2001, http://creoleways.com/2001/06/05/guadeloupe-jacky-dahomay-contre-les-derives-syndicales; and Dahomay, "Le LKP et les 'tontons macoutes': Une mise au point," *Médiapart*, March 11, 2009, http://blogs.mediapart.fr/blog/jacky-dahomay/110309/le-lkp-et-les-tontons-macoutes-une-mise-au-point.

73. Within Guadeloupe there is a general mistrust of centralized political power, as seen in the 2003 referendum on establishing an *assemblée unique*; see chapter 1, note 22 above.

CHAPTER TWO

1. In chapter 3, I discuss these initiatives, and their failures, in more depth.

2. "Social dialogue" is a common term in the context of labor relations. According to the International Labor Organization, it represents "all types of negotiation, consultation or simply exchange of information between, or among, representatives of governments, employers and workers, on issues of common interest relating to economic and social policy. . . . The concept of social dialogue and its definition vary from one country to another and from one region to another and continue to evolve." In France social dialogue became the main paradigm for labor relations during the Sarkozy era, a development which informs Lukas's comment. Sarkozy institutionalized social dialogue in the name of "flexicurity," a vague neologism marrying "flexibility for firms, and security for workers." See Donna Kesselman, "The Future of Good Jobs and the Crisis of Their Representations in France," paper delivered at the International Labour Process Conference, Rutgers University, March 2010.

3. I purposefully translate *nèg mawon* as "rebel slave" rather than "runaway slave" because the model of marronage that I discuss here encompasses forms of resistance beyond flight.

4. See, for example, Erin Mackie, "Welcome the Outlaw: Pirates, Maroons, and Carib-bean Countercultures," *Cultural Critique* 59, no. 1 (2005): 24–62.

5. Michel-Rolph Trouillot, *Silencing the Past: Power and the Production of History* (Boston: Beacon Press, 1995), 25. On the shifting narrative form of postcolonial history, see David Scott, *Conscripts of Modernity: The Tragedy of Colonial Enlightenment* (Durham, NC: Duke University Press, 2004). For other important takes on the politics of his-torical narration in the Caribbean, see Richard Price, *First-Time*; Richard Price, *Travels with Tooy: History, Memory, and the African American Imagination* (Chicago: University of Chicago Press, 2008); and Stephan Palmié, *The Cooking of History: How Not to Study Afro-Cuban Religion* (Chicago: University of Chicago Press, 2013).

6. David Scott, *Refashioning Futures: Criticism after Postcoloniality* (Princeton, NJ: Princeton University Press, 1999).

7. Césaire's views on political autonomy, sovereignty, and independence were not static. Although independence was not an imperative for him in the 1940s, he did later recognize its appeal and was himself at times seduced by its promises. However, he was certain that France would not engage in a democratic devolution of power for the Antilles and, more importantly, he felt that Martinicans were not ready to un-dergo an insurrectional search for political independence. For more, see his 1978 speech, "Discours des trois voies ou des cinq libertés," reprinted in *Politiques Publiques*, June 29, 2013, http://www.politiques-publiques.net/Aime-Cesaire-Discours-des -trois.html.

8. I should reiterate that my focus here is on the narrative purchase of maroons, and not on the politics surrounding present-day maroon communities. As Kenneth Bilby has shown, historical narratives of marronage are often divorced from how present-day maroon communities are both treated and imagined by their contemporaries. For more, see Kenneth Bilby, *True-Born Maroons* (Gainesville: University Press of Florida, 2005), 24–66.

9. Bilby, *True-Born Maroons*; Richard Price, *Rainforest Warriors: Human Rights on Trial* (Philadelphia: University of Pennsylvania Press, 2011).

10. See, for example, Richard Burton, *Le roman marron: Études sur la littérature martini-quaise contemporaine* (Paris, France: L'Harmattan, 1997).

11. Gabriel Debien, "Le marronage aux Antilles françaises au XVIIIe siècle," *Caribbean Studies* 6, no. 3 (1966): 3–43.

12. For a detailed discussion of these legal codes and their shifts over time, see Bernard Moitt, "Slave Resistance in Guadeloupe and Martinique, 1791–1848," *Journal of Caribbean History* 25, no. 1–2 (1992): 136–60.

13. Moitt, "Slave Resistance," 58.

14. As Debien notes in "Le marronage" (at p. 4), grand marronage dominated the reports of militia commanders and state officials.

15. Debien, "Le Marronage," 7.

16. Josette Fallope, *Esclaves et citoyens: Les noirs à la Guadeloupe au XIXe siècle dans les processus de résistance et d'intégration: 1802–1910* (Basse-Terre: Société d'histoire de la Guadeloupe, 1992), 209, 210, 409.

17. Moitt, "Slave Resistance," 66.

18. For a discussion of the problem with this typology, see Jerome Handler, "Escaping Slavery in a Caribbean Plantation Society: Marronage in Barbados, 1650s–1830s," *New West Indian Guide* 71, no. 3–4 (1997): 183–225; and Jean Fouchard, *The Haitian Maroons: Liberty or Death* (New York: E. W. Blyden Press, 1981).

19. See, for example, Carolyn Fick's discussion of the debates over "escapist" or "restorationist" marronage versus "revolutionary" marronage. Carolyn E. Fick, *The Making of Haiti: The Saint Domingue Revolution from Below* (Knoxville: University of Tennessee Press, 1990), 7-8.

20. For more on the debates over the role of marronage in the Haitian Revolution see Fick, *Making of Haiti;* and David Patrick Geggus, *Haitian Revolutionary Studies* (Bloomington: Indiana University Press, 2002), esp. chapter 5. For an analysis of the ideological underpinnings animating these debates, see Trouillot, *Silencing the Past,* 103-7.

21. C. L. R. James, *The Black Jacobins* (New York: Vintage Books, 1989), ix. For more on how James's narrative of the Haitian Revolution speaks to the political imperatives of his time, see Scott, *Conscripts of Modernity.* On the problems of Haitian exceptionalism, see Michel-Rolph Trouillot, "The Odd and the Ordinary: Haiti, the Caribbean, and the World," *Cimarrón: New Perspectives on the Caribbean,* 2, no. 3 (1990): 3-12; and Yarimar Bonilla, "Ordinary Sovereignty," *Small Axe* 13, no. 3 (2013): 152-65.

22. On ideas of sovereignty as nondomination, interdependence, and relational autonomy within the context of Native American studies, see Iris Marion Young, "Two Concepts of Self-Determination," in *Ethnicity, Nationalism, and Minority Rights,* ed. Stephen May, Tariq Modood, and Judith Squires (Cambridge: Cambridge University Press, 2004); Jessica Cattelino, *High Stakes: Florida Seminole Gaming and Sovereignty* (Durham, NC: Duke University Press, 2008); Taiaiake Alfred, "Sovereignty," in *Companion to American Indian History,* ed. Philip Deloria and Neal Salisbury (Malden, Mass: Blackwell, 2002).

23. In the case of Jamaica, even after emancipation maroons continued to cooperate with the colonial state by suppressing peasant insurrections. See Bilby, *True-Born Maroons.*

24. For more on methodological nationalism as a naturalization of the nation-state form, see Andreas Wimmer and Nina Glick Schiller, "Methodological Nationalism and Beyond: Nation-State Building, Migration and the Social Sciences," *Global Networks* 2, no. 4 (October 2002): 301-34; Frederick Cooper, *Colonialism in Question: Theory, Knowledge, History* (Berkeley: University of California Press, 2005); Jane Burbank and Frederick Cooper, "The Empire Effect," *Public Culture* 24, no. 2 (2012): 239-47; Gary Wilder, "From Optic to Topic: The Foreclosure Effect of Historiographic Turns," *The American Historical Review* 117, no. 3 (2012): 723-45; and Gary Wilder, *Freedom Time: Negritude, Decolonization, and the Future of the World* (Durham, NC: Duke University Press, 2015).

25. See, for example, Édouard Glissant, *Le discours antillais* (Paris: Seuil, 1981), 104, 154; Dany Bébel-Gisler, *Leonora: The Buried Story of Guadeloupe* (Charlottesville: University of Virginia Press, 1994), 5.

26. For a careful survey of the trajectory of the maroon within Antillean literature, see Marie-Christine Rochmann, *L'esclave fugitif dans la littérature antillaise: Sur la déclive du morne* (Paris: Karthala, 2000). As Rochmann suggests (74-75), although the figure of the maroon had already emerged within the historical canon, it is not until the 1950s that the "mythic maroon" narrative becomes dominant. See also Burton, *Le roman marron.*

27. See Richard Price and Sally Price, "Shadowboxing in the Mangrove," *Cultural Anthropology* 12, no. 1 (1997): 3-36; A. James Arnold, "From the Problematic Maroon to a Woman-Centered Creole Project in the Literature of the French West

Indies," in *Slavery in the Caribbean Francophone World*, ed. Doris Y. Kadish (Athens: University of Georgia Press, 2000); and Burton, *Le roman marron*.

28. For a discussion of the problems with this claim, see Jerome Camal, "From Gwoka Modènn to Jazz Ka: Music, Nationalism, and Creolization in Guadeloupe" (PhD diss., Washington University, 2011), 104.

29. See "L'ARC: Le glas du GLA?" in *Magwa: Magazine Gwadloupeyen Anticolonialiste*, special edition, supplement no. 17 (November 1987): 35–52.

30. Richard Price, *Maroon Societies: Rebel Slave Communities in the Americas* (New York: Anchor Press, 1973), xiii.

31. Miguel Barnet and Esteban Montejo, *Biografi a de un cimarrón* (La Habana: Instituto de Ethnología y Folklore, 1966).

32. Miguel Barnet, "The Untouchable Cimarrón," *New West Indian Guide* 71, no. 3–4 (1997): 281–89, at 282 and 284.

33. Abeng is also the title of a 1984 novel by Michelle Cliff, itself the product of a slightly different problem-space. For more, see Ronald Cummings, "(Trans)Nationalisms, Marronage, and Queer Caribbean Subjectivities," *Transforming Anthropology*, 18 (2010): 169–80.

34. See, for example, Jean Fouchard, *Les marrons du syllabaire* (Port-au-Prince: Editions Henri Deschamps, 1953); Yvan Debbasch, "Le marronage: Essai sur la désertion de l'esclave antillais," pts. 1 and 2, *L'Année Sociologique* (1962): 1–112, (1963): 117–95; Jean Fouchard, *Les marrons de la liberté* (Paris: Edition de l'Ecole, 1972); Leslie F. Manigat, "The Relationship between Marronage and Slave Revolts and Revolution in St. Domingue–Haiti," *Annals of the New York Academy of Sciences* 292, no. 1 (1977): 420–38.

35. Richard Laurent Omgba and André Ntonfo, eds., *Aimé Césaire et le monde noir* (Paris: L'Harmattan, 2012), 19.

36. See, for example, Rochmann, *L'esclave fugitif*.

37. See, for example, Auguste Armet, "Aimé Césaire, homme politique," *Études Littéraires* 6, no. 1 (1973): 81–96.

38. Patrick Chamoiseau, "Nous sommes ses fils rebelles," *Le Journal du Dimanche*, April 20, 2008.

39. Raphaël Confiant, *Aimé Césaire: Une traversée paradoxale du siècle* (Paris: Stock, 1993).

40. An important exception here is Gary Wilder, who has consistently questioned the false divide between Césaire's literary and political oeuvre, viewing them both as acts of poetic reinvention. See Gary Wilder, "Aimé Césaire: Contra Commemoration," *African and Black Diaspora: An International Journal* 2, no. 1 (2009): 121–23; "Untimely Vision: Aimé Césaire, Decolonization, Utopia," *Public Culture* 21, no. 1 (2009): 101–140; *Freedom Time*; and "Thinking with Aimé Césaire," in the online forum on "Legacies of Césaire," 2013, http://cesairelegacies.cdrs.columbia.edu /political-legacy/thinking-with-aime-cesaire.

41. See James Clifford, "A Politics of Neologism: Aimé Césaire," in *The Predicament of Culture* (Cambridge, MA: Harvard University Press, 1988); and Colin Dayan, "Out of Defeat: Aimé Césaire's Miraculous Words," *Boston Review* (2008).

42. Aimé Césaire, *Discourse on Colonialism* (New York: Monthly Review Press, 2000), 83.

43. Nathaniel Mackey, "Other: From Noun to Verb" in *Discrepant Engagement: Dissonance, Cross-Culturality, and Experimental Writing* (Cambridge: Cambridge University Press, 1993), 265–67.

44. To appreciate the power of Césaire's neologism, it is necessary to understand that the term *nèg* carries a historical and political weight that goes beyond the simple word *black* or even *Negro*. It is more of a racial slur than a racial category.

45. Euzhan Palcy and Annick Thébia-Melsan, *Aimé Césaire: A Voice for History* (San Francisco: California Newsreel, 1994).

46. See Mackey, "Other: From Noun to Verb," for more on how Césaire's effort reflected a tendency within black folk expression to use what Zora Neale Hurston described as "verbal nouns." Mackey also shows how Césaire's efforts resonate with Amiri Baraka's discussion of cultural appropriation and how the musical verb *swing* was objectified as a noun. One could similarly argue that in turning *marronage* into a verb, Césaire sought to de-objectify the figure of the maroon.

47. Clifford, "A Politics of Neologism," 181.

48. See, for example, Georges Trésor, "Le guadeloupéen et la loi," *Études Guadeloupéennes* 7 (1995): 3–39; Georges Combé, "Esclavage et mentalities," *Études Guadeloupéennes,* 12 (2001): 52–64; and André Lucrèce, *Société et modernité* (Fort-de-France: Éditions de l'autre mer, 1994).

49. Trésor, "Le guadeloupéen," 38.

50. Ibid.

51. Katherine Browne, *Creole Economics: Caribbean Cunning under the French Flag* (Austin: University of Texas Press, 2004).

52. Combé, "Esclavage," 57. For a similar argument in the context of Puerto Rico see Fernando Picó, "The Absent State," in *None of the Above: Puerto Ricans in the Global Era,* ed. Frances Negrón-Muntaner (New York: Macmillan, 2007).

53. André Lucrece, in *Société et modernité,* goes so far as to describe these acts as the product of maroon traditions.

54. Combé, "Esclavage," 57.

55. Trésor, "Le guadeloupéen," 39.

56. See chapter 3 for more on this.

57. See Richard Burton, "Debrouya Pa Peche, or Il y a Toujours Moyen De Moyenner: Patterns of Opposition in the Fiction of Patrick Chamoiseau," *Callaloo* 16, no. 2 (1993): 466–48; Renée K. Gosson, "For What the Land Tells: An Ecocritical Approach to Patrick Chamoiseau's Chronicle of the Seven Sorrows," *Callaloo* 26, no. 1 (2003): 219–34.

58. *Clap Noir: Le Site du Cinéma Africain,* January 22, 2008, https://web.archive.org /web/20080122074627/http://www.clapnoir.org/fiches_films/films/neg_maron.htm.

CHAPTER THREE

1. Karl Marx and Friedrich Engels, *The Communist Manifesto* (London: Penguin, 2002).

2. Direction du travail, de l'emploi et de la formation professionnelle de la Guadeloupe, *Les conflits collectifs en 2002.*

3. This discrepancy is often attributed to a greater perceived need for labor unions in Guadeloupe, given local employers' reluctance to apply basic labor legislation, such as the thirty-five-hour workweek. Indeed, a study conducted by the local labor department found that the majority of labor conflicts were carried out to demand the application of existing labor legislation.

4. As shown in chapter 4, even just the rumor of a barricade can cause disruption and chaos.

5. Moudong was the name of an important group of maroons.

6. These workers went on strike to protest the AFB's attempt to replace their local contract with a new national-level contract that would have resulted in decreased pay and the elimination of local holidays such as Carnival and Abolition Day. Union leaders argued that the new national contract was an example of the dismantling of French labor rights, which they argue has accompanied France's insertion into the European Union.

7. Barricades are emblematic symbols of protest within French traditions of struggle dating back to the French Revolution. See, for example, Mark Traugott, "Barricades as Repertoire: Continuities and Discontinuities in the History of French Contention," in *Repertoires and Cycles of Collective Action*, ed. Mark Traugott (Durham, NC: Duke University Press, 1995). Their contemporary symbolic purchase in Guadeloupe is comparable to that of burned-out cars, which have also become important symbols of dissent, most notably during the infamous 2005 riots in the French *banlieues*.

8. Victor Turner, *Dramas, Fields, and Metaphors: Symbolic Action in Human Society* (Ithaca, NY: Cornell University Press, 1974). As Turner suggests (at p. 38), the first phase of a social drama is "signalized by the public, overt breach or deliberate non-fulfillment of some crucial norm regulating the intercourse of the parties." He referred to this as a "symbolic trigger" of confrontation or encounter.

9. Ellen Schnepel cites some interesting figures in this regard, stating that due in part to the historical differences between Martinique and Guadeloupe—notably Martinique's having "escaped" the French Revolution (as discussed in chapter 1)—the plantocracy in Guadeloupe is more heavily dominated by outside interests than in Martinique. By 1960 only 14.35 percent of Guadeloupe's sugar industry was held by local interests (as opposed to 88.87 percent in Martinique); 23.30 percent was held by Martinican elites, and 62.35 percent by *métropolitains*. Schnepel also notes the importance of the Syro-Lebanese community in the local economy. See Ellen Schnepel, *In Search of a National Identity: Creole and Politics in Guadeloupe* (Hamburg: Helmut Buske Verlag, 2004), 10, 47. See also Gérard Lafleur, *Les libanais et les syriens de Guadeloupe* (Paris: Karthala, 1999).

10. For more on how the békés imagine themselves through these pre-republican frames, see Emily Vogt, *The Ghosts of the Plantation: Historical Representations and Cultural Difference among Martinique's White Elite* (Chicago: University of Chicago, 2005).

11. Direction du travail, de l'emploi et de la formation professionnelle de la Guadeloupe, *Les conflits collectifs en 2002*.

12. These statements echo the longstanding position that elites have had on the project of departmentalization. As explained in chapter 1, elites have often opposed French integration, partly to avoid French labor regulations and protections, and have historically favored independence or even annexation to the United States.

13. During my time in Guadeloupe, there was a television show called *Entreprendre* on Canal 10 devoted to these discussions. For more on Canal 10 and its role in labor struggles, see chapter 4.

14. Similar workplace occupations have become common in places such as Argentina; for more see Avi Lewis and Naomi Klein, *The Take* (New York: First Run Features, 2006); Alejandro Pizzi Ignasi and Brunet Icart, "Autogestión obrera y movilización social: El caso de las empresas recuperadas argentinas en la Ciudad de Buenos Aires y Provincia de Buenos Aires," *Latin American Research Review* 75, no. 1 (2014): 39–61.

15. *Bokits* are a type of fritter sandwich sold in Guadeloupe, mostly by street vendors.

16. In the final chapter, I examine the twists and turns of the 2009 negotiations.

17. I use the French term *le piquet* to highlight the importance of the picket site as a suspended space of community, as opposed to the US-style picket line, which invokes the idea of movement. In the United States, picket lines emerged as a response to the use of vagrancy laws to arrest striking workers. These laws, originally meant to ensure a steady labor supply by punishing idleness and unemployment, were used to arrest sit-down strikers during the 1930s. See William Chambliss, "The Law of Vagrancy," in *Criminal Law in Action*, ed. William Chambliss (New York: John Wiley & Sons, 1984); Ahmed White, "A Different Kind of Labor Law: Vagrancy Law and the Regulation of Harvest Labor, 1913–1924," *University of Colorado Law Review* 75, no. 3 (2004): 667–744; Ahmed White, "The Crime of Staging an Effective Strike and the Enduring Role of Criminal Law in Modern Labor Relations," *WorkingUSA: The Journal of Labor and Society* 11, no. 1 (2008): 23–44. See also Jeffrey Adler, "A Historical Analysis of the Law of Vagrancy," *Criminology* 27, no. 2 (1989): 209–29.

18. To preserve the anonymity of the workers I interviewed, I have used pseudonyms for them and for the Sucré company, and have obscured the time and details of the conflict in question.

19. The base salary is significant because it has an impact not only on workers' current salary but also on the amount of their pensions. As demonstrated by recent labor conflicts throughout the world, battles over pensions are increasingly becoming a central area of concern for the labor movement and a central target of reform for employers and governments.

20. Jennie Smith discusses similar notions in her study of the Gwoupman Peyizan movement in Haiti, which is based on similar ideas of collective agricultural practices, food preparation, and consumption. See Jennie M. Smith, *When the Hands Are Many: Community Organization and Social Change in Rural Haiti* (Ithaca, NY: Cornell University Press, 2001). *Koudmen* actions were also central to the nationalist movement in Guadeloupe during the 1970s, particularly during their struggles to seize agricultural lands from the large sugar estates. For more, see Union des travailleurs agricoles, "Les occupations de terres en guadeloupe," *Les Temps Modernes* 39, no. 441–42 (1983): 1974–87.

21. Many in Guadeloupe believe that workers are compensated by unions while they are on strike. It is true that unions will often take up collections to help strikers, particularly around the holidays, and fundraising events are frequent (including selling lunches at the picket site). The money generated by these events, however, is not comparable to an actual salary.

22. On the notion of bodily hexis see Pierre Bourdieu, *Outline of a Theory of Practice* (Cambridge: Cambridge University Press, 1977).

23. Victor W. Turner, *The Ritual Process: Structure and Anti-structure* (Ithaca, NY: Cornell University Press, 1982), 45.

24. *Selections From the Prison Notebooks of Antonio Gramsci*, ed. and trans. Quintin Hoare (London: Lawrence and Wishart, 1972), 10.

25. For a discussion of the difference between agents and actors in historical action, see Michel-Rolph Trouillot, *Silencing the Past: Power and the Production of History* (Boston: Beacon Press, 1995), 23.

26. Though he never mentions it explicitly, one can assume that Max is informed here by the idea of the "new man" as developed by Ernesto Che Guevara; see Che Guevara, *Socialism and Man in Cuba* (New York: Pathfinder Press, 2009).

27. My conversation with Max about the long strike and its importance in creating new relationships of community and solidarity took place more than a year before the

Sucré strike. Our conversation was not about any strike in particular, but about what he understood to be the importance of any long strike. It was not until much later that I realized how his description resonated with the narratives of the Sucré workers.

28. I found it to be a common pattern that many union members, particularly delegates, were also involved in local community organizations and held various positions of leadership outside the union. For more see chapter 2.

29. It is unclear if by *société* Denis is referring to the wider society or to the Sucré franchise, which had the legal status of a *société anonyme*. Either one is possible.

30. His decision to write a memoir suggests that he recognized his role as both an actor and a narrator of history, reflecting what Trouillot describes as the "double-sided" nature of historicity. However, the reason Denis thought it could be published only in the future was that (unlike me) he refused to use pseudonyms for his colleagues, whom he viewed as historical actors, even if they were not yet ready to assume that role.

31. I discuss the use of the labor courts in chapter 4.

CHAPTER FOUR

1. In the Caribbean, the descendants of South Asian indentured workers are locally referred to as "Indian" or "East Indian" (as opposed to West Indian). For more on the role of East Indians in the Caribbean, see Viranjini Munasinghe, *Callaloo or Tossed Salad? East Indians and the Cultural Politics of Identity in Trinidad* (Ithaca, NY: Cornell University Press, 2001); and Aisha Khan, *Callaloo Nation: Metaphors of Race and Religious Identity among South Asians in Trinidad* (Durham, NC: Duke University Press, 2004).

   From 1854 to 1885 an estimated 45,000 Indian workers arrived in Guadeloupe. Initially these workers were recruited from French territories, particularly Pondicherry, Mahé, and Karaikal. However, when local planters deemed that a larger labor supply was needed, the French government petitioned England for permission to recruit workers from British territories in India. This arrangement was formalized in the Treaty of Paris signed on July 11, 1860. At present Guadeloupe has the fourth-largest Indian community in the Caribbean, with nearly 50,000 residents of East Indian descent within a population of 420,000. This is significantly higher than in Martinique, where Indian immigration was less significant due to different post-emancipation patterns. For more, see Ernest Moutoussamy, *La Guadeloupe et son indianité* (Paris: Editions Caribéennes, 1987); Jean-Pierre Sainton, "Notes pour l'étude de la question de l'intégration politique des descendants d'indiens en Guadeloupe au cours de la 1er moitié du XXe siècle," *Bulletin de la société d'histoire de la Guadeloupe* 138–39 (2004): 139–60; Singaravélou, *Les indiens de la Caraïbe* (Paris: L'Harmattan, 1987); and Ellen Schnepel, "The Creole Movement and East Indians on the Island of Guadeloupe, French West Indies," in *The East Indian Odyssey: Dilemmas of a Migrant People*, ed. Mahin Gosine (New York: Windsor Press, 1994).

2. Eddy Nedeljkovic, "La grève organisée par l'UGTG n'est pas parvenue à paralyser la Guadeloupe," *Le Monde*, June 9, 2001.

3. On the notion of a deliberating public, see Michael Warner, "Publics and Counterpublics," *Public Culture* 14, no. 1 (2002): 49–90.

4. For more on the impact of decentralization in the Antilles, see Derek MacDougall, "The French Caribbean during the Mitterrand Era," *Commonwealth & Comparative Politics* 31, no. 3 (1993): 92–110; William Safran, "The Mitterrand Regime and Its

Policies of Ethnocultural Accommodation," *Comparative Politics* 18, no. 1 (1985): 41–63; William Miles, "Deja Vu with a Difference: End of the Mitterrand Era and the McDonaldization of Martinique," *Caribbean Studies* (1995): 339–68; Jean Crusol, "Assimilation, Nationalism, and Decentralization in Martinique, Guadeloupe, and Guiana," *The Caribbean and World Politics: Cross Currents and Cleavages*, ed. Jorge Heine and Leslie François (New York: Holmes & Meier, 1988).

5. At the time of my fieldwork each of the French overseas departments had a local RFO affiliate. These affiliates offered some local programming, including small segments in Creole, but were still very much dominated by the network's centralized programming structure.

6. One of Canal 10's hosts, Ibo Simon, started a major controversy after repeatedly using his television show as a space in which to voice xenophobic comments regarding Haitian migrants in Guadeloupe. His influence was such that he was eventually tried for inciting hate crimes in 2001. For more, see Philippe Zacaïr, "The Trial of Ibo Simon: Popular Media and Anti-Haitian Violence in Guadeloupe," in *Haiti and the Haitian Diaspora in the Wider Caribbean*, ed. Philippe Zacaïr (Gainesville: University Press of Florida, 2010).

7. The ubiquitous phrase *n'importe quoi* literally means "no matter what" but is often used in Guadeloupe (and France more generally) to refer to out-of-line behavior. When someone is spouting nonsense, they are saying *n'importe quoi;* when they are acting outrageously they are doing *n'importe quoi.* The use of this term often came across as a demand for restraint, control, and submission to norms. In fact, a common critique of the union was that they often do *n'importe quoi* to achieve their demands.

8. In the final chapter of this book, I describe a reversal of this distancing during the 2009 strike as callers became part of the "we" and engaged in public deliberation over the kind of action that "we" the Guadeloupean people rather than "they" the UGTG should engage in.

9. For more on *koudmen*, see chapter 3.

10. Madassamy's lawyers argued that the first charge was covered by a presidential amnesty and thus could not be grounds for incarceration, and that on the other two charges, Madassamy had yet to appear before the final authority for sentencing, the Judge d'application de peines (JAP).

11. As Begoña Aretxaga demonstrates in her study of Irish politics, the source of women's power within nationalist movements often does not stem from their own engagement but from that of their sons, over whose sacrifices they grieve. See Begoña Aretxaga, *Shattering Silence: Women, Nationalism, and Political Subjectivity in Northern Ireland* (Princeton, NJ: Princeton University Press, 1997), 110.

12. Allen Feldman, *Formations of Violence: The Narrative of the Body and Political Terror in Northern Ireland* (Chicago: University of Chicago Press, 1991), 237.

13. Anny Dominique Curtius, "Gandhi et Au-Béro, ou comment inscrire les traces d'une mémoire indienne dans une négritude martiniquaise," *L'Esprit Créateur* 50, no. 2 (2010): 109–123.

14. Ellen Schnepel, *In Search of a National Identity: Creole and Politics in Guadeloupe* (Hamburg: Helmut Buske Verlag, 2004); Lisa Outar, "L'Inde Perdue, l'Inde Retrouvée (India Lost, India Found): Representations of Francophone Indo-Caribbeans in Maryse Condé's *Crossing the Mangrove* and Ernest Moutoussamy's *A la Recherche de l'Inde Perdue*," *South Asian Diaspora* 6, no.1 (2013): 47–61. The extent of the integration of Indo-Caribbeans should not be overstated here. Indian communities

continue to be concentrated in certain geographic areas, they remain largely connected to the agriculture industry, and their entry into commerce is limited to certain sectors, particularly construction and transport.

15. See, for example, Jean Bernabé, Patrick Chamoiseau, and Raphaël Confiant, *Éloge de la créolite* (Paris: Gallimard, 1989).

16. The visibility of Saint-François as a center of indianité is due in large part to the role of local politician and poet Ernest Moutoussamy, who served as mayor of the commune from 1989 to 2008 and as a deputy for Guadeloupe in the French National Assembly from 1981 to 2002. Moutoussamy is an accomplished poet, novelist, and essayist who has written numerous works about the Indian presence in Guadeloupe. See, for example, Moutoussamy, *Guadeloupe et son indianité*, and *A la recherche de l'Inde perdue* (Paris: L'Harmattan, 2004).

17. Anny Dominique, "À Fort-de-France les statues ne meurent pas," *International Journal of Francophone Studies* 11, no. 1–2 (2008): 87–106.

18. Stephanie Serac, interview with Ernest Moutoussamy, RFO Radio Guadeloupe, June 7, 2007, http://web.archive.org/web/20070607224823/http://guadeloupe.rfo.fr/imprimer.php3?id_article=62.

19. When asked what was the difference between Indians from Guadeloupe and Indians from India, Moutoussamy deflected the question by contrasting Indo- and Afro-Guadeloupeans, suggesting that Afro-Guadeloupeans lost many of their African-based traditions due to the cultural stripping process of slavery, while Indo-Guadeloupeans managed to retain their original practices. Afro-Caribbean populations are thus imagined as "culture creators," while Indo-Caribbean populations are imagined as "culture bearers." For more on this in the context of Trinidad, see Viranjini Munasinghe, "Culture Creators and Culture Bearers: The Interface between Race and Ethnicity in Trinidad," *Transforming Anthropology* 6, no. 1–2 (1997): 72–86.

20. Madassamy was frequently referred to as simply Mada. This nickname was particularly meaningful given that the island of Guadeloupe is often, and increasingly among young people, referred to as Gwada.

21. Interestingly, the dockworkers' strike ended up outlasting the Madassamy affair by several months, becoming its own dramatic "affair."

22. These conditions of economic distress and malaise are an extreme version of what is also increasingly found in mainland France, where youth also face alarming levels of unemployment and few employment prospects.

23. The similarity between the *banlieue* uprisings outside Paris in 2005 and the union strikes was not lost on my informants. During the time of the French riots, many of them assured me that Antillean émigrés were actively involved in the demonstrations.

24. The legal precedent for force-feeding prisoners dates back to the French-Algerian War, which the union lawyers were quick to highlight at public meetings.

CHAPTER FIVE

1. For a broader discussion of the debates in the French mainland, see Christine Chivallon, "Resurgence of the Memory of Slavery in France: Issues and Significations of a Public and Academic Debate," in *Living History: Encountering the Memory and the History of the Heirs of Slavery*, ed. Ana Lucia Araujo (New Castle: Cambridge Scholars Publishing, 2009); Doris L. Garraway, "Memory As Reparation? The Politics of Remembering Slavery in France from Abolition to the Loi Taubira (2001)," *International Journal of Francophone Studies* 11, no. 3 (2008): 365–86; Catherine Reinhardt, "Slavery and Commemoration: Remembering the French Abolitionary

Decree, 150 Years Later," in *Memory, Empire and Postcolonialism*, ed. Alec G. Hargreaves (Lanham, MD: Lexington, 2005): 11–36; Nelly Schmidt, "Commémoration, histoire et historiographie: A propos du 150me anniversaire de l'abolition de l'esclavage dans les colonies françaises," *Ethnologie française* no. 3 (1999): 453–60; Françoise Vergès, "'I Am Not the Slave of Slavery': The Politics of Reparation in (French) Postslavery Communities," in *Frantz Fanon: Critical Perspectives*, ed. Anthony C. Alessandrini (London: Routledge, 1999); Françoise Vergès, *La mémoire enchaînée: Questions sur l'esclavage* (Paris: Albin Michel, 2006).

2. On the silence in France around colonialism and slavery, see Maeve McCusker, "Troubling Amnesia: The Slave Trade in French and Francophone Literature and Culture," *Eighteenth-Century Life* 35, no. 1 (2011): 221; Ann Laura Stoler, "Colonial Aphasia: Race and Disabled Histories in France," *Public Culture* 23, no. 1 (2011): 121–56; M. Lazreg, "Mirror, Mirror, Tell Me Who I Am: Colonial Empire and French Identity," *Public Culture* 23, no. 1 (2011): 177–89; Catherine Benoit, "La Caraibe ou l'impensé de l'anthropologie francaise," in *A la périphérie du centre: Les limites de l'hégémonie en anthropologie*, ed. Michelle Daveluy and Louis-Jacques Dorias (Montreal: Liber, 2009); Helene Champagne, "Breaking the Ice: A Burgeoning Post-Colonial Debate on France's Historical Amnesia and Contemporary 'Soul Searching,'" *Modern & Contemporary France* 16, no. 1 (2008): 67–72; Nélia Dias, "Double Erasures: Rewriting the Past at the Musée du Quai Branly," *Social Anthropology* 16, no. 3 (2008): 300–311; Christine Chivallon, "La quête pathétique des postcolonial studies ou la révolution manquée," *Mouvements*, no. 3 (2007): 32–39; Cécile Vidal, "The Reluctance of French Historians to Address Atlantic History," *The Southern Quarterly* 43, no. 4 (2006): 153–89; Pascal Blanchard, Nicolas Bancel, and Sandrine Lemaire, *La fracture coloniale: La société française au prisme de l'héritage colonial* (Paris: La Découverte, 2005); S. Dulucq and C. Zytnicki, "Penser le passé colonial français," *Vingtième Siècle, Revue d'Histoire*, no. 2 (2005): 59–69; Myriam Cottias, "Le silence de la nation: Les 'vieilles colonies' comme lieu de définition des dogmes républicains (1848–1905)," *Outre-mers* 90, no. 338–39 (2003): 21–45; Myriam Cottias, "Nos ancêtres les gaulois: La France et l'esclavage aujourd'hui," *Cahiers Sens Public*, no. 2 (2009): 45–56; Myriam Cottias, "Et si l'esclavage colonial faisait histoire nationale?," *Revue d'Histoire Moderne et Contemporaine* 52, no. 4, supplement (2005): 59–63.

3. Marie-José Jolivet, "La construction d'une mémoire historique à la Martinique: Du schoelchérisme au marronnisme," *Cahiers d'Études Africaines*, 27, no. 107–8 (2008): 287–309.

4. Édouard Glissant, *Le discours antillais* (Paris: Gallimard, 1997), 823.

5. For more on "Schoelcherisme," see Jolivet, "La construction d'une mémoire historique"; and Nelly Schmidt, "Schoelcherisme et assimilation dans la politique coloniale française: De la théorie à la pratique aux Caraïbes entre 1848 et les années 1880," *Revue d'Histoire Moderne et Contemporaine* 35, no. 2 (1988): 305–40.

6. André Schwarz-Bart, *A Woman Named Solitude* (New York: Atheneum, 1973); Roland Anduse, *Joseph Ignace: Le premier rebelle* (Pointe-à-Pitre: Jasor, 1989); Maryse Condé, *An tan revolisyon: Elle court, elle court la liberté; Pièce de théâtre* (Guadeloupe: Conseil régional de la Guadeloupe, 1989); Daniel Maximin, *Lone Sun* (Charlottesville: University of Virginia Press, 1989).

7. For an analysis of these projects and the impact on the landscape, see Nick Nesbitt, "The Vicissitudes of Memory: Representations of Louis Delgrés," in *Voicing Memory: History and Subjectivity in French Caribbean Literature* (Charlottesville: University of Virginia Press, 2003); Laurent Dubois, "Solitude's Statue: Confronting the Past in

the French Caribbean," *Outre-mers* 94, no. 350–51 (2006): 27–38; and Catherine Reinhardt, *Claims to Memory: Beyond Slavery and Emancipation in the French Caribbean* (New York: Berghahn Books, 2006).

8. For more, see David Murray, "The Cultural Citizen: Negations of Race and Language in the Making of Martiniquais," *Anthropological Quarterly* 70 (1997): 79–90.

9. Christine Chivallon, "Rendre visible l'esclavage: Muséographie et hiatus de la mémoire aux Antilles françaises," *Homme* 108 (2006): 7–42, at 15.

10. Richard Price, *The Convict and the Colonel* (Boston: Beacon Press, 1998), 184. For a similar argument regarding Puerto Rico, see Isar Pilar Godreau, "Changing Space, Making Race: Distance, Nostalgia, and the Folklorization of Blackness in Puerto Rico," *Identities: Global Studies in Culture and Power* 9, no. 3 (2002): 281–304.

11. Christine Chivallon, "Mémoires antillaises de l'esclavage: Vers une anthropologie du postcolonialisme?," *Ethnologie Française* 32, no. 4 (2002): 601–12, at 608.

12. Church records indicate that a large bell with the inscription "Liberté" was installed in 1848 at the top of the stairs as a commemorative gesture after emancipation. The steps, however, are apparently unrelated to this memorial and were built much earlier with the financial support of the local *habitations* (plantations). In 1998, an additional monument to emancipation was added at the bottom of the stairs in the shape of a large drum, as were the small plaques with the name of African tribes. I am grateful to Raymond Gama for sharing these records with me.

13. Reinhardt, *Claims to Memory*, 138.

14. Michel-Rolph Trouillot, *Silencing the Past: Power and the Production of History* (Boston: Beacon Press, 1995), 27.

15. Christine Chivallon, "Mémoires antillaises de l'esclavage," 602. See also Dany Bébel-Gisler, "The Incomplete Past of Slavery: The African Heritage in the Social Reality, Subconsciousness, and Imagination of Guadeloupe," in *From Chains to Bonds: The Slave Trade Revisited*, ed. Diene Doudou (New York: Berghahn Books, 2001).

16. For a discussion and critique of this view, see Richard Price, "An Absence of Ruins: Seeking Caribbean Historical Consciousness," *Caribbean Review* 14, no. 3 (1985).

17. Édouard Glissant, *Caribbean Discourse*, trans. Michael Dash (Charlottesville: University of Virginia Press, 1989), 64. See also Arcadio Diaz Quiñones, *La memoria rota* (San Juan, PR: Ediciones Huracan, 1993).

18. Nicholas B. Dirks, "History as a Sign of the Modern," *Public Culture* 2, no. 2 (1990): 25–32.

19. The union declares a new slogan at each of their union-wide congresses, which are held every three years.

20. The hope was that this kind of political and cultural organization could reach out to students, unemployed youth, and other nonunionized sectors of the population. However, despite the desire of the organizers to expand their struggles beyond the rank and file of the union, the overwhelming majority of those involved in the project are still UGTG leaders and workers. Thus NONM consists mostly of union members who swap their union T-shirts for NONM shirts to engage in nonunion activity. For more on the organization, visit http://www.mouvman-nonm.org/.

21. *Nonm* is arguably a gender-neutral word, but many of the women involved in NONM joke sarcastically that the focus of the organization is on the men because women are already *à la vanguard* in their political development. There was relative gender parity among the membership of the organization, but during my fieldwork the positions of leadership were for the most part held by men (as is the case of the UGTG generally).

22. I conducted extensive interviews with Gama about these events, but he did not organize them alone. One of the other main organizers is the local activist and poet Carlomann R. Bassette. For more on his views of Guadeloupean history, see Carlomann R. Bassette, *Des enjeux et défis politiques à Trois-Rivières de Guadeloupe* (Port-Louis: Éd. Lespwisavann, 2008). See also Laurent Dubois, *A Colony of Citizens: Revolution and Slave Emancipation in the French Caribbean, 1787–1804* (Chapel Hill: University of North Carolina Press, 2004), 124–25.

23. *Lespwisavann, Istwa & Sosyété*, http://www.lespwisavann.org/.

24. Raymond Gama, "Historien guadeloupéen ou historien de l'histoire de la Guadeloupe?," *Lespwisavann, Istwa & Sosyété*, online journal (March 2007): 7–12.

25. For more, see Hayden V. White, *Metahistory: The Historical Imagination in Nineteenth-Century Europe* (Baltimore: Johns Hopkins University Press, 1973); Michel de Certeau, *The Writing of History: European Perspectives* (New York: Columbia University Press, 1988); Tzvetan Todorov, *The Morals of History* (Minneapolis: University of Minnesota Press, 1995); Michel-Rolph Trouillot, *Silencing the Past*; Stephan Palmié, *The Cooking of History: How Not to Study Afro-Cuban Religion* (Chicago: University of Chicago Press, 2013); and David Scott, *Conscripts of Modernity: The Tragedy of Colonial Enlightenment* (Durham, NC: Duke University Press, 2004).

26. Trouillot, *Silencing the Past*, 49.

27. On issues of authenticity in historical representations, see Richard Handler and Eric Gable, *The New History in an Old Museum: Creating the Past at Colonial Williamsburg* (Durham, NC: Duke University Press, 1997).

28. The presence of French foods is so prevalent that there are currently initiatives in local schools to introduce children to the taste of local fruits and vegetables, which some argue are becoming *oubliés* or *méconnus* (forgotten or unknown). See Daniel Osard, "À la découverte des saveurs du terroir," *France-Antilles*, October 15, 2003. For more on the politics of food in the Antillean imagination, see Valérie Loichot, *The Tropics Bite Back: Culinary Coups in Caribbean Literature* (Minneapolis: University of Minnesota Press, 2013).

29. A 2006 study by the French National Institute for Statistics and Economic Studies found that 79 percent of the labor force in Guadeloupe drives to work in personal vehicles. See "Guadeloupe: Déplacements domicile-travail," *Antiane Eco* 72 (January 2010): 11.

30. Jerome Pruneau, Stéphanie Melyon-Reinette, and Danielle Agnès, "'Maché an masla!': Ethnographie de l'usage symbolique du corps 'charnel' dans le carnaval guadeloupéen," *Caribbean Studies* 37, no. 1 (2009): 45–64.

31. This lack of physical representation might speak to the organizers' desire to preserve the importance of the act of walking itself, rather than abstracting the experience of the walk into a material representation of the terrain covered. As de Certeau argues, the fixation of pedestrian pathways onto city maps constitutes a form of forgetting in which "the trace . . . is substituted for the practice." In other words, the importance of the act can be obscured by foregrounding the specificity of the terrain covered. See Michel de Certeau, "Walking in the City," in *The Practice of Everyday Life* (Berkeley: University of California Press, 1984), 87.

32. These statements were made during an interview on the TV segment "Pawol Cinc et Quat" on the TV station L'Une.

33. For more on walking as a kind of speech act, see Michel de Certeau, "Walking in the City."

34. See, for example, Martin Japtok, "Sugarcane as History in Paule Marshall's 'To Da-Duh, in Memoriam,'" *African American Review* 34, no. 3 (2000): 475–82; and Gastón Gordillo, *Landscapes of Devils: Tensions of Place and Memory in the Argentinean Chaco* (Durham, NC: Duke University Press, 2004).

35. The historian Adeline mentions in her anecdote is most likely Raymond Gama, whom I discuss above. Adeline does not cite him by name, instead recounting her story of "walking with a historian" as if this had become a quotidian act.

36. As Trouillot suggests, the category of archives goes beyond government-sponsored institutions to include other, less visible institutions and practices that "sort sources and organize facts." He describes archives as "sites of mediation" that bridge the distance between what happened and what is said to have happened and argues that "in that sense, a tourist guide, a museum tour, an archaeological expedition, or an auction at Sotheby's can perform as much an archival role as the Library of Congress." Trouillot, *Silencing the Past*, 52.

37. Renato Rosaldo discusses the truth effects of these forms of historical evidence when he suggests that for the Ilongot, "the trees themselves bore silent, yet culturally incontrovertible, testimony to the truth of the tales of the past." Rosaldo, *Ilongot Headhunting, 1883–1974: A Study in Society and History* (Stanford, CA: Stanford University Press, 1980), 44. A similar argument has been made in relation to the artifacts and mise-en-scènes of "living history" museums, where the "tangible presence" of the living tableaux (and how organizers emphasize this presence) generates an epistemological status of truth that marks them as "the real thing." See Eric Gable, Richard Handler, and Lawson Anna, "On the Uses of Relativism: Fact, Conjecture, and Black and White Histories at Colonial Williamsburg," *American Ethnologist* 19, no. 4 (1992): 791–805, at 795.

38. For more on this, see Comité guadeloupéen d'aide et de soutien aux détenus, *Le procès des guadeloupeens: Dix-huit patriotes devant la cour de l'état francais* (Paris: L'Harmattan, 1969); and Raymond Gama and Jean Pierre Sainton, *Mé 67 . . . Mémoire d'un événement* (Pointe-à-Pitre: Societé guadeloupéenne d'edition et de diffusion, 1985).

39. The definition for *acheminer* in the Petit Larousse Illustré (2005 edition) reads as follows: "Transporter vers un lieu. Se diriger vers un lieu. Avancer, progresser vers l'aboutissement de quelque chose. 'S'acheminer vers un resultat.'" (To transport to a place. To move towards a place. To advance, to progress towards the successful conclusion of something. 'To move toward a result.')

40. Édouard Glissant, *Caribbean Discourse*, 161–62.

CHAPTER SIX

1. I would argue that the LKP is not unique in this regard; their movement echoes the kind of politics that have been developing around the globe over the past two decades, from the Zapatistas in Chiapas to the occupiers of Zuccotti Park.

2. The notion of a prefigurative politics—of a politics that anticipates and rehearses that which it seeks to create—has been said to be one of the defining characteristics of contemporary social movements. See, for example, David Graeber, *Possibilities: Essays on Hierarchy, Rebellion, and Desire* (Oakland, CA: AK Press, 2007); Francesca Polletta, *Freedom Is an Endless Meeting: Democracy in American Social Movements* (Chicago: University of Chicago Press, 2002); and Jeffrey S. Juris, *Networking Futures: The Movements against Corporate Globalization* (Durham, NC: Duke University Press, 2008).

3. For more on the politics of disappointment, see Jessica Greenberg, *After the Revolution: Youth, Democracy, and the Politics of Disappointment in Serbia* (Stanford, CA: Stanford University Press, 2014). On cynicism as a similarly productive stance, see Lori Allen, *The Rise and Fall of Human Rights: Cynicism and Politics in Occupied Palestine* (Stanford, CA: Stanford University Press, 2013).

4. Protests over gas prices began in Guiana, where gas was most expensive, at $1.77 per liter.

5. The prefect refused to meet with them, claiming that the delegation was too large for a proper dialogue. "Laisser passer les fêtes pour durcir le mouvement," *France-Antilles*, December 18, 2008, http://www.guadeloupe.franceantilles.fr/actualite/societe-social-emploi/laisser-passer-les-fetes-pour-durcir-le-mouvement-17865.php; "Un 'front' d'organisations sur Pointe-à-Pitre," *Carib Creole One*, December 17, 2008.

6. For the complete list of demands, see Union générale des travailleurs de Guadeloupe, "LKP: La plateforme de revendications," January 20, 2009, http://ugtg.org/article_700.html.

7. Édouard Glissant, "The Question," *Les Influences*, June 29, 2009, http://www.les influences.fr/Pouvez-vous-rappeler-au-nouveau.html.

8. See Juris, *Networking Futures.*

9. "4é jour d'une Guadeloupe en crise," *Carib Creole One*, January 23, 2009.

10. To listen to snippets of the song along with Coco's reflections about the inspiration for it see, "Dominick Coco: Jantiman," YouTube video, posted by Yenkinou, March 18, 2009, http://youtu.be/hEv1oMMqXT0.

11. Versions of the song, "La gwadloup sé tan nou," can be heard on several websites, including the UGTG's, http://ugtg.org/article_789.html.

12. The prominent Creole linguist Jean Bernabé has argued that "la Gwadloup sé tan nou" should not be translated as "Guadeloupe is ours" but as "Guadeloupe, it is ours." He argues that this slogan constitutes a hailing of both the political subject and the political space of Guadeloupe. I have retained his suggestion when transcribing the song lyrics but have used the shorter version for the title. For more, see Jean Bernabé, "Gwadloup sé tan nou, mais qui est ce 'nou'?," *Carib Creole One*, February 18, 2009.

13. "L'energie de la Guadeloupe n'est pas destructrice," *France-Antilles Guadeloupe*, March 19, 2009.

14. In many ways the concept of the *pwofitan* resonates with that of "the 99%" generated by the Occupy Wall Street movement.

15. In Guadeloupe the French government is referred to as *l'état*, local elected officials as *les élus*, and the local government bodies as *les collectivités.*

16. Daniel Dayan and Elihu Katz, *Media Events: The Live Broadcasting of History* (Cambridge, MA: Harvard University Press, 1992).

17. "Le Liyannaj kont pwofitasyon impose son rythme," *France-Guyane*, January 26, 2009, http://www.franceguyane.fr/actualite/economie-consommation/le-liyannaj-kont-pwofitasyon-impose-son-rythme-16751.php.

18. "Victorin Lurel, 'La Guadeloupe est au bord de la sédition,'" *Le Nouvel Observateur*, February 19, 2009.

19. James C. Scott, *Seeing like a State: How Certain Schemes to Improve the Human Condition Have Failed* (New Haven, CT: Yale University Press, 1998).

20. Deborah A. Thomas, *Exceptional Violence: Embodied Citizenship in Transnational Jamaica* (Durham, NC: Duke University Press, 2011), 230–34.

21. For more, see the work of Vanessa Agard-Jones, including "Bodies in the System," *Small Axe* 17, no. 3 (2013):182–92; and that of Catherine Benoît, including *Corps, jardins, mémoires: Anthropologie du corps et de l'espace à la Guadeloupe* (Paris: CNRS Éditions, 2000); and "Silent Performances in the Guadeloupean Dooryard Gardens: The Creolization of the Self and the Environment," in *Performance and Appropriation: Profane Rituals in Gardens and Landscapes*, ed. Michel Conan (Washington, DC: Dumbarton Oaks Research Library and Collection, 2007).

INDEX

The letter f *or* t *following a page number indicates a figure or table, respectively.*